D0586911

Understanding Globalization

SCHOOL OF ORIENTAL AND AFRICAN STUDIES
University of London

Please return this book on or before the last date shown

Long loans and One Week loans may be renewed up to 10 times
Short loans & CDs cannot be renewed
Fines are charged on all overdue items

Online: http://lib.soas.ac.uk/patroninfo
Phone: 020-7898 4197 (answerphone)

— 1 NOV 2007
— 3 DEC 2010

Understanding Globalization

Tony Schirato and Jen Webb

SAGE Publications
London • Thousand Oaks • New Delhi

SAGE Publications Ltd
1 Oliver's Yard, 55 City Road
London EC1Y 1SP

SAGE Publications Inc
2455 Teller Road
Thousand Oaks, California 91320

SAGE Publications India Pvt Ltd
B–42 Panchsheel Enclave
PO Box 4109
New Delhi 110 017

British Library Cataloguing in Publication data

A catalogue record for this book is available from the British Library

ISBN 0-7619-4793-0 (hbk)
ISBN 0-7619-4794-9 (pbk)

Library of Congress Control Number: 2002-1127787

Typeset by Mayhew Typesetting, Rhayader, Powys
Printed and bound in Great Britain by
TJ International Ltd., Padstow, Cornwall

Contents

1

The Idea of Globalization

What's in a name?

Globalization is the 'name' that is often used to designate the power relations, practices and technologies that characterize, and have helped bring into being, the contemporary world. What it in fact means, though, is less than precise. Armand Mattelart refers to globalization as:

> one of those tricky words, one of those instrumental notions that, under the effect of market logics and without citizens being aware of it, have been naturalized to the point of becoming indispensable for establishing communication between people of different cultures. (2000: 97)

He argues in the same place that globalization has a **hegemonic** role in organizing and decoding the meaning of the world. In a similar vein, John Beynon and David Dunkerley, in their general introduction to *Globalization: the Reader*, make the claim that 'globalization, in one form or another, is impacting on the lives of everyone on the planet . . . globalization might justifiably be claimed to be the defining feature of human society at the start of the twenty-first century' (2000: 3).

Certainly, struggles over its meanings, its effects and its origins are played out in a variety of ways and sites, from academe and the media, through governments and corporations,

1

to the streets of Seattle, Melbourne and Genoa. For some, globalization means freedom, while others see it as a prison. For some it means prosperity, while for others it guarantees the poverty of the developing world. And though the word itself has been in use only since the early 1960s, some writers see it as dating from the empires of the ancient world, while for others globalization is coterminous with the modern era and the processes of **modernization**, or even of postmodernization. It seems everyone has a stake in its meaning, and is affected by its **discourses** and practices, though there is no straightforward or widely accepted definition of the term, either in general use or in academic writings.

Globalization and the politics of naming

The intensity of debates over its meanings and applications can be understood if we take into account the importance of naming in the establishment of 'reality'. Mattelart points to this in his *Networking the World*, where he opens a chapter devoted to a critique of the politics of globalization by quoting the French philosopher Albert Camus's comment that 'Naming things badly adds to the misfortune of the world' (Mattelart, 2000: 97). At the time we commenced writing this book there was clearly a considerable amount of misfortune to be found globally. Wars were being waged in Palestine, Chechnya, Afghanistan, Kashmir, Algeria, Sri Lanka, Angola, the Sudan and in other places long forgotten, or never covered, by CNN. The number of people in the world living in poverty – which the World Bank defines as US$1 a day or less – was over 1.19 billion in 1998 (PREM, 2000), and increasing or at best remaining the same in Africa, Eastern Europe, Latin America and Central Asia (Nye and Donohue, 2000: 184). Crime and the management of crime contribute to this generalized misfortune: Pierre Bourdieu points out that 'California, one of the richest states of the US' spends more on its prison budgets than on the budget of all the universities combined, and that 'blacks in the Chicago ghetto only know the state through the police officer, the judge, the

2

prison warder and the parole officer' (Bourdieu, 1998a: 32). Unemployment too continues to impact on people's lives across the globe: in the week following the 11 September attacks on the Pentagon and the World Trade Center, over 100,000 airline employees in the United States, and many more around the world, were made redundant, with little prospect of regaining their jobs in the short to medium term. Clearly these are, in Camus's terms, 'bad things', which increase the level of misery for many people. But how their status is weighed and valued in the public imagination and in the eyes of power brokers varies tremendously according to how they are named, and to the contexts of their reportage.

We saw an extreme expression of this **politics of naming** in the media responses to the terrorist attacks on the United States on 11 September 2001, the destruction of New York's Twin Towers, the assault on the Pentagon, and the loss of thousands of lives. In the United States, but also in the United Kingdom, Europe, Canada, Japan, Australia and New Zealand, the media networks ran virtually non-stop coverage of the event, with other programming effectively suspended. All other news (about politics, economics, entertainment, or sport) was virtually ignored, or treated peripherally, rating a serious mention only if it could somehow be connected with the attacks. International politics, for instance, was represented by stories of British Prime Minister Tony Blair pledging to support the United States; finance news dealt with the market collapse, seeing it as a consequence of the political uncertainty surrounding American President George W. Bush's response to the attacks. Entertainment was covered in stories about musicians like Celine Dion 'singing for the victims and their relatives'; and sports news was reduced to depictions of baseball teams 'playing for' America and/or New York.

The Western media were clearly of the opinion that something groundbreaking had taken place; as CNN put it, this was 'a day of unfathomable death, destruction and heartbreak' (CNN, 2001b). Comparisons were made with historical events such as the bombing of Pearl Harbor, though most media commentators followed President George W. Bush in characterizing the attacks as the first twenty-first-century war. Newspaper articles employed apocalyptic headings ('One with the world at last'; 'Our charmed life has gone forever') and lamented that 'On September 11, the world changed' (Goodman, 2001: 31). This change supposedly involved the loss, for Americans, of their innocence and security; although as Slavoj Zizek observed, 'when a New Yorker commented on how, after the bombings, one can no longer walk safely on the city's streets, the irony of it was that, well before the bombings, the streets of New York were well-known for the dangers of being attacked or, at least, mugged' (Zizek, 2001).

The significance of the event and the media's response for the wider story of globalization is that it worked as a profound instance of the politics of naming. What was, effectively, an appalling but localized disaster became international news – for a time, almost the only international news. And the language used in the reportage, and in statements by politicians and other world leaders, signals the efficacy of naming in bringing things into social reality, and in foreclosing, or shutting out, other 'realities'. Shocking as these events were, the 11 September attacks did not involve particularly high fatalities compared with many contemporary wars and acts of violence. The attacks on New York and the Pentagon resulted in the loss of what was initially reported as 6,500 lives (later reduced to around 3,000). By contrast, tens of thousands of people died in Russia's two invasions of Chechnya; some 19,000 Eritrean soldiers were reported as killed in the two-year war with Ethiopia (*Afrol News*, 2001); CNN reported that war-related deaths in east Congo were estimated to have reached 2 million by June 2001; and many hundreds of thousands have lost their lives in conflicts in Cambodia, the Balkans, East Timor, Iraq/Iran, Somalia and Ethiopia/Eritrea. But the reportage of these events came nowhere near the treatment of 11 September, possibly the most widely publicized event since World War II.

The response to the 11 September attacks, and the ideas and actions mobilized by the responses, are exemplified by Jean-Marie Colombani's article 'After this act of terrorism we are all Americans' in the *Guardian Weekly* of 20 September 2001

4

(initially published in *Le Monde*). Colombani's article, which more or less encapsulates the reactions of the Western media, required that 'we' (the CNN audience, the readers of Western newspapers) repress any doubt both as to who we are, and to what the attacks meant:

> At a moment like this, when words fail so lamentably to express one's feeling of shock, the first thought that comes to mind is that we are all Americans, all New Yorkers . . . As during the darkest hours of French history, there is absolutely no question of not showing solidarity with the United States and its people, who are so close to us, and to whom we owe our freedom. (2001: 33)

This necessarily denies the possibility that his readers might identify with anyone but the United States, and collapses multiple forms of marking and identification into a tub of Americana. Colombani continues:

> The US, isolated because of its unrivalled power and the absence of any counterweight, has ceased to be a pole of attraction. Or, to be more accurate, it seems to attract nothing but hatred in some parts of the world. . . . In today's monopolistic world a new and apparently uncontrollable form of barbarity seems poised to set itself up as a pole of opposition. (2001: 33)

There are a number of things happening here, the most obvious of which is the editing out of other contexts for the 11 September attacks. Colombani also fails to identify other contemporary misfortunes, such as the slaughter of Bosnian Muslims in Srebenica, as having comparable weight or significance; he would not and could not have declared, then or now, that 'after this we are all Bosnian Muslims'. But perhaps most significantly, he sets up a dichotomy, with 'us' opposed to them – the uncontrollably barbarous. The reason behind this is what Bourdieu (1998a: 19) refers to as the 'false universalism of the West', which he describes as a claim to **universalism** which is 'no more than a nationalism which invokes the universal (human rights, etc.) in order to impose itself'. The attacks and deaths in the United States can move Colombani to call for Europeans to identify with Americans not just because of shared historical links, but more importantly because American society and its way of life are understood as standing in for 'universal' qualities or characteristics – humanity, reason, freedom, human rights, democracy and the 'good of mankind' – as opposed to the monstrosity, barbarity, madness and intolerance of its enemies.

This editing out of one broad spectrum of social issues, perspectives and values, and editing in of another as the only valid reality, is associated with the principle of **foreclosure**. Foreclosure is usually associated with psychoanalytical theory: Freud uses it with regard to the Oedipus complex, whereby a male child is required to repress desire for his mother and foreclose that aspect of his identity and desire as a requirement of his entry into 'normal' (patriarchal) society. Judith Butler refers to it in her discussions of the way in which 'normative heterosexuality' is understood as the basis and condition of subjectivity, and other possibilities of sexuality/subjectivity are foreclosed. So foreclosure can be understood as a process whereby certain feelings, desires, ideas and positions are both unthinkable with regard to, and simultaneously constitutive of, an identity. Foreclosure is also at the basis of the politics of naming, as we can see from Colombani's article ('After this act of terrorism we are all Americans'), because the process of foreclosure requires that 'we' (the CNN audience, the readers of Western newspapers) repress any doubt both as to who we are and as to what these attacks meant. The politics of naming thus simultaneously creates one reality, and forecloses another.

How is it possible to name one set of values as universal and foreclose another set while still holding to the notion of a globalized world predicated on such principles as freedom and democracy? Cultural theorists such as Ernesto Laclau, Chantal Mouffe and Claude Lefort have written, apropos of democracy, that it functions, theoretically, as an 'empty set' which allows no single group (a class, an ethnicity, a gender, a religion) to 'fill it up' or inflect it with their particularities. What Colombani's article points to is the process whereby the universal, supposedly a non-inflected set just like democracy, is already filled with content – in this case, Western and/or American values, institutions and politics. And it is this inflection that allows Colombani to give the attacks on the United States a universal weight or meaning while denying a similar weight or meaning to the experiences of Bosnian Muslims or Afghani refugees.

The name of globalization

Much the same can be said, of course, about the 'empty set' that is globalization. Despite the obvious difficulties in understanding what is meant by 'globalization', we can identify a number of positions that seek to explain and describe it. The many definitions in the literature range from the purely economic (interest rates, exchange rates, mobility of finance) and the rate of human movement (refugees, migrants, mobile professionals) to the effects of power (the collapse of nation-states, technological surveillance, 'action at a distance'). But the many ways of thinking and writing about globalization can be collapsed into a small number of categories, which we will outline in a very broad brushstroke approach here.

The writers David Held and Anthony McGrew identify two main groups or 'sides' in the debate, whom they name the **'globalists'** and the **'sceptics'**. Globalists, they argue, are believers, in the sense that for them 'globalization is a real and significant historical development' (2000: 2) – the effect of real structural changes in the past few centuries. The sceptics, on the other hand, consider that what we are experiencing at present is simply a continuation of trends that developed in the period of European colonial expansion, peaked during the period 1870-1914, and were interrupted by the two great wars and the 'cold war' of the twentieth century; so, for them, globalization is principally ideological, present more in the discourse than in reality.

Both sides in the debate, however, keep the market economy central to how globalization is viewed, and how it proceeds. Andreas Busch offers a very similar classification, identifying writers on globalization as either 'liberals' – who start from the premise that globalization is unquestionably real, and move on to insist that it brings only benefits to all – or 'sceptics' – for whom global tendencies necessarily have negative political and economic outcomes (Busch, 2000: 30–1). He adds a third category, though: the 'moderately optimistic'. This group breaks with the other two (and, therefore, with Held and McGrew's globalist/sceptic division) by imputing considerably less importance to the economic sphere. At the same time, the 'moderately optimistic' category straddles the views of the other two groups by generally agreeing that there are globalizing tendencies which can be identified and measured, but that they are not as all-encompassing as the literature might imply; and nor are they operating without resistance, and without exceptions (Busch, 2000: 33).

In the chapters that follow, we will outline these ideas about what globalization means and for whom it takes on its meanings, and offer a critique of the central ideas and practices associated with it. In the process we will develop our own explanation for globalization, and trace its trends, patterns and movements across a number of domains, including history, technology, nationality, identity, media, the public sphere and economics. We start by considering the **Marxist** approaches of Immanuel Wallerstein, and Hardt and Negri, and draw on their ideas to discuss the relationship between history, ideology and globalization. Then we depart a little from this established category by examining a second strand of thought which comes from theorists we could designate **Neomarxist**, such as Mattelart, Castells, Baudrillard, Virilio and Appadurai. Their examination of the processes of globalization centres around the extent to which technological developments have brought about a change in the way societies, states, cultures and individuals function and understand themselves. The third perspective which informs our discussion of globalization is exemplified by the work of writers such as Pierre Bourdieu and Zygmunt Bauman. These writers work in the tradition of Neomarxism, and give more emphasis to the cultural than to the economic aspects and effects of globalization. While they share the notion that globalization has a history, and that technological developments have dramatically affected everyday life, they stress that these changes are explicable in cultural terms, specifically in terms of the politics of naming. That is, they argue that the changes are located within, and can be evaluated in terms of, powerful discourses that shape everyday life; discourses which simultaneously name, and thus help bring into being, what they are supposedly designating or describing.

'The global' and its meanings

Most analysts accept the importance of the technological, economic, cultural and political changes associated with the term 'globalization', but very few agree as to what these changes mean or if, taken together, they add up to something that 'really exists' for everyone – as access to technology, as a world view, or simply as an instrumental name and set of discourses. In order to address the question, we first have to qualify it with two additional questions: for whom is globalization 'real', and in what ways? For the S11 (anti-globalization) demonstrators who protested in Seattle, Melbourne and Genoa, there was no doubt that globalization existed and was responsible for most of the misfortunes of the world, from environmental degradation and vandalism, to the worldwide exploitation of workers. For them it was a reality which had changed the world, with negative consequences for their lives.

But to what extent are these consequences a result of globalization, or of the set of processes, values, technologies and politics associated with it? The protesters might well define it in terms of the power and influence of global capitalism, embodied in the practices of transnational corporations, the World Bank, and the International Monetary Fund (IMF); or characterize it as the various political, economic and cultural ways in which American hegemony has imposed itself upon the world; or point to the ways in which the IMF and the World Bank, operating as *de facto* arms of American free-trade policies, have effectively undermined the sovereignty of developing nations.

But the politicians who were the targets of the demonstrations would have had a very different understanding of the word 'globalization', an understanding shared, by and large, with spokespersons of the media, bureaucracies and business. When George W. Bush, Tony Blair and Silvio Berlusconi dismissed the protesters in Genoa as selfish malcontents who didn't understand the benefits globalization was bringing, particularly to the poorest and most underprivileged of the world's peoples, they were effectively repeating a discourse that was constitutive of Bill Gates's dream of 'frictionless capitalism', or Ted Turner's prophecy that the spread of CNN would eliminate war from the world: 'With CNN,' he announced, 'information circulates throughout the world, and no one wants to look like an idiot. So they make peace, because that's smart' (Mattelart, 2000: 95). Globalization may or may not be 'the defining feature of human society at the start of the twenty-first century', but importantly a large number of powerful people (from business, bureaucracies, government and the media) consistently assert that, contrary to what the protesters believe, it is the answer to, rather than the embodiment of, 'the misfortunes of the world'.

Still, before we could accept any of these explanations as evidence of the existence of something new called 'globalization', we would need to convince ourselves that the activities of capitalist institutions and/or American hegemony, and the technology associated with them, have changed and proliferated sufficiently over the last thirty or so years to justify talking about them, as do Beynon and Dunkerley, as 'impacting on the lives of everyone on the planet'. There are arguments both for and against the claims made by the protesters. Beynon and Dunkerley, for instance, argue that although globalization is not a new phenomenon, it takes a number of forms in the contemporary world which mark it off, quantitatively and qualitatively, from its antecedents. These forms include the usual suspects such as the technological compression of time and space; the spread of human rights, democracy and intercultural understanding; a 'new and voracious phase of Western capitalism'; the 'imposition of Americanized culture'; electronic imperialism; disparities with regard to the ownership and production of and access to information; and the 'concentration of ownership of global media production and transmission in the hands of a small number of (mostly American) corporations' (Beynon and Dunkerley, 2000: 2).

As evidence for globalization, this characterization is unsatisfactory for two main reasons. First, there is nothing to suggest that these social, political and cultural forms, taken together or considered separately, are either constitutive of or inform any kind of universalization. There are many groups of people throughout the world, especially in Africa, South America and parts of Asia, for whom time and space are still experienced much as they were by their cultures a century ago. And to speak of democracy as a universal is not just to ignore obvious exceptions such as China, but also to conflate radically different versions of democracy (as practised, for example, in Zimbabwe, the United States and Fiji). As for the homogenizing effects of Western and particularly American culture, this ignores the argument put forward by some cultural theorists that local cultures have been particularly adept at transforming hegemonic cultural forms for their own purposes. Michel de Certeau, for instance, describes the way in which the indigenous people of South America may have appeared to the Spanish conquerors to have submitted to the Christianity they had imposed upon them, but in fact those conquered and converted were using Christian rituals and practices in ways that were very far from the Spaniards' intent (1984: xiii).

The second objection is that, as Armand Mattelart has demonstrated in a number of books (such as *The Invention of Communication*, *Mapping World Communication* and, most particularly, *Networking the World*), many of the forms identified by Beynon and Dunkerley were already discernible in the imbrication of the development of communication technologies and imperialist policies and practices in the late nineteenth century. We see them, for instance, in the choice (or imposition) of Greenwich time, in 1884, as the standard for the calculation of world time; or in the dividing up of the world, in 1870, into spheres of influence between British, French and German (and later American) news agencies. Mattelart argues that the cultural, social and political forms of contemporary life are not new; rather they have been intensified and quickened by what he calls the 'originating' aspect of globalization, which involves the use of communication technology to bring about the integration of world financial markets:

> Globalization originated in the sphere of financial transactions, where it has shattered the boundaries of national systems. Formerly regulated and partitioned, financial markets are now integrated into a totally fluid global market through generalized connections in real time. The financial sphere has imparted its dynamics to an economy dominated by speculative movements of capital in a context of constant overheating. With the expansion of the speculative bubble, the financial function has gained autonomy from the so-called real economy and supplanted industrial production and investment. (2000: 76)

Mattelart's position is interesting: he is sceptical with regard to both the emancipatory claims made for globalization – the idea that it improves human rights, or promotes democracy – and the notion that the **ideology** and cultural politics behind it are new. To exemplify this, he points to a number of striking parallels between the discourses and practices of nineteenth-century imperialism and those of the American hegemony. But at the same time he subscribes to the 'reality' of globalization in the sense that he accepts that there is a form of global activity – understood as the imbrication of communication technology, financial markets and flows, the media and other forms of information transmission, and a 'corporate management' ethos – which has accomplished the 'unification of the economic field and, by extrapolation . . . account[s] for the general state of the world' (2000: 75).

How does this take place? A prominent example of this phenomenon in action was the so-called 'Asian economic crisis' of 1997–98. World financial markets had been flowing into Asian stocks, realty and currencies because of the perception (fuelled by the successes of the 'tiger economies' of Singapore,

South Korea and Taiwan) that quick and even spectacular short-term profits could be made. There was no more logic to this activity than there was to the South Pacific 'bubble' in the eighteenth century or the rush for African colonies in the nineteenth. In each case, the economies in question were overheated and running large current account deficits. Once a number of businesses in the region defaulted on loan payments, there was a mass withdrawal of capital which caused local corporations to go under, workers to be laid off and currencies to fall dramatically in value. As Mattelart suggests, the keys to what happened were the speed, mass and reach of both the transmission of information and the circulation of capital. The resultant social and political consequences were drastic: in Indonesia, for instance, the government's attempt to implement IMF-sponsored economic reforms (which included cutbacks in public spending), coupled with the weakness of the Indonesian rupiah (which made it harder for people to buy food), led to riots directed against ethnic Chinese, who constituted a significant part of the local business community. Erratic and dramatic capital flows not only brought about the deaths of thousands of Chinese, they also created political instability throughout the South-east Asian region: only the stronger economies (Singapore, for instance) escaped without some form of sociopolitical disruption.

Mattelart's argument is that, in the contemporary world, social, cultural and political issues, including the sovereignty of states, are predicated – if not entirely dependent – upon this new phenomenon of capital flows, and the technology which makes it possible. Advances in communication technology, **informationalism**, the hegemony of American and Western culture, and the proliferation of institutions concerned with, or involved in, global governance have meant that states, groups and individuals are becoming 'increasingly enmeshed in worldwide systems and networks of interaction' and 'relations and networks of power', so that 'distant occurrences and developments can come to have serious domestic impacts while local happenings can engender significant global repercussions' (Held and McGrew, 2000: 3). But this is a long way from accepting the position held by some theories of globalization, which is that flows of capital, culture, media, images and ideas have severed the connection between territoriality and identity, eroded the functions and power of the state, homogenized societies and cultures, and recontextualized lives and events in terms of global, rather than local, meanings and agendas.

If we look, for instance, at the reactions to the 11 September attacks on the World Trade Center and the Pentagon, there was certainly a great deal of rhetorical commitment to the notion of a 'global response to terrorism'. The leaders of states such as the United Kingdom, Australia, Pakistan, Japan and Russia, for instance, all offered the United States both discursive and material support. And newspaper editors, television reporters and politicians in the West were quick to embrace the Manichaean distinction between the 'allies' and the 'forces of barbarism and terror'. But this distinction soon became symptomatic of a general splintering of the facade of global unity into local interests, values and conflicts. Sometimes this occurred inadvertently, as when George W. Bush invited all nations (presumably including Islamic ones) to join him in a 'crusade' (a term from which he hastily resiled). The 'allies' and their 'global war on terrorism' took on an even more Western/anti-Islamic inflection a few days later when Italian Prime Minister Silvio Berlusconi told reporters that the situation was all about the superiority of 'our' (Western) civilization, and the inferiority of Islam. India followed up by trying to include Pakistan's support for Kashmiri Muslim separatists in the terrorist category; Russia invited the West to join its own crusade in Chechnya; Israel used the moment to justify its refusal to respect Palestinian statehood; and Prime Minister Mahathir of Malaysia took advantage of the occasion to round up and imprison Islamic opponents.

This strong anti-Islam rhetoric, fuelled by the media, was gradually directed more specifically at the Taliban. The front page of *The Weekly Telegraph* (3–9 October 2001), for instance, showed a photograph of 'The haunted face' of a former Taliban secret policeman above the caption 'I was a Taliban torturer – I crucified people'. But within a week of the attacks six people, including a Sikh, had been murdered in the United States –

supposedly because they were of 'Arabic appearance' – and mosques were attacked in the United Kingdom and Australia. In Pakistan, that country's official support for the war against terrorism was undermined by scenes of large demonstrations, violently repressed, against America. And in Australia the inflection reached particularly farcical proportions when the governing Liberal Party, determined to win an upcoming election at any cost, countenanced and contributed to the characterizing of the Taliban regime in Afghanistan as barbaric and an enemy of civilization, while simultaneously demonizing a boatload of Afghanis who sailed into Australian waters to claim refugee status. Prime Minister John Howard campaigned for his re-election on the twin platforms of promoting and contributing to the communality of global interests, while steadfastly protecting Australian territorial sovereignty against intrusions from the unwanted masses emanating from across that same globe.

Local or global?

We posed the question earlier as to whether or not there was a reality behind the claim that lives and activities in the contemporary world could be understood in terms of, or were informed by, the processes associated with globalization? The question perhaps needs to be rephrased to address what Held and McGrew refer to as the 'puzzle' of 'the disjuncture between the widespread discourse of globalization and the realities of a world in which, for the most part, the routines of everyday life are dominated by national and local circumstances' (2000: 5). This disjuncture is played out most obviously in the different agendas, explanations and understandings that are brought to the meetings of organizations such as **G-8** and the World Trade Organization, as we saw above in our discussion of the views taken by protesters compared with that of the politicians. The kind of discourse and politics offered by politicians and corporations are often read, not just by protesters, but also by theorists of globalization, as symptomatic of, and shorthand for, what we call 'neocolonialism' or 'neoimperialism'; a position

David Held and Anthony McGrew (2000: 5), in their description of different versions of 'global scepticism', characterize as Marxist in orientation. They write that, for Marxists:

> The history of the modern world order is the history of Western capitalist powers dividing and redividing the world up into exclusive economic zones. Today, it is argued, imperialism has acquired a new form as formal empires have been replaced by new mechanisms of multilateral control and surveillance, such as the G7 and World Bank. As such, the present epoch is described by many Marxists not in terms of globalization, but instead as a new mode of Western imperialism dominated by the needs and requirements of finance capital within the world's major capitalist states. (2000: 5)

The most obvious objection to this position is, of course, the one directed at Marxism in general; that is, it assumes that social, cultural and political activity is explicable in terms of the overdetermining order of the economy. But if we consider the work of a number of important cultural theorists – Jean Baudrillard, who writes about the current era in terms of its tendency to **hyperreality**; Paul Virilio, who analyses the social, cultural, political, environmental and military implications of contemporary changes to time and space; Michel Foucault, who traces the workings of power; Manuel Castells, whose concern is informationalism; or Arjun Appadurai, who addresses the relationship between technology, media, culture and identity – it is apparent that important changes are happening in the contemporary world which are not reducible to explanations about the transformation of capitalism, even though they may linked with or informed by it.

The disjuncture between the global and the local is also evident in a number of the more identifiable features of globalization – the proliferation of non-government organizations (NGOs), the use of computers and the internet to pursue political and social agendas, the increase in fundamentalist religious groups (including in the United States); and what we might term the '**turn to the local**' in politics and culture, which can be seen in the emergence of the Zapatistas in Mexico, ethnic conflicts in Eastern and Central Europe, and anti-EU sentiment in the United Kingdom. These do not seem readily explicable through reference to conventional theories of a globalized world, with universal values, but rather in terms of the post-modern notion that power, rather than being concentrated in the hands of a small number of transnational corporations (TNCs), or a country such as the United States, has 'gone elsewhere'.

The relative diffusion of power, and the extent to which states, groups and individuals are becoming (in Held and McGrew's terms) 'increasingly enmeshed in worldwide systems and networks of interaction', was evident in the ways in which the United States and its allies, and President George W. Bush in particular, responded to the 11 September attacks. In his initial statements Bush was reasonably subdued, talking about the United States finding out which 'folks' had done this – a response which didn't go down well with many commentators in the media, or with many US citizens, who had clearly expected the President to 'talk tough', declare 'war on terrorism' and show the world the consequences of attacking the United States. Bush and his advisers quickly read and acted upon this sentiment, which resulted in the 'wanted, dead or alive' comment, the promises to strike against terrorism, and policies such as placing armed guards on commercial aircraft, and giving the military the option of shooting down planes they considered to be a threat to national security. But this gave rise to another unexpected response: Americans, already hesitant about flying, were suddenly faced with the prospect of shoot-outs inside aircraft, and being blown out of the sky by their own air force. The aviation and tourism industries, already in the process of shedding staff, were horrified; and this further exacerbated the free-fall of US and world markets.

And there were other local issues that overrode the global imperative. Just as Bush's attempt to build a coalition against global terrorism effectively 'ran away' from him, and was appropriated to further the interests of specific nations, so too in the American domestic sphere the rush on the part of journalists, sportspersons, entertainment celebrities and ordinary Americans to participate in the 'God bless America' phenomenon did not remain a purely patriotic gesture. Instead, there were two related developments, both seemingly antithetical to everything America stood for. The first was a crisis in the 'core business' of America, evidenced in the market collapse, the failure of corporations, and the decline in the dollar; the second was an increase in the power of the military, the CIA and the FBI at the expense of civil liberties.

In the months following the 11 September attacks Western nations increasingly backed away from their initial strong support for US retaliatory action, some US citizens began complaining about the restrictions on their freedom, the media (eventually) took an arguably more measured view of American military action, and Western leaders (including the former US Secretary of State Madeleine Albright) strongly criticized Bush's 'axis of evil' speech, and his plans to continue action against nations he designated as 'the enemy' (BBC News, 2002). Increasingly, Bush's actions seemed to be explicable in terms of their being a series of carefully staged performances of power and control which functioned to conceal the reality that no one person, state, alliance or sphere (not even Bush, capitalism, the 'free world', the West or America) was able to control or direct what was taking place.

We are in a sense back to Held and McGrew's 'puzzle' over the disjuncture between the discourses of globalization and the realities of localization, a disjuncture that is played out in the literature on globalization, and evidenced in the failure of authorized truths fully to silence alternative perspectives and actions. What we can identify in this disjuncture is that there is no clear chain of command operating within the globalized world. Despite imbalances of military and economic weight, power continually shifts from one site to another, and the world's regions, nations and organizations coexist more in an uneasy dynamic tension than in a vertical set of relations: in a grid rather than along a chain.

Just as there is no evidence that power is held in one site, unproblematically, so too no unproblematic, final or definitive statement can be made about globalization. Rather, what it means, and what effects it has, are determined and identified variously, depending on the perspective of those making such determinations and identifications. The politics thus associated with the use of the term 'globalization', and the problems this poses for researchers into the field, are of the same order as the problems and politics that John Frow has identified in his work on the term **postmodernism**. Because of the multiple and often contradictory positions held on postmodernism, he writes, 'It begins to look as though the very engagement with the term represents a trap: as though your words, whatever their content, have nothing to do but to roll through the clown's mouth into the groove waiting to receive them' (1997: 22). Frow goes on to write that, given the difficulty of engaging with such an established term, it might be better 'to practice a strategy of avoidance: to dismiss the concept as a non-concept, imprecise, incoherent, contradictory, lacking any real historical significance' (1997: 22). But he rejects the temptation to avoid the concept because:

> the very persistence of the word, however irritating this may be, seems to indicate that something is at stake, something that cannot be brushed aside as a theoretical fashion . . . It may be that the term is the index of a real epochal shift . . . or it may be that it indicates something less well defined, more obscure and more heterogeneous but nevertheless of genuine theoretical and practical interest. (1997: 23)

Though he is referring only to postmodernism, the same could be said of globalization: if a term is being used so often, in so many theatres, and with such profound effects, it is worth paying attention to it. In this book we attempt to do just this: to pay attention to the term and to the politics of its deployment and its effects. But rather than attempting to craft a unitary and definitive statement about globalization, we will suggest, following Hardt and Negri's description in their book *Empire* (which we discuss in the next chapter) that it should be understood as a kind of grid of power, one which incorporates globalists and sceptics, liberals and Marxists, libertarians and fundamentalists, First and Third World nations and their economies, and so on, all within a dynamic and often agonistic relationship.

Conclusion

In this chapter we have focused on the politics of naming as it applies to globalization, and discussed the extent to which naming not only brings the thing named into social existence, but forecloses other possibilities. We have also outlined the multiplicity of perspectives held on globalization, and the various definitions deployed in making sense of the term, and of the politics and practices associated with it. But while theorists from a range of disciplines – including international relations, politics, media studies, economics, cultural studies, sociology, developmental studies, communication, geography and history – have offered different explanations and evaluations of the processes associated with globalization, there is still general agreement that any discussion of the term needs to take into account the following issues: technology and changes in the way people experience and understand time/space; the ways in which such changes have influenced capitalism; globalization as ideology; globalization as a form of colonialism; the relationship between global forces and the sovereignty of the state; global (in)security and the actualities and possibilities of global governance; the media and the idea of a global 'public sphere'; and the emergence, throughout the world, of a coalition of forces opposed to different aspects of globalization.

We will consider all these theories and issues, in detail, in the chapters that follow, and attempt to devise a way of analysing the logic of the 'grid' that is the concept of global-ization. In the next chapter we will contextualize the agonistics over the meaning of globalization by making comparisons between relevant historical precedents, most particularly with the period 1870–1914, and the technological, economic, social, political and cultural changes of the last thirty years.

2

Globalization: History and Ideology

In our previous chapter we suggested that globalization could be understood as a set of technologies, institutions and networks operating within, and at the same time transforming, contemporary social, cultural, political and economic spheres of activity. But we also stressed that globalization is as much a set of ideas, and ways of discussing these ideas, so that the changes, and the consequences associated with them, need to be contextualized within what we termed 'the politics of naming'. In other words, it is the evaluation and interpretation – the naming – of those technologies, institutions and networks as socially, culturally, economically and historically identifiable phenomena that in a sense bring globalization into being, or make it real to most people.

The efficacy of this naming process depends, predominantly, on power relations. If the United States, for instance, named a state or organization as 'terrorist', this could have serious consequences for the people who had been so named because the United States has the political, economic and military means to render that naming effective – to make its views a widely shared reality. But as theorists such as Michel Foucault have demonstrated, the workings of power are not simply a matter of relative military or economic muscle; rather, they are very much tied up with, and dependent upon, the institutions, knowledges and discourses which legitimate them. In this chapter we look at the ways in which the discourses of **neoliberalism** make use of history to naturalize and define the project of globalization. And in particular we look at how this attempted naturalization of globalization is connected with, and largely driven by, institutions and groups associated with the logic of neoliberalism.

A precedent of sorts comes out of the work of Edward Said, who in writing about nineteenth-century European colonialist activities points out that these activities were facilitated not just by the military power of European nations, but more importantly by a body of knowledge and a form of reason that legitimated them, and which he calls 'Orientalism'. **Orientalism** provided the thinking tools through which the world could be conveniently divided up into us/them, rational/irrational, centre/periphery, the West/the rest. Central to Orientalist discourses, logics and world views was a reading of the present in terms of its relation to the past and to the future, so that European states justified their intervention in places such as China, India and Egypt in terms of what we can call a 'teleological' reading of history. In other words, they saw all the activities of the present and the past as moving ineluctably towards a necessary future in which their own world views, religious beliefs, social and economic practices, values and principles would be universally shared. How this worked in practice was that while the European colonialists might well acknowledge that China, India and Egypt were the sites of great cultural and technological achievements which had shaped the present, they would insist that the torch of civilization had now passed on to Europe. The contemporary Orient and its peoples, cultures and societies, they would argue, were backward, decadent and irrational, and so the future of civilization depended upon Europe bringing the 'light of reason' to 'areas of darkness' (which generally meant Asia, Africa, Australia, New Zealand, the Pacific; that is, everywhere that wasn't Europe). This meant that European intervention in, or subjugation of, other areas of the world was justified: such activities were really little more than 'history at work', and therefore inevitable, irreversible and, most importantly, universally beneficial.

What is neoliberalism?

A similar logic is operating today, in the form of a body of knowledge and form of reason that underpin international relations and understandings and that can be termed 'neo-liberalism'. We define this as the movement towards, and the coming into being of, a particular idea of freedom as unfettered circulation, particularly of capital and goods.

Neoliberalism, like Orientalism, categorizes the world in terms of the politics of difference. But where the older approach drew a fairly simple division between the Occident and the Orient, neoliberalism divides the world several ways. Mike Moore, director-general of the World Trade Organization (WTO), pointed out this hard face of 'free' trade, and the gulf between the discourse of neoliberalism and its practices, in a documentary screened on Australia's SBS television channel on 11 September 2001 (a few hours, in Australian time, before the news of the World Trade Center attacks hit the airwaves). In pointing out the many problems in the free-trade principle, he noted that each nation in the WTO has one vote; but while, say, Morocco may be able to afford to send only one delegate, the United States and other powerful nations will send a battery of experts further supported by communication technology, and so will inevitably be advantaged in any negotiations. And while the WTO officially forbids trade barriers, it cannot ban import taxes, which makes it difficult or impossible for poorer nations to trade in the areas where they should have a comparative advantage – textiles, for instance, or agriculture, which are precisely the areas protected by wealthy countries.

Moore discussed the case of Moroccan tomato growers, who ought, under WTO rules, to have free access to markets in Europe, but have been bound by a series of restrictions which mean they can export their products to Europe for only six months of the year, and this mainly during the cold months – when of course they can't export, because they have limited means of storage. The lack of technology and chemicals means they can't produce year-round, and can't manage their export by holding back stock for later sale. European producers, on the

23

other hand, have both technology – and will, for instance, grow tomatoes year-round in greenhouses – and storage, and so are considerably advantaged. And because Morocco lacks the capacity to impose effective trade restrictions, its producers are liable to be swamped year-round with European products – including, ironically, canned tomatoes. Free trade, manifestly, works only when and as it suits the wealthy; and is 'free' only for those already on the trade train – and yet it continues to be mooted as 'good for us all', on the grounds that liberalization in trade ensures competition, which is essential for trade and hence for development. In short, free/competitive trade works to increase power differentials while supposedly bringing about universal development – much as Orientalism justified military, cultural, economic and social domination and exploitation in the name of (technologically driven) progress.

The neoliberal focus on the economy as central to the workings of society was made patently clear after the 11 September attacks on New York and the dip in the finance market across the Western world. The reopening of the New York Stock Exchange was promoted not just as a market moment, but also as a demonstration of America's resilience in the face of terrorism, complete with prayers, songs and demonstrations of nationalism:

> With minutes to go before the historic reopening, dealers put on a defiant show, clapping their hands as they pushed through the crowds, signalling their collective relief to be alive and to play their part in America's fightback against terrorism. . . . [Dick Grasso, chairman of the Exchange] called a two minute-long silence in memory of the estimated 5,000 people who lost their lives on September 11. The impeccably observed silence was ended by a rendition of 'God bless America', a song that has overtaken 'The Star-spangled Banner' as the national anthem over the past week. (Milmo, 2001)

This equation of the market with nationalism, and of the stock-broker with the warrior, isn't peculiar to America; the Australian

Treasurer, when asked about the effects of 11 September on Australia, said:

> My message to Australian consumers would be that we had a strong growth in June, our housing cycle is going well, our interest rates are going low, they are at historical lows and, so, in relation to all of those matters, it is quite a good time to .. continue your spending. And I know the events have been terrible, they have shocked the world, they have shocked us all, but that is no reason to change your buying behaviour. (Costello, 2001)

This contextualizing of human suffering and death in terms of our 'buying behaviour' can be seen as an exemplar of neo-liberalism – it aspires to the liberation of money and entrepreneurship from social contexts and their obligations. The freedom of neoliberalism is a freedom that, as philosopher Michael Polanyi puts it, aims to liberate us from everything, even 'from obligations toward truth and justice, reducing reason to its own caricature: to a mere rationalization of positions that were actually predetermined by desire and were held – or secured – by force alone' (Polanyi and Prosch, 1975: 14).

In other words, the central mechanism of neoliberalism is not freedom *per se*, but an unbounded economy; its central logic is that individuals, ideas and the movements of the market are inextricably bound together; and its central project, according to many theorists, is 'the creation of a global free market and the consolidation of Anglo-American capitalism within the world's major economic regions' (Held and McGrew, 2000: 5); or, more bluntly, 'the ideology of rule by the world market' (Beck, 2000: 100).

Neoliberal discourses, like those associated with Oriental-ism, are predicated on a particular and limiting notion of history: for both these ways of understanding and managing power relations, history is confined to only a few 'stories'. The story for Orientalism is about the steady decay of Oriental cultures and the inevitable rise of Europe; for neoliberalism, it is the story about a 'freedom' which sweeps everybody and everything along in its wake. Pierre Bourdieu writes about the way in which neoliberalism abstracts itself from history, behaving as though all history can be explained in terms of neoliberal discourses and practices, when he describes neoliberal ideology as an 'initially desocialized and dehistoricized "theory"' with the 'means of making itself true' (1998a: 95). In other words, neoliberalism claims to explain history, but prevents history from explaining or accounting for neoliberalism. This, of course, is very effective in establishing the dominance of its discourses, because if its historical grounding is manifest, then it can't be seen as ahistorical, inevitable or irreversible.

Globalization and history

History is thus a very useful and important adjunct to, and aspect of, the politics of naming, which explains why debates about the meaning of globalization invariably revolve around, and appeal to, the notion of history. Armand Mattelart addresses this in a number of his books (specifically, *Networking the World*, *The Invention of Communication*, *Rethinking Media Theory* and *Mapping World Communication*) where he performs what Foucault would call the **archaeological** exercise of demonstrating where neoliberalism and globalization came from. That is, he traces their genesis in social, political and cultural contexts and developments; identifies how they were tied in with, and worked to promote, technological developments; and shows how they were used at different times to further the interests of specific groups – especially capitalists, colonialists, governments and the military.

For Mattelart, globalization emerges out of the **Enlightenment** and liberalism, both of which, he argues, 'aimed at the construction of an unrestricted global arena' (2000: 1) to achieve universal democracy and/or a universal market. Mattelart locates the neoliberal project of globalization in a particular historical moment, and tied up with historical interests; and traces how this particularity came to universalize itself as the defining characteristic of Western society, politics and culture. This grounding of neoliberalism in historical practices undoes what Bourdieu identifies as the dehistoricizing of discourses, effectively preventing it from appearing ahistorical and hence inevitable.

An example of this archaeology can be seen in *Networking the World*, where Mattelart demonstrates how writers from across a variety of times, disciplines, political leanings and nationalities – from French Enlightenment writers such as Diderot, Rousseau and Voltaire to British economists such as Adam Smith and John Stuart Mill – drew a direct connection between the perfectibility of the human race and developments in science, technology and communications. While their utopian discourses and narratives took a variety of forms and inflections, generally they were predicated upon the emergence of infrastructure that facilitated communication flows – newspapers, roads, canals and later railways, undersea cables and international languages. But what is particularly striking is the very close relationship assumed by these writers between 'universal reason' and economic development. As Mattelart records, Adam Smith (the 'father' of economics) maintained that the growth of what he termed the 'universal mercantile republic' would overcome and replace the old relationship of military force between nations, and so, in the interests of stable trade, nations would cease to make war (Mattelart, 2000: 5). Rather than being identified as citizens of a (potentially military) state, we would become 'an economic community composed of consumers' (Mattelart, 2000: 6). This attitude was taken up and developed by writers who followed Adam Smith, and still has considerable valence at the beginning of the twenty-first century.

Still, by providing a 'family tree' for neoliberalism, and showing the long tradition of connecting reason, freedom, economic growth and international interaction, we can come to understand that there is nothing inevitable, or necessary, about the global neoliberal project. Rather, it is the outcome of a particular manner of thinking which was in the interests of, and justified the actions of, powerful institutions. What we see in studying the history of neoliberalism is the use of reason and a utopian discourse to justify the setting free of the economic field from social, national and humanitarian obligations.

There are three main ways in which history is put to work to make sense of globalization. Two come from avowed critics of globalization who can be categorized as either Marxist in origin (and hence focus closely on the economic sphere), or those with more heterogeneous concerns (who look equally at the cultural, social and governmental spheres). We will trace the first group by looking at the work first of Immanuel Wallerstein, and then of Michael Hardt and Antonio Negri, and the second by discussing aspects of the work of Pierre Bourdieu. Members of the third group take a perspective on globalization that can be termed 'sociohistorical', and whether or not they criticize globalization, they see it as a historical reality, and are concerned to identify the various contexts and contents of its processes. We will describe this approach to the use of history by tracing the work of those writers Held and McGrew have called the 'globalists'.

The first way: Marxist uses of history

The use of history to critique neoliberal versions of globalization has its origins in traditional Marxist theory, most particularly in the work of Immanuel Wallerstein who, like Mattelart, undertakes a kind of archaeology of globalization. Wallerstein traces the trends in human societies, and argues that the defining characteristic of all social systems is the division of labour in a sphere of economic exchange. There are, he writes, only two ways in which societies are organized: as what he calls **minisystems** where division of labour and economic exchange occur only within a discrete group – we might think here of traditional and isolated hunter-gatherer societies – which, he writes, were always rare and are now virtually non-existent; and **worldsystems**. This is a central tenet of his view of history and of globalization; he argues that, except for the occasional minisystems, economic exchange has always been able to occur across political and cultural barriers (2000: 233). This doesn't mean, of course, that he identifies just one pattern of world-systems; rather, he offers a catch-all definition – 'a unit with a single division of labour and multiple cultural systems' (2000: 233) – but distinguishes various ways of operationalizing it. Most particularly, he distinguishes between contemporary patterns and the world-systems of the ancient world, where imperial might dominated economic exchange, and the economic structure worked redistributively (transferring goods and wealth from the empire to the imperial centre). The modern form of world-system is capitalist rather than military-imperial, and is genuinely international and distributive; in the place of military forces and trade routes we now have tentacles of trade and exchange criss-crossing the globe.

This modern form, Wallerstein argues, emerged in Europe along with the social changes (the movement away from feudalism), global exploration and the rise of trade that began during the sixteenth century. The crucial aspect here was that the motive force behind economic (and, as a consequence, social, cultural and political) activity was capitalism of and for itself, as opposed to economic activity of and for an empire, nation or state:

> capital has never allowed its aspirations to be determined by national boundaries in a capitalist world-economy, and . . . the creation of 'national' barriers – generically, mercantilism – has historically been a defensive mechanism of capitalists located in states which are one level below the high point of strength in the system. (Wallerstein, 2000: 235)

In other words, the various forms of European expansion that occurred from the sixteenth century onward, and the competition between states, can be understood not just as the results of the imperial aspirations of various European nations, but as effects of their relative positions within the world economy.

This 'archaeology' becomes particularly interesting for contemporary students of globalization when Wallerstein describes the bases for the stability of the world-system. There are, he writes, three main reasons for its (relative) stability. Probably the least important of these is also the most obvious – the military strength of economically dominant states. The other two are far more relevant to our discussions about, and understanding of, contemporary globalization. Firstly, he argues that the world-system is structured in terms of three main strata, or categories – core, semi-periphery and periphery – and that nations and regions are categorized as such on the basis of their relative position within the world economy, and on their specific internal political and economic characteristics. What is significant about this categorization is that the upper stratum can maximize their economic benefit by using the lower stratum, and maintain stability by playing the lower strata off against one another. In a sense this is an extension of the old colonial game of limiting the possibility of local people organizing resistance against the colonizers by setting up one local group as preferred subjects, and using them to police the other local groups – thus effectively disrupting traditional ways of coexistence, and incidentally setting in place ongoing patterns of aggression, the antagonistic relations between the Shona and Matabele people of Zimbabwe being a case in point. In the contemporary 'global' context, the upper strata are more likely to undertake the same sorts of practice by establishing trade blocs, which forces poorer nations to undercut one another to win preferential status.

This 'playing off' will only work if there is a general belief in the legitimacy of the system, and a commitment to it; and this is the second reason Wallerstein provides for its ongoing stability. If groups or individuals feel that 'their own well-being is wrapped up in the survival of the system as such' (2000: 237), then they will be motivated to protect and maintain its stability; and it is the work of ideology to 'convince' the members of the world-system that its structures and patterns are both legitimate and natural. Wallerstein is relatively sceptical about the extent to which ideology is able to work for members of the lower stratum, but the commitment and belief of the middle stratum (which is both exploiter and exploited) is crucial.

We can see this process in action in the political, cultural and social activities that followed the 11 September attacks in the United States in 2001. Responding to the attacks, the United

States co-opted states like Britain, Australia, Japan and Canada – its closest allies and part of Wallerstein's 'core' stratum – in its 'war against terrorism'. This core group can also, generally, be assumed to have an ideological investment in the maintenance of the world-system, since they reap considerable benefits from the *status quo*. But it is not enough for the core to wield their power alone; and if this initial co-optation had been all that the United States had done, it would only have polarized the international community by setting Christianity against Islam, the North against the South, the West against the rest, and so on. The United States was determined to put together a global front; and particularly concerned that this front should incorporate the 'semi-periphery' – Islamic states (such as Pakistan, Indonesia and Saudi Arabia) and 'developing' states (Indonesia again, and Uzbekistan) – to provide material, strategic or discursive support. These groups/states can be assumed to have a certain investment in the status quo, and a willingness (or necessity) to support the core by working against the periphery – the groups that were demonized and remained 'the enemy' (Hamas, the Taliban, Iraq, Syria, Iran, the Islamic Jihad). The alliance of the semi-periphery not only justifies the actions of the core, but also 'proves' the success of global capitalism and internationalism by drawing out a demonstration of commitment from those who are not obviously advantaged by its terms.

Wallerstein's tracing of the conflictual nature of global organization and relations goes some way to problematizing the continued argument that free trade is good for all. But world-systems theory doesn't provide a satisfactory explanation of globalization, because it effectively subsumes all social, cultural and political spheres and activities under, and explains them in terms of, the sphere of economic relations. A more comprehensive Marxist account of the complexities of the relationship between the economic, political, cultural and social spheres is Michael Hardt and Antonio Negri's *Empire* (2000).

We argued in the previous chapter that the various practices, institutions and discourses associated with globalization can be understood as a machine-like grid of power which incorporates and transforms politics, economics and the social (and its many aspects such as culture, civil society and subjectivity). Michael Hardt and Antonio Negri analyse and historically locate this phenomenon in terms of what they call the system and hierarchy of **Empire**. Their work informs all of the areas we cover in this book, but most particularly those of capitalism, sovereignty, subjectivity and the media, and we will deal with their specific 'takes' on these topics in the relevant chapters. At this point, however, we want to provide a brief introduction to the concept of Empire, and explain its relation to our understanding of globalization.

The first and most important point that Hardt and Negri make is that Empire is different from previous forms of state-driven imperialism:

> In contrast to imperialism, Empire establishes no territorial centre of power and does not rely on fixed boundaries or barriers. It is a decentred and deterritorializing apparatus of rule that progressively incorporates the entire global realm within its open, expanding frontier. Empire arranges hybrid identities, flexible hierarchies, and plural exchanges through modulatory networks of command. The distinct national colors of the imperial map of the world have merged and blended in the imperial global rainbow. (Hardt and Negri, 2000: xiii)

Empire must be understood as a move beyond, and as something irreducible to, state sovereignty. While it is acknowledged that a state such as the United States, for instance, occupies a considerably privileged position within Empire, this is largely because the United States, as it is constituted (as an ever-expanding and heterogeneous society largely driven by capitalist imperatives), is very different from the old European imperial powers, and provides a kind of template for Empire. But everywhere else the inability of nation-states to control or manage their economic, political, social and cultural affairs is a symptom of the more or less terminal decline of state sovereignty, and the ascent of Empire. Indeed, for Hardt and Negri, globalization *is* Empire. Empire, then, can be understood as the political form of globalization – although, as Hardt and Negri suggest, the logic of global capitalism pervades the social, cultural and political spheres to such an extent that any formal separation of, say, the economic from the political, is effectively meaningless.

Hardt and Negri attribute four main characteristics to Empire. Firstly, they understand it as both a system and a hierarchy; that is to say, it is like a machine with its own logic (values, imperatives and modes of operation), which organizes the global world and orders it within this logic (through decisions about where investment is to flow, which government is to be supported, or which areas are to be networked).

Secondly, Empire processes cultures, crises, resources and power formations in order to reproduce and extend itself. Every conflict or form of difference is incorporated into Empire, which in turn serves as another push towards, and justification of, the global extension of its power and authority. Empire is able to do this because it presents itself as universal, ahistorical and inevitable; that is to say, as the only solution to, or authority able to mediate conflict, crisis, inequity, violence, poverty, injustice and suffering. Empire is both a universal form of reason (associated with concepts and values such as the Enlightenment, civilization, democracy and human rights) and an ineluctable, and therefore uncontestable, grid of power (resistance is futile – history is over).

Thirdly, and in keeping with the logic of the erasure of time and space supposedly brought about by developments in communication technology, Empire is decentred and boundless. As we suggested earlier, Empire relies neither on fixed boundaries nor on centres of power. The United States may occupy a privileged position within Empire, but power is diffused throughout the many apparatuses, organizations and agents. The United States is only one of a number of identities (including nation-states, institutions of global governance, NGOs and transnational corporations) which influence the exercising of power; and the United States is itself affected by Empire – for example, by being subject to the fluctuations of the market. The real-time electronic flow of investment capital is a symptom of the way in which Empire has overcome, and has no need of, spatial categories.

Fourthly, and perhaps most importantly, Empire is constituted by, and constitutive of, the imbrication of the economic, political and cultural aspects of contemporary life. In order to explain how this is carried out, Hardt and Negri make use of the Foucauldian distinction between older and more contemporary disciplinary regimes. In the old order, normativities inculcated through the work of institutions such as hospitals, schools and prisons attempted to delimit what could be thought; there were external forms of control and discipline. In the newer 'society of control', however, control of behaviour and thought is internalized: subjects are now produced through, and continuously tied into, networks which more or less serve to affirm and naturalize the logics of Empire. The economic and political values and imperatives that characterize Empire saturate not just cultural texts, but also the sites such as the media and communication networks which largely constitute the civic space of the contemporary global world.

The second way: cultural theory and history

While writers such as Bourdieu and Mattelart would concur with Wallerstein, and Hardt and Negri, in critiquing the relationship between neoliberal ideology and the exploitative and hegemonic sociopolitical practices associated with various forms of colonialism, they take somewhat different approaches. Bourdieu specifically rejects what he calls the 'fatalism' (1998a: 50) of Marxist readings of history, and draws a parallel between traditional Marxism and neoliberalism, arguing that the flows of power and the movements of history are not (as both these positions would hold) tied directly and unequivocally to the economic sphere. Rather, they are relatively heterogeneous, dynamic and open-ended. To address this, he brings his critical attention to areas outside the strictly economic, targeting the state, the media, the arts, education and other fields of sociocultural activity, and drawing on means other than economic analysis – such as the effects of discourses, the weight of **cultural capital**, or various forms of **symbolic violence** – to explain domination and the exercise of power. The term he gives to the combination of discourses, ideas and values that both naturalize and reproduce power imbalances is **doxa**. Bourdieu explains the term in this way: 'By using doxa we accept many things without knowing them, and that is what is called ideology' (Bourdieu and Eagleton, 1994: 268); or, as Zygmunt Bauman defines it, doxa is simply 'an evidence not debated and undebatable' (1998: 99). If something is simply accepted, simply undebatable, then it can seriously disadvantage people without their being able to resist the circumstances that distress them; it is seen as 'just the way things are', and people submit to it the way they submit to the weather: not necessarily happily, but all the same adjusted to the circumstances.

Doxa is a useful way to 'read' the sociopolitical world, in order to bring into question all the unspoken, undebated assumptions that underpin the practices of the dominant; and for Bourdieu, the most influential and pervasive doxa in the contemporary world is neoliberalism. He looks to language and the media as central factors in the process by which it has become established as a doxa, quoting various reports to the effect that a company which sacks its workers is 'slimming', or being 'flexible', or mobilizing a 'bold social plan' (1998a: 30–1). This sort of reportage effectively positions economic activities as the central, or indeed only, activities that are worthy of attention; other areas – education, health, the national interest – are rendered secondary or overlooked. And the process of naming that brings about this taken-for-grantedness is based on euphemisms which direct attention away from the negative social effects of economic competition and the goal of maximum profit, and which is consequently difficult to critique. If there is general agreement that 'boldness' and 'flexibility', for instance, are good things, then it is difficult to resist the actions of a company which aggressively assaults the rights and needs of workers or the developing world, or which overrides the concerns of particular nations. Being laid off, or breathing the poisoned air at Bhopal, may cause us individual distress, but it is often easier to displace the source of that distress from the actions of a capitalist system to somewhere else: my own bad luck, my own incompetence, a mistake . . . And in this way, Bourdieu writes, certain discourses and practices become established as doxa, and everyday people in their everyday lives tend simply to accept them, and to accommodate themselves to the distress they may be caused.

This process of becoming accommodated to the 'ontologizing' of the global market mentality as that which drives progress, civilization and universal emancipation can be seen in the discourses of authorized speakers; we might identify here politicians such as Thatcher, Gore, Bush and Blair, or writers like Francis Fukuyama. But it can also be found in the work of academic proponents of the benefits of globalization, even when they seem to make no overt reference to, or even seem to be arguing against, the 'grand narratives' of globalization. In 'The end of the nation state', for instance, Kenichi Ohmae dismisses Fukuyama's (often repeated) characterization of our time as having reached 'the end of history' with the end of the Cold War and the 'triumph' of capitalism. Ohmae writes, 'Nothing could be further from the truth' (2000: 238) because with the development of global capital and communication technologies, there is a massive rise in the numbers of people from around the world who are actively, even aggressively, participating in 'history' to demand:

> a decent life for themselves and a better life for their children. A generation ago, even a decade ago, most of them were as voiceless and invisible as they had always been. This is true no longer: they have entered history with a vengeance and they have demands – economic demands – to make. (2000: 239)

What is interesting in Ohmae's argument is the notion that all these people want to be 'globalized', or at least share the benefits of globalization. This presumes that all people and cultures necessarily subscribe to a capitalist, commodity-driven world view, and that peoples and cultures outside capitalism have necessarily lived, as he writes, in 'obscurity' and 'isolation'. It also presumes that they enter the stage of history only when they give voice to their desire to embrace capitalism and its benefits. What Ohmae's account does is mimic those Orientalist discourses identified by Said, in which peoples and cultures can be understood and evaluated only in terms of their relation to the 'civilized West'. And just as it was the 'moral duty' of colonialism to rescue China, India, Egypt and other parts of the world from ignorance and savagery, similarly the market takes on the more or less 'spiritual duty' of sharing the benefits of development with those 'living in obscurity in forest and desert and rural isolation' (Ohmae, 2000: 239).

Another less overt but in some ways equally symptomatic exemplification of the way in which neoliberal discourse informs the analysis of globalization and its processes can be found in Elaine Ciulla Karmack's 'Globalization and public administration reform'. Karmack gives an account of what she terms the attempts of governments to reform public bureau-cracies and institutions in the 1980s and 1990s, noting, to her surprise, that 'These countries have different histories and different electoral systems; they are at different stages of devel-opment and yet . . . they are employing a set of reform concepts and strategies that are remarkably similar' (2000: 229). What she is referring to here are the 'reforms' initiated by Margaret Thatcher in Britain and Ronald Reagan in the United States; reforms copied, and sometimes outdone, by zealots such as the governments in New Zealand and Australia. But it is not really surprising that the strategies employed by different govern-ments were so 'remarkably similar'. The bottom line of neoliberalism is to 'get government out of business' or, more generally, away from controlling or intervening in the affairs of business; and each government was driven by the same neo-liberal ideology. Secondly, and as a corollary, each government's reforms involved the reasonably predictable neoliberal goals of downsizing or privatizing public institutions, services and utilities such as airlines and telecommunications. The third issue is that a failure to embrace the imperative to 'reform' bureau-cracies could involve negative consequences for those failing to comply. As Jeff Garten, author of *The Lexus and the Olive Tree*, wrote, 'The world needs to walk away from countries unwilling to make serious changes' (cited Nye and Donohue, 2000: 232), and few nations with an investment in the world system would be willing to have that system walk away. So we are less surprised than is Karmack by the similarity of reforms undertaken by the governments concerned.

The extent to which neoliberal ideology 'speaks' Karmack – and thus renders her unable to provide an objective critique of these practices – is exemplified by the way she unquestioningly reproduces the characterization of a former Treasury Secretary of New Zealand of government involvement in airlines and other services as 'a problem'. She writes:

> As capitalism and market mechanisms gained popularity throughout the world, the contrast between the perceived clarity and efficiency of a competitive market and the multiple, obscure goals and inefficiency of government monopolies no doubt added to the general belief that government was not performing as it should. (2000: 235)

Here we can see that Karmack sets the 'perceived clarity and efficiency' (of private capital) against the 'obscure goals and inefficiency' (of government) without identifying what is at stake in the privatizing of infrastructure, or measuring the effects of the extension of the market into all aspects of life. In this, she provides an example of doxa, and of what Bourdieu describes as 'desocialized and dehistoricized theory', at work: she not only presumes the teleologically driven, beneficial effects of privatization but simultaneously edits out the negative social effects associated with it. Consider Karmack's description and characterization of what she terms the 'pathbreaking' efforts of the New Zealand government in the 1980s:

> A Labor government in New Zealand started the country along a dramatic road to recovery. It cut subsidies, reduced taxes, and opened its economy to trade. Not only did it privatize previously owned state industries – it did not stop

there. New Zealand has gone further than any other country in the world in privatizing its government. (2000: 233)

Karmack doesn't explain specifically what the reforms have achieved – she simply states that they have become 'nearly as popular an export as sheep' (2000: 248). There is no reference to the human costs of such policies (high unemployment and underemployment, or the loss of services under a user-pays system), or their more recent consequences, which have included the near demise of Air New Zealand (which, ironically, was forced to seek financial support from the government), the virtual extinction of the national rail system, the collapse in early 1998 of the power grid in its major city, Auckland, inequities in the health system, and the demoralization of the tertiary education sector, to name a few. Karmack doesn't seem to feel the need to explain how or why the privatization of government is necessarily a good thing. But in a sense, of course, she doesn't have to: history, explicable in terms of what Bourdieu calls the 'fatalistic doctrine' (1998a: 50) which is built on the imbrication of the concepts of freedom, liberation, deregulation, acts as her guarantor.

The third way: globalist perspectives

It is not only critics of globalization and neoliberalism who appeal to, and make use of, history. David Held and Anthony McGrew point out that some globalist perspectives also recognize that analysis of the development of globalization:

> involves drawing on a knowledge of what differentiates these discrete phases, including how such systems and patterns of global interconnectedness are organized and reproduced, their different geographies and histories, and the changing configuration of interregional power relations. (2000: 7)

They refer to writers such as Modelski, Hodgson, Bentley, Frank and Gills, Mazlish and Buultjens, and Clark, but we could include names such as Russell Robertson, Kevin O'Rourke and Jeffrey Williamson in this category of what we term the 'third way' of using or appealing to history as a means of explicating globalization. Its recognition of the constantly changing patterns of international relations, and the tensions necessarily raised by interaction, runs counter to the neoliberal ideology that globalization can be understood as a 'preordained logic' leading to 'a single world society or global civilization' (Held and McGrew, 2000: 7). From the globalist perspective, globalization is certainly a 'reality'; history provides plenty of evidence, from the period of European 'discovery' of the world to the present, of trends and tendencies towards the establishment of patterns of global interconnectedness which have transformed societies and cultures worldwide.

But history, as these theorists point out, also makes it clear that the processes of globalization are more or less contingent. That is to say, they produce different effects on different groups at different times. For instance, we cannot simply equate the military imperialism of the eighteenth and nineteenth centuries with contemporary Western cultural imperialism. Nor has there been steady and inevitable movement towards a globalized world: the processes of globalization have been resisted – for instance, by nationalism movements in the twentieth century; rolled back – as was the case with the end of the *belle époque* and the beginning of World War I in 1914; or 'taken elsewhere' – as in Michel de Certeau's example of the native South Americans' particular version of Christianity. The usefulness of history, from this perspective, is that it confirms the existence of globalization as a long-term phenomenon, and also allows analysts to isolate and differentiate what is specific to its contemporary manifestations.

The difference between this sociohistorical reading of globalization and that offered by neoliberalism can be summed up by saying that neoliberalism understands globalization as an embodiment of the spirit of freedom which drives history; sociohistorical globalism, in contrast, stresses the ways in which history drives, shapes and transforms (and sometimes curtails) globalization. But how does the globalist approach differ from the work of critics such as Bourdieu and Mattelart? The most useful way of understanding this is through reference to their varying relation to the notion of 'critique', as Foucault understands it; that is, as 'something akin to an investigation into what we are (how we think, what we value, how we understand ourselves, how we treat others). But it also means thinking about what else we might be – how we could be different from ourselves' (Danaher et al., 2000: 10).

Critiquing globalization

When discussing the extent to which these writers engage in critique, we need to consider the notion of foreclosure, which we introduced in our previous chapter. This is what analysts such as Karmack and Ohmae are practising when they edit out the social consequences of a market-dominated world (such as Karmack's argument that private capital is efficient), or universalize a particular set of values and agendas (Ohmae's idea that people in the forests and deserts 'want to be like us'). These two aspects of foreclosure – the universalizing of 'us', and the exclusion of 'them' – do not come about without effects; they are tied up with a politics, which, many writers argue, leads inevitably to resistance, and indeed to the sorts of terrorist action we saw on 11 September 2001.

An alternative approach to the sociohistorical aspects of globalization, and one which is closer to Foucault's notion of critique, can be seen in the writings of a number of contemporary theorists who have addressed terrorism and its roots, and critiqued the media characterization of terrorists as irrational cowards or misguided zealots. Pierre Bourdieu, for example, locates the motive force of terror in the despair of those excluded, by Western claims to universal reason and justice, from reason and justice (1998a: 20). For Jean Baudrillard, terrorism is the inevitable outcome of our world system: 'Wherever exchange is impossible,' he writes, 'what we encounter is terror' (1993: 128); and effectively it 'punches a hole between first and third worlds' (1993: 82). If the First World will not engage on the

41

terms it itself promulgates – freedom and equality – then, Baudrillard writes, we can expect only this sort of response, one which makes terrifyingly visible the way in which the discourses of globalization have foreclosed their circumstances. What Bourdieu and Baudrillard do here, in contrast to the globalists, is what we referred to as 'critique', because they firstly undertake a 'historical analysis of the limits imposed on us', and then experiment with the possibility of going beyond' those limits (Foucault, cited in Danaher et al., 2000: 10–11). Critique as practised by writers such as Baudrillard, Bourdieu and Mattelart can be understood as the analysis and evaluation of, and an attempt to intervene with regard to, a problem or issue. In this case, what is at stake is the relationship between history, neoliberal ideology and the contemporary practices of globalization. Their critique is oriented towards something political and practical; that is, they attempt to understand the limits that constitute what we are, in order to find ways of going beyond those limits.

This 'practicality' sets them apart from most sociohistorical accounts of globalization, which tend to be informed by what Bourdieu refers to as the 'scholastic point of view' (1998c: 127). What he means by this is that scholarly work can be a kind of language game almost exclusively involved in and for itself, rather than undertaken with a practical dimension and designed to enable us to understand and deal with problems and difficulties. The 'scholastic' approach can be found in numerous accounts of globalization as/and history, and what distinguishes these researches from those characterized by critique is the building up of (usually historically comparative) data about such matters as the levels of world economic integration, or the extent to which increases in integration have brought about a concomitant decrease in social and economic inequalities. The pre-eminent concerns of these accounts, whether they emanate from the disciplines of history, sociology, economics or communications, are twofold. Firstly they seek to identify, analyse and evaluate the available evidence in order to come to some conclusions to questions such as whether globalization exists or not; whether it is a new phenomenon or can be traced back to, say, the Crusades; whether there was greater economic integration in the *belle époque* period of 1870–1914 than in history to that point, and subsequently. And secondly, they attempt to identify and evaluate the consequences of proliferating global forces and processes on everyday social, cultural, political and economic activities.

Two presumptions are behind this approach. The first is that economic, cultural and social changes are carried along or brought about by irreversible technological development. This is what Jonathan Crary refers to as 'technological determinism', in which 'an independent dynamic of mechanical invention, modification, and perfection imposes itself on to a social field, transforming it from the outside' (1990: 8). The second presumption is that this process of change is susceptible to 'scientific explication'; that is, it is consistent, systematic and explicable, and can be detected through rigorous historical and statistical analyses and comparisons. Held and McGrew's discussion of the globalist approach is an example of this scholastic point of view in practice. They write that globalist analysts 'attempt to establish a more systematic specification of the concept of globalization' by drawing on 'socio-historical modes of analysis' to measure social, political and economic change:

> To understand contemporary globalization involves drawing on a knowledge of what differentiates [its] discrete phases, including how such systems and patterns of global interconnectedness are organized and reproduced, their different geographies and histories, and the changing configuration of interregional power relations. (2000: 6–7)

The interesting thing about their account is that while they are clearly attached to the notion of a rigorous, scientific line of inquiry, expressed in terms such as 'systematic specification' or 'socio-historical modes of analysis', the notion of whether there is in fact a reality of globalization is never interrogated. Rather than starting with an analysis of social and economic practices, and then working out the motivations for such changes, they start with the presumption that globalization exists and has particular effects, and then gather evidence to prove that it does in fact exist. Held and McGrew are at pains in this characterization to stress that the globalists are very different from the promoters of neoliberal discourse, writing that 'at the core of the globalist account lies a concern with power: its instrumentalities, configurations, distribution, and impacts' (2000: 8). But the process of slipping, seamlessly, from the position that globalization unproblematically exists, though it may be informed by changes in the organizing and exercising of power, to a position whereby these changes are assigned the truth and value of the name of globalization is in itself part of the doxa of globalization. In other words, if one of the ways power is exercised in the contemporary world is through the production, dissemination and inculcation of a perspective or category which is the starting point for all analysis and debate about the 'realities' of that contemporary world, then academic 'debates' and 'globalist accounts', no matter how scientific or rigorous, can simply function as one of the mechanisms through which doxa (and consequently power differentials) is produced and imposed.

What all this indicates is that because the dominant discourses of what is meant by globalization are so well entrenched (regardless of how the S11 protesters, or Moroccan farmers, or other critics may define it), it is very difficult to objectify the term, to place it at arm's length from oneself, and continually apply a critical attitude to one's own thinking and understanding about the notion. As we pointed out in the previous chapter, the effect of the politics of naming is to bring something into social reality. Unless scholars engage closely and critically with the established terms and concepts they use in their work, they may risk ontologizing the ideas behind those terms, and fall into an unproblematic acceptance of the doxa associated with their field, as we suggest is what tends to happen in globalist accounts of history and globalization. But, as John Frow points out, this doesn't mean we should avoid using terms and concepts such as 'globalization'; there is a practical reason for engaging closely and critically with the term, and with the various positions and logics associated with it: 'rather than simply taking up one of those predefined positions and pursuing all its consequences as though you were discovering rather than repeating them, you should devise a way of analysing the logic of the grid itself' (1997: 23).

Conclusion

In the following chapters we attempt to do something of this kind – to devise a way of analysing the logic of the 'grid' that is the concept of globalization. We have already picked up on Francis Fukuyama's insistence on the 'end of history', and pointed out the extent to which 'history' is put to work to support one or other perspective on global politics and on relations of value. In the next chapter we take up Paul Virilio's claim that 'We are not seeing an "end of history", but we are seeing an end of geography' (Virilio, 2000: 9) because of the rapidity of communication technology. We address this by examining the relationship between contemporary communication technology, informationalism, and changes to the ways in which time/space can be understood.

3

Technology, Informationalism and Space/Time

The world changed radically over the twentieth century, and more so over the past few decades: much of this change is associated with the development of new technologies. One outcome of this is the reduction of the effects of space and time on everyday life and on trade. Through communication technologies we talk to one another, view news and documentaries about other parts of the world and other cultures, revisit history, and share in the cultural production of other social groups. Through other technologies we can rapidly traverse the globe physically, transmit information almost instantaneously, and send goods around the world in hours or days, rather than months. The speed of transmission, and the mobility of capital, mean that both space and time seem to have been truncated, or to have collapsed entirely.

Not surprisingly, then, technology is one of the most prominent of the many areas used to characterize globalization, and the new communication technologies in particular are seen by many people as having radically changed the way the world works. One of the foremost analysts of globalization, Manuel Castells, in fact identifies twentieth-century technology as having brought about 'one of those rare intervals in history . . . the transformation of our material culture' (2000a: 29). Castells is not alone in making this claim: for many analysts, the processes we call 'globalization' can be reduced to, or simply understood in terms of, the consequences of the development of new communication technologies. The problem with this approach (which, it must be pointed out, does not necessarily characterize Castells's work) is that it decontextualizes technology, editing out the various forces and fields that both bring it into being and deploy it. In this chapter we examine the discourses on the relationship between technology and globalization, and discuss the tensions that are evident in writings on informational technology. Just as in the previous chapter we made the point that unless the idea of globalization is interrogated there is little point in gathering data to 'prove' its existence, so too we here interrogate the often rehearsed argument that the new order of globalization has collapsed space and time.

What is 'technology'?

Technology, in Freud's thinking, is simply an extension of our natural organs to get things done. If we take this line, we can argue that whenever people use anything other than their bodies to navigate the world and interact with others, they are effectively deploying a form of technology. Technology, in this viewpoint, 'is not an object, it is always a means to an end' (Rybczynski, 1983: 213).

This still has valence when we think about the association between technology and globalization, because although technology is no longer attributed simply to basic tools, for instance, or even nineteenth-century machines, it is still developed and deployed to get things done – as 'a means to an end'. And in fact it could be argued that there has been little change in at least the Western imaginary in our understanding of technology from the days of the Renaissance, when humanists such as Leonardo da Vinci insisted on a connection between technological development and 'progress'; or, more precisely, between progress and the ability to control technology (Rybczynski, 1983: 12). This was very explicit in the kinds of ideological narratives that Michael

Adas identifies as being seminal to Western colonial discourses of the nineteenth century. Adas writes that:

> As early as the 1830s, European colonial administrators and missionaries came to view railroads, steamships, and Western machines in general as key agents in their campaigns to revive 'decadent' civilisations in Asia and uplift the 'savage' peoples of Africa. Lord William Bentinck, the reform-minded Governor-General of India in this period, viewed the steamboat as a 'great engine of moral improvement'. . . . A decade later an editorial in *The Times* of London boasted that a combination of good government and the introduction of Western technology, particularly through railway construction, made it inevitable that the British would become 'the greatest benefactors the Hindoo race had known'. (1989: 224)

There was, thus, a clear connection between technological developments and neoliberal discourses of freedom, progress and benefit, and what is essential to these accounts is that behind them can be found what we might term the 'guarantee of technology': a guarantee that technology would transform the world for the better. Armand Mattelart refers to a host of writers (such as Geddes, Bellamy, Cabet, Chevalier and Saint-Simon, and even going back to Francis Bacon in the seventeenth century) who celebrated the ways in which science and technology would bring into being utopias marked by productive, attractive and fair working conditions, the abolition of child labour, universal emancipation, the domestication of climates, equality, an expanded public sphere, and the disappearance of poverty, ignorance, class, and cultural misunderstandings. And he finds much the same religious and utopian spirit in the works of modern writers such as Marshall McLuhan with his promise and prophecy of a 'global village', and the political scientist Daniel Bell, who believed that science and technology had made Western culture and institutions affluent, rational and free, and therefore politically homogeneous and stable, and had taken them into a 'post-ideological' phase – that is, beyond politics.

Freedom and progress thus continue to be main actors in the 'story' of technology, but this story retains the old anxieties (exemplified by Ned Ludd and his revolutionary followers) about the frightening, uncontrollable aspects of technology. Along with the celebratory statements, there were also voices of resistance concerning the increasing use of technology in Europe during the eighteenth and nineteenth centuries, ranging from 'apocalyptic visions of the damaging effects of rail and tunnels burrowing into the countryside and turning it into Swiss cheese' to fears that sending troops into battle by rail would make them effeminate (Mattelart, 1996: 103).

The late twentieth century was marked by similar fears of physical danger: along with the celebratory comments about the collapse of space and time effected by communication technologies are reports on what Paul Virilio terms '*instant transmission sickness*, with the rapid emergence of the "Net junkies", "Webaholics" and other forms of cyberpunk struck down by IAD (Internet Addiction Disorder)' (Virilio, 2000: 38). And just as the post-Enlightenment age had its share of techno-sceptics, many contemporary theorists have expressed reservations about, or rejected outright, this utopian reading of technology-driven society. Mattelart refers to Jean-François Lyotard's influential report *The Postmodern Condition*, which draws attention to the inevitable antagonism between the ideology of 'communication transparency' and the roles, responsibilities and functions of the state, and to Jacques Ellul's 'dissention' with regard to the 'progressive value' of new technology: 'For Ellul . . . the wired-up society is a new form of social management, in which what predominates are collections of individuals with no interaction other than that created by and through technology' (Mattelart, 1994: 143).

It is important in analysing the role and effects of technology on the contemporary world not to fall into what Jonathon Crary calls **technological determinism**. He raises this issue in *Techniques of the Observer*, a book about vision and technology in the nineteenth century, where he describes the (then) widely held notion of technology as 'an independent dynamic of mechanical invention, modification, and perfection [which] imposes itself on to a social field, transforming it from the outside. On the contrary,' he writes, 'technology is always a concomitant or subordinate part of other forces' (Crary, 1990: 8). He addresses the role of optical devices to explore this notion that technology is a product of its social context, rather than its producer, describing them as:

> points of intersection where philosophical, scientific, and aesthetic discourses overlap with mechanical techniques, institutional requirements, and socioeconomic forces. Each of them is understandable not simply as the material object in question, or as part of a history of technology, but for the way it is embedded in a much larger assemblage of events and power. (1990: 8)

Just as a history of the use of technology cannot be reduced to a description of technical changes (for optical devices, the gradual development of tools such as the camera obscura, the stereoscope, photography and 'moving pictures'), so too it is misleading to try to make sense of the notion of globalization purely or even predominantly in terms of technical changes or developments. This is not to suggest that technology isn't an important aspect of globalization; it is not unreasonable to claim that developments in communication technology (especially computers, fibre optics and digitalization) have significantly changed the social, cultural, political and economic spheres of activity in many areas of the world. But there is a difference between pointing out that technology has affected the way many people live and think, and going on from there to argue that technology equals globalization. Indeed, an argument could be made that technology has tendencies which are equally counter-globalization; dividing the world neatly into the haves and have-nots, producing the superpower we know as the United States, while ensuring that most people will remain outside the network of power, if not the network of communication. And another argument could be made that though technology may usher in an era of instantaneous networking, and a new global democracy, it equally engenders the sorts of violence we have already seen in New York, Jerusalem and Bosnia. The American novelist Don DeLillo wrote, in an essay on 11 September:

> Technology is our fate, our truth. It is what we mean when we call ourselves the only superpower on the planet. The materials and methods we devise make it possible for us to claim our future. We don't have to depend on God or the prophets or other astonishments. We are the astonishment. The miracle is what we ourselves produce, the systems and networks that change the way we live and think. But whatever great skeins of technology lie ahead, ever more complex, connective, precise, micro-fractional, the future has yielded, for now, to medieval experience, to the old slow furies of cutthroat religion. (DeLillo, 2001: 37)

Society and technological change

The point, then, is to identify the social role of technology, the ways in which it is accommodated by the social, political and economic fields, and the limits on its effects. We will discuss the Coen Brothers' film *O Brother, Where Art Thou?* (2000) to pick up the question of the relationship between technological changes and the sociocultural sphere. The film follows, very loosely, the narrative of Homer's *Odyssey*; in case viewers missed the inter-textual reference, the main character and leader of the group (played by George Clooney) is called Ulysses (the Latin form of Odysseus) Everett McGill. Like Odysseus he is on a journey home (though, where the Greek hero was a returning warrior, McGill and his companions are escaping convicts). Like Odysseus, his journey is marked by encounters with super-stition and the supernatural. (One of their number claims to have been taught to play the guitar by the devil in exchange for his immortal soul.) The characters they meet along the way also allude to the *Odyssey*; they include sirens, a blind seer and McGill's own neglected wife, Penelope. And the teleological premise of the *Odyssey* is certainly evident in that, as was true of the original Odysseus, each of McGill's encounters along the journey may seem capricious and arbitrary, but necessarily propels him towards his wife, his home and his destiny.

But where Odysseus's destiny was to take back his realm and re-establish his leadership, McGill is caught up under a more modern narrative. Paul Virilio quotes a 'west coast guru' as saying, 'techno is our destiny, the freedom high-tech machines give us is the freedom to be able to say "yes" to their potential' (Virilio, 2000: 26); McGill's destiny is intimately tied to the newly emerging communication technologies, of which he is a mouthpiece. Despite the context in which he finds himself – the deeply impoverished and largely rural state of Mississippi during the Great Depression – and despite the very cumbersome forms of technology they encounter and use – upright radios, lumbering Ford pickups and sedans, chuffing trains and operator-assisted telephones – he insists on their value, and their role in humanity's future. He understands the new devices as being coterminous with progress, reason and rationality and, in the best tradition of nineteenth-century optimism, tells his companions that science and technology are going to build infrastructure and networks that will link everyone, and in the process sweep away misunderstandings, superstition, poverty and injustice.

What makes this Coen Brothers' film interesting, from our perspective, is that rather than subscribing to the notion of technology operating more or less independently as a vehicle for progress and the dissemination of reason, it demonstrates how it is intertwined with wider social and cultural issues. It shows this by focusing on popular music and its dissemination, firstly by means of the (fairly) new recording technologies and then through radio. When McGill and his companions, as part of a ruse to avoid recapture, record an old-time song ('Man of Constant Sorrow') it reaches a mass audience via the radio, and catapults them to what we would now call cult status. They aren't initially aware of their fame, because their whole attention is caught up with the process of their journey to freedom and with avoiding the lawmen and other obstacles in their course – pointing to the way in which we can be caught up in and by technology.

The connection between journey-as-progress, technology and its social contexts becomes most evident towards the end of the film. An election is being fought for the governorship of the state, between the (corrupt) incumbent and a Huey Long-style populist who holds traditional electioneering gatherings in local settings and to a relatively small audience. The incumbent, who is facing defeat, seizes on the sudden popularity of McGill and his companions – now known as the Soggy Bottom Boys – and aligns himself with them and their technology-induced fame, and their status as celebrities. His challenger takes the opposing position, rants against the group, and publicly announces their criminality, on the (not unreasonable) assumption that this will mean the incumbent will lose the election, tarred by his association with wanted criminals. Instead, in a foreshadowing of the connection between celebrity and politics, the fame of the Soggy Bottom Boys legitimizes the incumbent, and the challenger is the one tarred and run out of town. The technological developments that allowed the Soggy Bottom Boys to become famous are really connected not at all with progress and reason in this example, but with a fleeting popular mood, and with political self-interest.

Technology and social change

The second critical perspective on technology that is presented by *O Brother* is in the penultimate scene: Ulysses is caught up in a flood when the valley where he spent his idyllic youth is being transformed into a lake to supply power for surrounding areas. This literal flood acts as a very direct metaphor for the flood of technology, reason and progress that was part of the 1930s discourses of social progress. The Coen Brothers capture this moment of technological and social change by showing the waters sweeping away buildings, animals, people and various artefacts – gramophones, guitars, furniture, tools, clothes and, curiously, hundreds of containers of pomade. In a sense the scene of a community and its artefacts being swept along and away by overwhelming 'flows' points to the kinds of effects of globalization outlined by theorists such as Beck, Castells and Mattelart, in their suggestion that technology unleashes forces and flows which are impossible to ignore or withstand. But the scene also harks back to the ideas of earlier writers – Smith, Mill, Voltaire, Diderot and Rousseau – that we looked at in our previous chapter, and their conviction that scientific developments will enable the perfectibility of the human race. The promises of technology include greater ease in living, greater rates of production, and greater human interaction across borders due to the new and rapid forms of communication. And they include the greater permeability of national boundaries and the related flow of people, goods and ideas across the globe, so that they can circulate rapidly and freely across the borders of time and place. In the film the sight of gramophones and guitars swirling and spinning along can be read as pointing to the way communication technology sent local music (blues, Appalachian folk, country) circulating not only throughout America, but also around the world, in the process transforming genres, styles and practices worldwide. But it also points to the anxieties attendant upon both technologization and globalization: the objects and people 'circulating freely' in the flood water are in fact being swept along helplessly, spinning out of control.

What this announces is the imbrication of technology, popular culture and the process of commoditization. Technology is not a clear and straightforward motive force for progress, but rather the conduit which allows a country-blues song to be taken from its sociocultural context – a rural lament about suffering in a local world of Deep South poverty and racism – and transformed into a commodity that denotes a nostalgic attachment to another time and place. And this commoditizing and popularizing of the record is enhanced, not by the reason and rationality that are meant to accompany technology and the free circulation of things and ideas, but by its association with the exotic – with criminality and superstition.

Technology thus informs and helps shape the many social and political changes that are part of the temporary moment, but it does not constitute an explanation of them, nor does it direct them along the path of reason or progress. Slavoj Zizek writes:

the way computerization affects our lives does not depend
directly on technology, it results from the way the impact of
new technology is refracted by the social relations which, in
their turn, co-determine the very direction of technological
development. (Zizek, 1996: 198)

If for 'computerization' we simply read 'technology', we can
take from this the point that social and cultural factors determine technological development at least as much as technology
determines cultural development. McGill's experiences are not
of someone formed and tossed about by technological systems
and devices, but of someone formed by a cultural, social, political and economic history, and inflected by technology. This
offers a very different emphasis from that of technological
determinism, because it means we can see technology as operating within a context, transforming and being transformed by
the 'larger assemblage of events and power' in which it is being
utilized and given meaning. We can still identify this process at
work whenever celebrity and media recognition translate
directly into capital. Professional athletes, popular musicians
and movie actors are all under the same logic that shaped the
career of the Soggy Bottom Boys, and the social and political
groups associated with them. That is, technology (in the form of
media networks) both makes their fame and exploits it.

An advertisement for the ESPN cable network, for instance,
shows various baseball players posed or in slow motion, and
looking appropriately heroic, dramatic or imposing. The caption
reads 'ESPN – Making Legends'. The point is that ESPN's
coverage of baseball to a global audience enhances the recognition value of players; they – their names and deeds – are
circulated to hundreds of millions of people via cable technology, which helps them acquire the 'larger than life' status the
caption has announced. For the players this translates into more
lucrative contracts, advertising deals, product endorsements,
and for ESPN it means larger audiences and hence more
advertising revenue. The direct relationship between technology
and other contexts – especially the economic – is very apparent
here. But no matter how pervasive or powerful it may be,

technology and the ideas of rationality associated with it do not determine public attitudes. Rather, technology informs and helps shape those attitudes by circulating images, messages and meanings associated with particular events and social sites.

Technology and cultural convergence

This role, to circulate information, is central to general understandings of what communication technologies allow. We pointed out earlier that the processes associated with globalization can be understood as a pledge of faith in the ability of science and technology to bring into being the 'freedom of circulation' of ideas, goods and peoples. This is where technology comes to be seen as having a value independent of the contexts in which it is involved or deployed; that is, it supposedly makes barriers, differences and contexts irrelevant. Everyone, the story goes, can be logged on to the internet and communicate with one another without regard to difference in the vast democracy of that 'neutral' space. But in fact, as we describe above, far from being neutral, technology and the information it produces are always already tied up with the society and culture in which they are produced and/or deployed. Technology is not like an immutable language. Each culture in which a technological device is used places its own signature on the object/system, using it in locally specific ways. Indian trains, for instance, are very different from British or South American trains, and even the internet has its own inflections, from the language of use to web page displays, in different countries and regions across the globe.

An example of the problems associated with the notion of a universal/universalizing technology can be seen in a Sony television advertisement, which features a pair of Western (actually American) women in an exotic desert location (possibly India), looking on while a shaman performs visual magic. The women take a digital photograph of the event, transfer the information to their computer, and e-mail the image to a wheelchair-bound Stephen Hawkins-like professor. He is alerted to the arrival of the message by his computer ('Professor, you have mail'), and downloads the image of the 'exotic magic'. The caption/ voiceover announces, quite simply, 'We are all connected.'

This is, effectively, an example of the technological determinism that Crary warns us about. The advertisement demonstrates the way in which technology allows an event (here, the shaman's performance of magic) to be taken out of time and place, since in a few seconds the 'real' of the here and now of an exotic foreign location is available to a person back in the United States. But the overcoming of time and space is only one aspect of the 'magical' value of technology. Communication technology, the advertisement insists, brings cultures together. It allows us to ignore the limitations of our bodies (if the professor can't move to the world, the world can be brought to the professor), and keeps us alert to the constant flow of the world to us ('You've got mail').

But this is a limiting view of technology and its effects. There is a famous joke featuring the Lone Ranger where he and his faithful companion Tonto are surrounded by 'hostile Indians'. The Lone Ranger says, with alarm, 'Tonto, old friend, we're really in trouble this time.' To which Tonto replies, 'Whadd'ya mean, "we", paleface?' Tonto is pointing out a flaw in the Lone Ranger's thinking, one which presumes a 'we' that is never necessarily 'we'. Relationships, like technology, are never neutral, but in fact are contingent, and based in the Lone Ranger's case at least partially on differences in race, culture and interest, and on imbalances of power – the cowboys are always supposed to win – a differential which disappears in the joke.

The shaman in the Sony advertisement could take the Tonto option, and point out that he is not part of the 'we' who 'are connected' by technology, an objection which undercuts the notion that technology is essentially neutral, progressive and emancipatory, or that it collapses time, place, context and differences. The advertisement is located in a particular sociopolitical context in which the Americans have the wealth that allows them to produce and access technology, and the local people have not; the Americans can travel across borders and cultures and transcend geographical barriers, while the local people are tied to locale; the Americans can take their pick of the commodities and experiences offered by cultures across the world, while the local people can only 'give of themselves'. The point is that the final statement 'We are all connected' implies that the process of connecting equals or initiates 'community', but in fact the only people connected are the Americans. The power differential that defines the relationship between the two groups of people isn't collapsed or transcended, but accentuated, through the possession and deployment of technology.

To a certain extent what happens in the advertisement is very similar to conventional tourism – Westerners travel to an exotic locale, grab a few souvenirs, and send them home. But there are aspects of the advertisement's narrative that highlight other markers of difference and inequality. The fact that the images being sent home are directed to a professor gives the activity a quasi-scientific status; and if the community apparently produced by the technology really exists, it is a community which is marked by deep differences. There are 'subjects' (the professor-scientist, the tourists-anthropologists), and there are the 'objects' which they are examining (the exotic local culture, the magical shaman). There are different orders of knowledge (science versus superstition), and though it could be argued that these orders are collapsed broadly into the category of magic, there is a great difference between 'scientific' magic (technology) and 'native' magic. Though the shaman can perform spectacular tricks, Western technology actually sends images through the ether and so is much more powerful magic. What the advertisement implies, finally, is that Western technology will override local superstition. It will not wipe it out exactly, since it has the value of the spectacular, the strange, the exotic; but will put it in its place as a kind of cultural show for tourists.

Globalizing technologies

While we thus reject the notion that technology is the motive force of social and cultural change, it is still central to the processes of globalization; and so when making sense of, evaluating and contextualizing the processes and discourses of globalization it is important to consider the question of technology. Particularly, what we need to take into account are those forms of communication technology that have come to be associated so strongly with globalization: how they are different from previous technologies, their supposed effects, and how they function within the 'larger assemblage of events and power' (Crary, 1990: 8) in which they are embedded. The 'usual suspects' on the list include computers, electronic mail, the internet, digital, cable and fibre optic technologies, mobile telephones, satellite technology, television, film, and telephone or video conferencing. Each can be located within the general categories of digitalization, networking and information processing.

Digitalization is probably the most important technological advance in the area of communications. The term refers to the process whereby information is produced as a universal binary code, and is thus able to circulate more freely and at greater speed across communication technologies, and not just within them. It is central to networking potentialities because it is characterized by growing convergence, and thus brings together different media (telephone, television, computers) and types of texts (pictures, sounds, words). In other words, digitalization means greater flexibility, because communication technologies are no longer text-specific, and can 'talk' to each other. Manuel Castells writes:

> the information technology paradigm is based on flexibility. Not only processes are reversible, but organizations and institutions can be modified, and even fundamentally altered, by rearranging their components . . . a decisive feature in a society characterized by constant change and organizational fluidity. (2000a: 61–2)

This also speeds up and facilitates information processing, because the changes in speed and mass associated with developments in communication technology allow greater amounts of information to be stored and circulated, and moved across mediums at 'real time' speed. Virilio writes about this in relation to the objects of technology themselves: the 'proliferation of "great lights in the sky"' at one end of the continuum, and 'Faster, smaller, cheaper' at the other. He writes:

> this NASA slogan could shortly become the watchword of globalization itself. But with one nuance, since the *speed* and *smallness* in question would no longer refer to devices designed to conquer extra-terrestrial space, but to our geography at the moment of its sudden temporal compression. (Virilio, 2000: 66; emphasis in original)

These developments are part of what Manuel Castells calls 'A technological revolution, centred around information technologies' which 'is reshaping, at an accelerated pace, the material basis of society' (2000a: 1): the way we communicate with each other, the way we get things done, and the way we fit ourselves to time and space, or (increasingly) time and space to ourselves. Castells argues that the technologies are thoroughly pervasive across society, 'an integral part of all human activity' (2000a: 61–2) and hence part of everyday life. But this begs the question of whose everyday life is being considered? What is apparent is that, regardless of the claims made about the pervasiveness of the new paradigm, only a very small percentage of the world's population is actually in the loop of the network society. Writing about the inequities of worldwide access to computers, the internet and cyberspace, probably the most recognizable – and supposedly universalized – areas of the information superhighway, Eisenstein demonstrates the extent to which they are culturally, racially, demographically, class- and gender-specific:

> Eighty-four per cent of computer users are found in North America and Northern Europe. Sixty-nine per cent are male, average age thirty-three, with an average household income of $59,000 . . . The racial elitism of cyber communities is palpable. In the US, only 20 per cent of Afro-Americans have home computers, and a mere 3 per cent subscribe to online services. Rather than a highway, the Internet seems like a segregated private road. (Eisenstein 2000: 212)

And he goes on to point out, more generally, that:

> Approximately 80 per cent of the world's population still lacks basic telecommunication access . . . There are more telephone lines in Manhattan than in all of sub-Saharan Africa. The US has thirty-five computers per hundred people, Japan has sixteen; Taiwan has nine. Ghana, on the other hand, has one computer per thousand people. . . . only about 40 per cent of the world's population even has daily access to electricity. (2000: 212)

Of course Castells is very much aware of these inequities; his argument, however, is that this technological revolution, like the industrial, mechanical and electronic revolutions that went before, does in fact penetrate human life and human activity, not as an outside force 'but as the fabric in which such activity is woven' (Castells, 2000a: 31). Let's look at Castells's informational technology revolution, and examine the extent to which it could be said that it constitutes the weave of the fabric of everyday life, both for the 'technology-rich' and for the 60 per cent of the world's population who lack daily access to electricity.

Castells and other writers (including Paul Virilio, Arjun Appadurai and Armand Mattelart) argue that the informationalism associated with the 'new' technologies has had a pervasive and irreversible impact upon the way the world understands time and space, which in turn has transformed all the main spheres of human activity – economic, cultural, social and political. If we look at economic activity, for instance, it might seem reasonable to think that the central questions in relation to globalization are whether or not we can speak of a truly integrated world economy, or whether labour is free to circulate across state borders; and it might seem reasonable to think that we should make comparisons between the percentage or volume of investment within or outside the OECD countries. But, although all these issues are considered significant within academic debates about the reach (or 'thickness') of global processes, what Castells and other analysts see as primary issues are the ways in which the speed and mass of information flows, tied in with computerized regimes of investment in, say, world currency markets, can have unforeseen, chaotic and devastating effects across the world – culturally, politically and socially.

One reason this is so important to cultural analysts, especially in relation to the question of the effects of technology on everyone's everyday life, is that information flows can affect the financial market quite independently of other seemingly more important factors like the long-term performance, wealth or resilience of a national economy. Because of the incredible speed with which financial transactions can be made across the globe and the integration of the global financial market, the market itself is extraordinarily volatile. And, as Castells writes:

> Since currencies are interdependent, so are economies everywhere. Although major corporation centres provide the human resources and facilities necessary to manage an increasingly complex financial network, it is in the information networks connecting such centres that the actual operations of capital take place. Capital flows become at the same time global and increasingly autonomous vis-a-vis the actual performance of economies. (2000b: 259)

The 'Asian crisis' of 1997-98 to which we referred in Chapter 1 is one example of this phenomenon; the computer program-driven withdrawal of funds from Asian markets and currencies threatened the sovereignty of the South Korean state, created internal political upheaval in Malaysia and initiated anti-Chinese pogroms in Indonesia. A more recent example occurred during the aftermath of the 11 September attacks in the United States. Markets around the world reacted negatively to the threats of terrorist action and to the possibility that the West would become embroiled in a protracted war, but what was equally significant was the way in which the quick availability of information worked to devastate the aviation and related industries. Early on in the aftermath of 11 September, figures became available which showed heavy cancellation of immediate and intermediate flight bookings, both within the United

States and around the world. Airline share prices crashed, some companies went under, services were cancelled or severely reduced, and airline workers across the world were made redundant. This created a domino effect in related industries such as tourism, sport and the arts, all of which rely on people being willing or able to travel nationally and internationally, and depend on subsidies from, and sponsorship agreements with, carriers. The 'flow on' effects were felt not just with regard to related industries, but also in national and international spheres of politics and culture.

What these experiences and examples suggest is that Castells is essentially correct to claim that information and other technology exerts a considerable influence, at least potentially, over the everyday activities and lives of people around the globe, regardless of whether or not they are in affluent or developing countries, or have access to that technology. 'Real time' movements of large amounts of capital facilitated by computer technology can, for instance, throw an Indonesian worker out of a job and deprive that person's family of their livelihood, and can create social and political crises and instability.

Technology and knowledge

But what does this tell us about the relationship between this imbrication of information technology with everyday life, on the one hand, and the ideological claims about its emancipatory and progressive dimension, on the other? Let's consider this question by taking up the question of the actual effects of globalizing technologies, and **global convergence**.

Castells points to the fact that corporations have become part of interdependent, information-dependent networks, which means that while those corporations enjoy the benefits of 'just in time' information and computer-generated projections, for instance, at the same time they are tied into, and become dependent with regard to, the logics, flows and rhythms of the network. The network reproduces itself, more or less endlessly, and those within have no choice but to 'reproduce' in its wake. As Virilio writes:

> Like some gigantic implosion, the circulation of the general accident of communication technologies is building up and spreading, forcing all substances to keep moving in order to interact globally, at the risk of being wiped out, of being swallowed up entirely. (Virilio, 1997: 71)

Attempting to think or act outside the logic of the network is virtually impossible because, as the Sony advertisement tells us, 'we are all connected'. So even if one component of the network were to decide, for instance, that 'just in time' information was not the most useful or effective way of operating, it would be bound to continue using it regardless, precisely because everyone else in the network (its suppliers, technicians, distributors, parts manufacturers and financial consultants) continued to do so.

There is also a sense in which the availability and use of new information and communication technology can be understood in terms of the notion of a fetish, rather than as something that is required or needed to facilitate decision making or increase productivity. After all, there is only so much information which can be processed, in an intelligible way, in the short term. And in fact at some point the increased mass and complexity of information will necessarily have the opposite effect, rendering people more or less incapable of action or decision making, reducing executives to the helpless question 'How can I make sense of all this?' and requiring a level of informational analysis and literacy which is beyond most people.

As an example of how 'network logic' might not necessarily be the most effective or productive way of determining decisions or strategies, let's consider the situation of the airline industry after the 11 September attacks in the United States. Short to medium-term extrapolations from available information – data on booking cancellations, projections of future booking levels and patterns, event cancellations, share price fluctuations – led to massive retrenchment and service cutbacks, which seems reasonable enough, on the surface. But there was a way in which the ability to think outside this negative logic could have been useful in attracting cultural and, as a consequence, financial capital, despite the crisis. A company which, as part of its patriotic duty, refused to retrench staff or cancel services might not have necessarily gained financially in the short term, but the long-term benefits of the move, and the capital that went with it, might have considerably outweighed the negatives. An airline company taking this stance, for instance, could from that point on legitimately have styled itself as the only 'patriotic' airline. In other words, there is a logic available to decision makers that is not necessarily the logic of what has been termed 'economic rationalism' – which, in its hegemonic form within Western capitalism, tends to operate on the basis of an almost fetishistic attachment to cutbacks, downsizing and the short-term 'bottom line'.

Another, slightly more everyday, example of this situation of information saturation occurs regularly in American sports such as football and baseball. In the 2001 Baseball World Series between the Arizona Diamondbacks and the New York Yankees, Yankees pitcher Mike Mussina was throwing late in a tight game. The network on which the game was being shown produced a dizzying amount of information, familiar to fans and analysts of baseball, about Mussina's record against upcoming batters, his record against right and left-handers, his results in this World Series and in post-season games, his performance after having pitched a hundred balls, and so on. After considering all this, the commentators suggested that Mussina should be pulled from the game, as did the majority of fans on the network web site. Manager Joe Torre decided, however, to keep Mussina in the game – a successful move, as it turned out. Despite what looked like a fairly straightforward 'information-driven' decision, the Yankees manager either went against the information, considered only a very selective part of it, or, in the words of the commentators, 'went with a hunch'. What this hunch might have been based on, of course, was what Michael Polanyi calls 'tacit knowledge'; that is, Joe Torre was possibly making a decision based, not on the raw data he had before him, but on what he knew from his experience (about pitchers in this situation, or more specifically Mussina), which he might not have been able to articulate, or even be aware of himself ('I went with a hunch').

There are a couple of points that can be made here. The first is that information on its own is useless or worse; what is more important is the literacy to read and evaluate information. Secondly, not all information is equal. That is to say, certain information may be critical, and everything else less relevant. In the case above, what might be seen as critical information could be knowledge of the general upward trend (despite periodic dips) of the stock market, or perhaps sensitivity to the public need for reassurance and the restoration of normalcy. The less relevant information would then be the mass of data about the crash in ticket sales – a literate analyst might well see this as important, but short-term, and a shock that the company could weather. Again we can see the validity of Crary's insistence, cited earlier in this chapter, that technological devices and developments need to be understood not as things in themselves but as 'points of intersection where philosophical, scientific, and aesthetic discourses overlap with mechanical techniques, institutional requirements, and socioeconomic forces' (Crary, 1990: 8). It is interesting to consider, for instance, what is not produced, understood or deployed – in fact, what is literally unthinkable – as information.

The exclusion of this kind of information in analysis is part of a much wider tendency which Bourdieu refers to as the 'editing out of the human'. He notes what he calls the 'hegemony of the mathematical' which is typically used as the basis of policy decisions by corporations, governments and organizations of global governance, such as the WTO, the IMF and the World Bank. The IMF, for instance, could reduce 'the Indonesian situation' after the 1998-99 Asian crisis, to two sets of mathematical/economic indicators: 'problems' (falling currency value, increased balance of payments deficit, falling GDP) and 'solutions' (a decrease in government spending, cutbacks in civil bureaucracies). This is clear, straightforward and clean, and because of the 'scientific' authority associated with statistically and mathematically based information it appears a far more authoritative guide to the outcome of a human situation than 'human' (sociological, psychological, emotional and hence unreliable) data.

What Bourdieu's comments, and these examples, point to is another aspect of what we have called 'the politics of naming'. In this case it is terms such as 'information' and 'knowledge' that are being named – and named without any real inter-rogation of what is meant by the terms, and what effects their naming may have on human experience. In *The Writing of the Disaster* (1986) Maurice Blanchot asks what has become, in the contemporary world, an almost unthinkable question: 'Why do we need more knowledge?' Blanchot questions the assumption, so central to post-Enlightenment culture, that knowledge is both neutral (that is, it is 'out there', waiting to be discovered) and beneficial (the more we know the better we are, both indi-vidually and as a group). His point is that knowledge is never neutral or absolute, but is motivated by interest, and contingent. That is, knowledge is not simply waiting to be discovered or uncovered, but is in fact produced as the result of activity carried out in authorized and legitimate institutions or fields at specific historical points. What counts as knowledge changes markedly across periods and contexts, so that 'reason', for instance, does not mean the same thing in the thirteenth and in the nineteenth centuries: the Enlightenment, along with the advent of colonialism, the 'reason of state' and the growth of capitalism ensured that. Similarly, 'madness' (as Foucault has shown; see Danaher et al., 2000) changes its meaning quite regularly over history, depending on the current condition of institutions (were there secure hospitals available?), knowledges (involving, say, notions of deviance) and discourses (about how society ought to function, and who belonged as a valid member). Scientific work may appear to uncover 'the truth' (about the characteristics of the homosexual, the hysteric or the paedophile, for instance), but in effect the 'truth' of this uncovering (along with the categories it refers to) is a historical contingency. As Foucault makes clear, different objects of knowledge appear and then disappear again as social, cultural and political forces are transformed by economics, politics and even fashion.

Space and time

Let's look at one of the central claims made about information-alism (and contemporary communication technologies more generally) – that it changes the way we understand and experience time and space. We have said that knowledge is produced within a space/time nexus (the historical and cultural context of the knowledge), and we have also pointed out that communication technologies are understood to collapse time and space; thanks to these technologies, Virilio writes, 'continents have lost their geographical foundations and been supplanted by the *tele-continents* of a global communication system which has become quasi-instantaneous' (Virilio, 2000: 9). Consequently, he writes later in the same text, *'here no longer exists; everything is now'* (Virilio, 2000: 116).

This is played out in the narrative that informs the Sony advertisement we referred to earlier – 'You have mail' and 'We are all connected.' What was most interesting about that advertisement was the way in which it presented the fantasy of a community connected by communication networks – the 'we' of the caption – but only through implication and domination. That is, the fact that the Americans were there with their technology in a primitive, technologically deprived place demonstrated to the locals not that 'we' are actually all 'connected' but that their own world was drastically limited because of their attachment to space/place, and their inability to transcend its physical dimensions. Their limitations could, the insistent 'we' suggests, be overcome if 'they' became (like) 'us' – Americanized, Westernized, affluent, democratic, modern, technologized – but presumably not white.

The reality of the situation, however, is that, unless 'they become us', the shaman and his people are consigned and confined to the status of objects of a Western subject's gaze, interest and power. From this perspective the advantages which theoretically come with being networked work against the interests of the dominated. The access to volumes of information at high speed, and to facilities and educational opportunities, effectively functions to accentuate further the gap that separates affluent from developing states.

In fact, the gap is not just between affluent and developing states. Not everyone in America has access to the technology, scientific objectivity and actual mobility of the 'anthropologists/tourists' in the Sony story. Some are wheelchair-bound, like the professor, but thanks to training, intelligence and institutional networks able to travel virtually across space and time. But far more people are pinned down in a very specific space and time because of their economic, social and cultural constraints. Doreen Massey makes just this kind of point in her discussion of the notion of time/space compression:

> Different social groups have distinct relationships to . . . mobility: some people are more in charge of it than others; some initiate flows and movements, others don't; some are more on the receiving-end of it than others; some are effectively imprisoned by it. In a sense at the end of all the spectra are those who are doing the moving and communicating and who are in some way in a position of control in relation to it – jet setters, the ones sending and receiving the faxes and the e-mails . . . But there are also groups who are also doing a lot of physical moving, but who are not in charge . . . refugees from El Salvador or Guatemala . . . [or] those who are simply on the receiving end of time–space compression. The pensioners in a bed-sit in any inner city . . . not daring to go out after dark. And anyway the public transport's been cut. (2000: 58–9)

Being a member of an affluent, technologized society doesn't automatically provide access to its facilities or its advantages. A writer who has most particularly picked up on this problem, and discussed the effects of distribution of all forms of capital, is Paul Virilio. He characterizes the gap between affluent and other as one that simultaneously involves a transformation of time/space resources and facilities, and particularly sees the issue of the relation to time as the main marker of social position and potential: 'The global metropolitics of the future electronic information superhighways in itself implies the coming of a society no longer divided so much into North and South, but into two distinct temporalities, two speeds: one absolute, the other relative' (1997: 71).

Virilio is pointing here to something more insidious, and potentially more devastating, than the so-called North–South divide; he is referring to an endlessly perpetuated process of what he calls **endocolonialism**, as distinguished from the earlier form, **exocolonialism**. In that form, there was an imperial centre (London, Paris, Washington) which controlled and directed politics, economic and social organization throughout the empire. Flows were only two-way: from the centre to the periphery, and from the periphery to the centre. Under endo-colonialism, by contrast, the old two-way flow has been replaced by a network of flows across the globe; and the old imperial centre/periphery has disappeared into a confusing congeries of power relations and connections. What appear to be free and interactive trade relations, Virilo would say, are in fact an utterly constricting set of obligations, tendencies and imperatives. An instance is, where workers in factories are required to work not according to human possibilities but according to the 'just in time' production systems that now dominate primary and secondary production. In fact, this means they have to work at a rate that will put most of them out of work. If they don't meet the demands, factories may be downsized, computerized, closed, moved offshore, outsourced. And when such structural issues mean they become unemployed, it is unlikely that they will be able to move away, to follow the work; instead, contemporary cities are marked by the presence of groups – ghettoes – of the long-term unemployed, who are captured by space, and for whom time ticks over according to a linear analogue rather than digital order. In this respect, Zygmunt Bauman writes:

> Globalization divides as much as it unites, it divides as it unites – the causes of division being identical with those which promote the uniformity of the globe. Alongside the

emerging planetary dimensions of business, finance, trade and information flows, a "localizing", space-fixing process is set in motion . . . What appears as globalization for some means localization for others; signalling a new freedom for some, upon many others it descends as an uninvited and cruel fate. Mobility climbs to the rank of the uppermost among the coveted values – and the freedom to move, perpetually a scarce and unequally distributed commodity, fast becomes the main stratifying factor of our late modern or postmodern times. (Bauman, 1998: 2)

So Bauman identifies a feature that is normally at the centre of neoliberal ideologies of globalization – mobility – as being the key, not only to global unification and homogeneity, but also to the production of new forms of difference and division as forms of disadvantage.

Conclusion

What writers such as Virilio and Bauman point to is an aspect of what we might term globalization's 'discontents'; and while those two writers tend to emphasize the extent to which many groups are, or are likely to be, economically disadvantaged by globalizing processes, there are many other issues and areas which are both subject to, and are being transformed by, new communication technologies, and by their own voices of discontent. We might identify here the survival of cultures, the independence and viability of the public sphere, state sovereignty, global (in)security and governance, individual and group identity.

In this chapter we have concentrated on technology and the culture of informationalism, but of course there are many different forms of contemporary communication technology which are lodged in amalgams of discursive contexts and relations (for instance, the relationship between satellite technology and the issues of state sovereignty or American cultural neocolonialism) which are equally important aspects of the 'grid' of globalization. In fact, none of the main spheres of human activity – economics, government, culture, civil society and everyday life and identities – is beyond, or independent of, these technologies, and the ideologies and politics with which they are imbricated. We will provide a detailed description and analysis of each of these areas, and the ways in which they have been subject to the grid of globalization, in the following chapters. In our next chapter we will deal with the economic sphere and, more specifically, with the relationship between technology and the development of what has become known as 'global capitalism'.

4

Global Capitalism

In our previous chapter we looked at one of the ways in which globalization is understood: as the relationship between the development of new communication technologies, on the one hand, and the contexts and politics of the use of that technology, on the other. In this chapter, we turn our attention to another popular way of understanding globalization: as an aspect of its effects on and in relation to the institutions, practices and strategies of **capitalism**.

We referred, in Chapter 2, to Hardt and Negri's concept of Empire, and their insistence that globalization needs to be understood as a grid of power strongly informed, if not driven, by the transformation of contemporary capitalism. For Hardt and Negri the advent of globalization has its beginnings in, and needs to be contextualized in terms of, a wider history of capitalist development. We will fill in some of that background history, and explain how, for Hardt and Negri, shifts in contemporary capitalist production are tied in, and almost synonymous, with changes in global relations of power.

For Immanuel Wallerstein and other advocates of world-systems theory, capitalism 'has always functioned as a world economy, and therefore those who clamor about the novelty of its globalization today have only misunderstood its history' (Hardt and Negri, 2000: 8). And certainly Hardt and Negri are under no illusions regarding capitalism's politics or pervasiveness, which they describe as having brought about a situation whereby:

> Today nearly all of humanity is to some degree absorbed
> within or subordinated to the networks of capitalist
> exploitation. We now see an ever more extreme separation of
> a small minority that controls enormous wealth from
> multitudes that live in poverty at the limits of powerlessness.
> (2000: 43)

After all, capitalism, within a Marxist framework of understanding (of which the book *Empire* is a product), is by virtue of
its own logic necessarily boundless and insatiable. The logic
works something like this. Capitalism operates through the
creation of surplus value, but that surplus value must always
find a market. Surplus value is created when the value of production exceeds labour and other associated costs. Surplus value
is only realized, however, through the process of consumption.
Surplus value is then (at least partly) returned to the capitalist
process as investment, which in turn creates more surplus value
and more goods for consumption. When home markets are
exhausted and unable to cope with what eventually becomes
capitalist overproduction, or when local labour costs restrict the
creation of surplus value, or when overproduction leads to
devaluation, capitalism is faced with a barrier to its mode of
operation. Sometimes this is accommodated by the development
of new home markets, or by increasing the labour pool and
cutting wages: but these are only short-term solutions.

The longer view demands that capital must go elsewhere, as
it did in the nineteenth century with colonialism. Colonies
provided the capitalist system of production with resources
(food, raw materials, precious metals and cheap labour), but
equally importantly it eventually provided new markets for the
consumption of commodities. In other words, the long-term goal
of capital is the capitalization of the entire world. This did not
necessarily occur consistently across the globe: certain areas
(such as Africa and parts of Asia) remained peripheral to capital,
serving as resources to be exploited, while others (such as Japan
and India) were quickly 'internalized' with regard to capital. As
well as overcoming the domestic barriers of falling surplus
value and rising labour costs, this process allowed the class

tensions associated with capitalist exploitation to be transported to the colonies, through the constitution of an unholy alliance of imperial capital and labour against colonial labour.

Hardt and Negri argue that the contemporary manifestations of global capital stem from a series of crises that began in the 1970s, and which threatened capital in much the same way that World War I, anti-colonial movements, and the inflexible structures and boundaries of the old imperial world brought an end to imperialist-driven capitalist expansion. The post-World War II period had been dominated by the **Keynesian**-inflected **Bretton Woods** system, which was characterized by a strong US military, political and economic hegemony with regard to the non-socialist world. This arrangement differed from the previous imperial system, in that the international monetary system was controlled by state institutions (national reserve banks) and international organizations (such as the International Monetary Fund and the World Bank).

During the 1970s this system went into crisis, according to Hardt and Negri, for two main reasons. Firstly, the Bretton Woods system was undermined by a series of related economic events and trends, including the United States' increasing trade deficits with Europe and Japan, the abolition of the gold–US dollar nexus, rampant inflation and trade wars. Secondly, the cost of the social gains made under the international version of the New Deal (that is, the implementation of a kind of new social contract, associated with the Roosevelt presidency in the United States, which guaranteed workers' rights, conditions and standard of living), coupled with what Hardt and Negri describe as the success of 'anti-imperialist and anticapitalist struggles in subordinate countries', effectively 'undermined the extraction of superprofits' (Hardt and Negri, 2000: 265).

According to Hardt and Negri, capitalism responded to this crisis in two ways. The first was straightforward and predictable, and involved an attempt at rolling back the conditions and costs associated with the New Deal regime, and undermining the power of organized labour in a variety of ways (for instance through anti-union legislation, and the increased use of technology within the production process). The second response was more innovative, and involved nothing less than an attempt to transform the nature of labour.

The names Hardt and Negri give to this second response are 'postmodernization' and 'the informatization of production', and it more or less corresponds to what other analysts, such as Manuel Castells, refer to as 'informationalism' (Castells, 1997). They locate this most recent transformation within the larger context of economic paradigm shifts, which are basically divided into three phases dominated by agriculture and raw materials, industry and manufacturing, and services and information respectively. The change from one paradigm to the next is usually characterized, they argue, by a relatively large-scale movement of labour; for instance, modernization involved the movement of labour from agriculture and mining to industry. The contemporary postmodern paradigm has seen a similar kind of migration, largely from industry to what are referred to as the service industries (such as health care, entertainment, education, advertising and finance). As Castells has indicated, service jobs differ from industrial work in a number of ways, most obviously in being less secure, more short-term, more mobile (for instance, not necessarily workplace-based) and generally less unionized. They also differ from industrial work, according to Hardt and Negri, in another important respect: 'they are characterized in general by the central role played by knowledge, information, **affect**, and communication' (2000: 285).

The pre-eminence of knowledge, information and communication in the globalized world – usually referred to as informationalism – is manifested in the increased production of what Hardt and Negri call 'immaterial goods'. The most obvious way of understanding this is to think of the way in which so many jobs, occupations and professions are tied in to, and effectively extend, networks – much as computers do. There are two main categories of this version of informationalism. The first category involves turning conventional industrial production into a service, largely through the use of communication technology. Workers in a factory, for instance, would 'share' the production process with technologies, and they would not necessarily provide finished products, but instead would supply parts or components of the end product. The second category, what Hardt and Negri, following Robert Reich, term 'symbolic-analytical services' (2000: 291), has a much higher value, and is likely to be better paid and more stable; examples include data analysis, financial planning and most research and development jobs and occupations.

The notion of affect, on the other hand, requires some elaboration. Hardt and Negri claim that the communication and media industries occupy a hegemonic place in the contemporary economic paradigm. Affective labour is concerned with 'the creation and manipulation of affect' (2000: 292); that is, the media and communication industries (but also health services concerned, say, with holistic care, and a variety of other industries devoted to the physical and psychical well-being of subjects) have taken on an important role in producing social relations, subjectivities, dispositions and what Bourdieu would refer to as forms of the **habitus** that are compliant with, and help reproduce, the structures, power relations and imperatives of Empire and capitalism. In other words, we could say that, in Foucauldian terms, affective labour has made an industry from, and works primarily to reproduce the effects and extend the pervasiveness of, **biopower**. We will treat this issue in more detail in Chapter 6.

Hardt and Negri's book is important for two major reasons: firstly, it allows us to contextualize in historical terms the relationship between capital and globalization; and secondly, it points to the way capital uses biopower to colonize and vampirize 'everyday life'. What it doesn't address, however, is the phenomenon, identified by Fredric Jameson in *The Geopolitical Aesthetic* (1992), whereby capitalism's alienation of the social is represented (ironically, in the capitalist-saturated media industry, in films such as *Alien* and *Videodrome*) as the ultimate totalizing threat to the social, a kind of insatiable machine that makes all human values and communities redundant. Certainly many of those taking part in the demonstrations at Seattle, Melbourne and Genoa that we referred to in Chapter 1 think of capitalism as if it were something sinister and 'out there'; a set of institutions (transnational corporations, the International

Monetary Fund, the World Trade Organization), or a collection of names (Bill Gates, Rupert Murdoch, George Soros), largely removed from, yet exercising a strong and insidious effect upon, ordinary people and everyday life.

This position is given credence by a wealth of statistical evidence documenting the growth of inequality in the contemporary world. For instance, 22 per cent of wealth in 1996 belonged to developing countries (which have 80 per cent of the global population); 15 per cent of income belonged to the poor (with 85 per cent of the world's population); and only a little over 1 per cent of global wealth was owned by the poorest 20 per cent of countries (Bauman, 1998: 70). Even those global institutions which ought to be very positive about the positives of globalization – the International Monetary Fund and the World Bank – express some concern. The IMF acknowledges that 'truly worldwide development . . . is not progressing evenly' (IMF, 2000). And the World Bank Briefing Papers (PREM, 2000) record the increasing inequality of income distribution across the globe, noting that 'in 1960 the average per capita GDP in the richest 20 countries in the world was 15 times that of the poorest 20. Today this gap has widened to 30 times.'

Arguments about globalization, and in particular the operations of global capitalism, tend to revolve around whether or not such activities are generally beneficial to all groups, or whether they simply reproduce – or even accentuate – existing inequalities, both within states and between affluent and developing states (such as the **G-8**, compared with most of sub-Saharan Africa). To examine this debate, and the gap between the promises of global capital and the actualities experienced by so many people around the world, we will first discuss what is meant by the terms 'capitalism' and 'global capital', and then move on to describe its working through global technological networks. We will look at the relation between corporations and nation-states in the production of goods and services and the distribution of income and wealth; and we will critically evaluate the extent to which this can be said to be an era of capitalist hegemony.

What is capitalism?

Capitalism is at the heart of the neoliberal ideology, being a system of economic and social organization based on private ownership of the means of production, and the separation of the economy and the state. Its founding principle is the pursuit of self-interest, which is achieved economically through competition between producers and producers, consumers and consumers. This competition, under capitalist logic, creates a state in which the right amount of goods and services at the right price are made available to meet consumer demand. The principle, in the simplest terms, is that increasing demand will put pressure on supply; prices will go up in response to the pressure; and demand will drop back, in the face of the raised prices, to reach an equilibrium with supply.

We can see this in the trade in fad goods among schoolchildren: at a moment in the school term, everyone suddenly wants to own marbles. The increased demand means that the playground value of the marble rises enormously; children with existing capital (such as extra pocket money, the ability to do favours, skill in playing marbles) will accumulate marble wealth and be able to use it to increase their consumption (swapping marbles for lollies, paying someone else to do their homework) and their status – they are the 'new rich'. But if they 'charge' too much for their marbles – if, for instance, they insist that they will give only one marble in exchange for a packet of crisps – then the exchange rate will seem unattractive to the other children, and they may have trouble doing business. There will then be, from their perspective, an oversupply of marbles in relation to the demand. They will have to be prepared to offer more, to trade up, as it were, until they reach the point where the number of marbles they are prepared to give matches the number of marbles others are prepared to receive for that bag of crisps. They may own the playground's wealth, but they cannot control the market. The point of this is that, under capitalism, the means of production are in private hands, and the levels of exchange, and the production of goods and services, are organized by the market and by the relation between supply and demand rather than through intervention (by 'governments' – here, parents or teachers).

The (economic) history of the twentieth century revolved around the struggle between capitalism and its two main competitors: fascism, where the means of production are in private hands, but the state plans and intervenes in production; and communism, where the state both owns the means of production and controls the outputs. Capitalism won a decisive victory over fascism with the end of World War II, and again over communism with the end of the Cold War. And it won, according to pundits, because it is the fairest, the most practical and the least ideologized approach to production. Certainly the huge failures in the former Soviet Union, for instance, or the state of the economy of North Korea would suggest that a command economy or ideology-driven market can have appalling consequences for consumers. But as we saw in the discussion of neoliberalism in Chapter 2, capitalism too is inescapably ideological; and even if it were not, 'pure' capitalism, in which the 'invisible hand' of the market is believed to bring about a dynamic equilibrium between supply and demand, can be just as devastating. Though the invisible hand can certainly even out any imbalances between supply and demand over time, this may only come about at great human cost. In a famine, for instance, there is excess demand – too many people, not enough food (at an affordable price, anyway). When enough people die of starvation, or flee to another country, demand will lessen and finally match supply; but this is not the sort of approach to outcomes that most governments would promote as ideal. Even the most avowedly capitalist system, that of the United States, does not rely on the invisible hand; the government intervenes actively in the form of tariffs and subsidies, and in negotiating trade associations with its neighbours and other favoured nations. Nor do (capitalist) corporations necessarily comply with the principle of free trade and free competition that is at the heart of capitalist logic: instead, major corporations do what they can to establish themselves as monopolies or, failing that, form associations with a few other powerful corporations so that together they can dominate the market, lobby government and control the invisible hand. In these sorts of practices we can hear the warning of the father of economics, Adam Smith, who put the invisible hand on the map. Though he promulgates *laissez-faire* capitalism, the ability of markets to self-correct, and the desirability of small government, he is never naive about the tendency of capitalists to operate against the market, and against the doctrines of pure capitalism:

> People of the same trade seldom meet together, even for merriment and diversion, but the conversation ends in a conspiracy against the public, or in some contrivance to raise prices. It is impossible indeed to prevent such meetings, by any law which either could be executed, or would be consistent with liberty and justice. But though the law cannot hinder people of the same trade from sometimes assembling together, it ought to do nothing to facilitate such assemblies, much less to render them necessary. (Smith, 1776/1937: 128)

Economic globalization

There is thus, in the highly individualistic sphere of operations that is capitalism, a constant tendency to converge, join others, and craft alliances, which means capitalism easily becomes a globalizing practice. Karl Marx prophesied this, writing that capitalism, driven as it is by the need for ever bigger markets and ever cheaper raw materials, would necessarily spread across the globe:

> The bourgeoisie, by the rapid improvement of all instruments of production, by the immensely facilitated means of communication, draws all, even the most barbarian, nations into civilization. . . . It compels all nations, on pain of extinction, to adopt the bourgeois mode of production; it compels them to introduce what it calls civilization into their midst, i.e., to become bourgeois themselves. In one word, it creates a world after its own image. (Marx, 1977: 225)

81

In other words, more than a century ago Marx had already foreshadowed the convergence of informationalism, production and communication technologies, neoliberalism and neocolonialism that we collapse under the term 'globalization'.

His reading of global capitalism is, of course, deeply negative; other 'readers' give highly celebratory, or at least neutral, accounts. The IMF, for instance, writes on economic globalization that 'It refers to the increasing integration of economies around the world, particularly through trade and financial flows' (IMF, 2000). But the article does bear out Marx's concern that global capitalism 'creates a world after its own image' because the IMF recognizes only one way to run an economy – the way of late twentieth-century capitalism. In all its analyses of national economies and production systems, the measure used is the measure of the West:

> Globalization means that world trade and financial markets are becoming more integrated. But just how far have developing countries been involved in this integration? Their experience in catching up with the advanced economies has been mixed. (IMF, 2000)

From the point of view of Western capitalism, then, integration means 'doing it my way' – the others have to 'catch up', rather than being able to introduce local systems and values into the world system. The World Bank similarly posits only one playing field, and one set of standards, in the global economy. In their 2000 Briefing Papers, World Bank delegates were given a brief history of global capitalism:

> it is important to recognize that economic globalization is not a wholly new trend. Indeed, at a basic level, it has been an aspect of the human story from earliest times, as widely scattered populations gradually became involved in more extensive and complicated economic relations. . . .
>
> The end of colonialism brought scores of independent new actors on to the world scene, while also removing a shameful

stain associated with the earlier 19th century episode of globalization. (PREM, 2000)

There are several points to draw from this World Bank narrative. Firstly, economic globalization is inevitable, in the sense that it has always been around in some form. Secondly, it may be negative in its effects – associated with the 'shameful stain' of nineteenth-century colonialism – but also provides a kind of commons, allowing 'independent new actors' to enter the stage and, presumably, bring in their interests and perspectives. But the stage is pre-established; the new actors don't really influence it, and can't really be heard:

> The extent to which different countries participate in globalization is far from uniform. For many of the poorest least-developed countries the problem is not that they are being impoverished by globalization, but that they are in danger of being largely excluded from it. The miniscule 0.4 percent share of these countries in world trade in 1997 was down by half from 1980. Their access to foreign private investment remains negligible. (PREM, 2000)

Again, the stage is set, and actors have to perform according to someone else's script. Although in terms of most official organizations (such as the WTO) every nation is equal, clearly some are more equal than others. We noted in Chapter 2 that while each member of the World Trade Organization has an equal vote, wealthy nations are much better equipped than are developing nations to put their vote to work, and make it count. And even outside the WTO and other transnational groups, there are pressures on nations to comply with the overall rules of the game: 'in a world of integrated financial markets, countries will find it increasingly risky to follow policies that do not promote financial stability' (IMF, 2000). If we accept that the economies of the world's nations are integrated, then clearly there are strict limits on what can and can't be done, and whose interests will be supported.

It is not just the 'poorest least-developed countries' which are interlopers or visitors in an already established sphere. The (now effectively deceased) Japanese 'economic miracle' is an exemplar of a developed nation which is also not quite the West, and which attributes its success not to its own values, cultural practices and traditional economic system, but to the extent to which it could become integrated within the global economic networks. The Berkeley Roundtable on Economic Integration cited as the first of several explanations for Japan's economic success the fact that it operated on 'a pattern of industrial "catch-up" shaped by import substitution and export promotion policies' (cited Sum, 2000: 118); in other words, Japan didn't experience an economic miracle because of economic genius, luck or something intrinsic in its culture, but because it played 'catch-up' with the West. Indeed, of the five principles it outlined for Japan's success, only one is expressly Japanese: the *keiretsu*, which are the networks of firms built around Japanese banks and corporations. All the others are the usual suspects of flexibility, high technology, government support and so on.

In short, both the IMF and the World Bank recognize clearly that economic globalization is highly uneven; both use the West as the measure of success; but neither seems to recognize or at least acknowledge that many of the problems of the developing world are not only problems in a Western classificatory system, but actually problems caused by the history of economic globalization. The depredations on Africa, for instance, can largely be sheeted home to that 'shameful 19th century episode of globalization', when Europe stripped the continent's resources and upended its cultural and social structures. And there were 'shameful' episodes in the twentieth century too: the regular famines in Africa, India and South-east Asia can be attributed in part to the Green Revolution of the 1960s and 1970s when traditional farming techniques and traditional crops were pushed aside to make way for supercrops of modified rice and wheat – which failed, inevitably, given the lack of liquid capital to purchase the necessary equipment, chemicals and irrigation necessary for their success, and left many producers worse off than they had been before.

Capitalism and commoditization

We pointed out earlier that anti-globalism protesters in places like Seattle, Melbourne and Genoa see economic globalization as necessarily 'bad', because it brings about the violation of traditional lifestyles, the hamstringing of the economies of developing nations, and a disastrously cavalier attitude to the environment. The Sienna Declaration, prepared by the board of directors of the International Forum on Globalization (IFG), and signed by over forty organizations in twenty countries, could be their mouthpiece. It reads:

> Rather than leading to economic benefits for all people, [economic globalization] has brought the planet to the brink of environmental catastrophe, social unrest that is unprecedented, economies of most countries in shambles, an increase in poverty, hunger, landlessness, migration and social dislocation. The experiment may now be called a failure.

This attitude to economic globalization, along with the point we made above that integration relies on the overlooking of the fact that most of the world can only hope to be the poor relations at the trade table, fuels the anti-capitalist sensibility played out in so many contemporary films. Fredric Jameson's *The Geopolitical Aesthetic* (1992) deals with these sorts of films, and the way they represent and play out the sense of a world of capitalist-driven, technological totalization and conspiracy, where every part of life is alienated, infiltrated and commoditized by institutions and agents operating within the global machine of capitalism. Jameson refers particularly to films such as *Alien*, *Three Days of the Condor* and *Videodrome*, and writes that such movies show, over and over, the intrusion of a capitalist logic into everyday life as a kind of colonizing, commoditizing force.

A very carefully detailed representation of this idea of the 'colonization' of everyday life by capitalism can be found in Jean-Pierre Jeunet and Marc Caro's 1995 film *The City of Lost Children*, which is a story about the attempt of an evil character called Krank and his gang of clones to steal the dreams of

children. Childhood, for the adult world, is understood variously – as a stage, a concept, a category; but, perhaps most of all,
it is understood as a dream of innocence, freedom and trust. As
such, childhood is a highly privileged state, at least in principle,
and is also highly marketable. Wide-eyed children are used by
advertisers to 'sell' banks, family cars and new government
policies, and by social groups to 'sell' their issues: family values,
universal education, regulation of paedophilia, and so on. *The
City of Lost Children* plays with these dreams and uses of childhood, and in the process complicates childhood's 'simplicity',
showing instead a world where adults are exploitative, dreams
become full of sinister intent, and innocence exists only to be
corrupted.

The opening sequence is an exemplar for the whole film. The
camera frames a realistic image of a traditional, charming
Christmas scene, where a small child, pyjama-ed and in bed in a
room filled with toys, watches wide-eyed as Santa emerges from
the chimney to offer him a wind-up toy. The child initially
seems taken with this; the sound track plays a lilting and lyrical
arrangement of strings; the impression is of the sanctity of
childhood and children's dreams of Christmas. But this illusion
quickly breaks down as one Santa after another emerges from
the chimney in a relentless reiteration that turns the enchant-
ment of Christmas to something threatening. A bass line comes
heavily in below the violins; the walls and ceiling and furniture
sway and melt; the Santas crowd the bedroom space, sipping
from hip flasks, touching everything in the room; the noise
builds to cacophony; and the reindeer shits on the floor. The
child bursts into frightened tears, scrambles out of his crib and,
keeping a fearful eye on the Santas, snatches up his teddy bear
from the shelf. The child's enchanted world has become a
nightmare.

In this first scene the movie's central threads are conveyed:
the nightmare that masquerades as children's dreams; the
commoditization and corruption of innocence in the service of
self-interest; and, above all, the disenchantment of the world
of childhood as it intersects with the world of the economy. The
capitalist thread of the movie pervades the milieu in one form or

another precisely because almost everybody in the film is marked out and treated, first and foremost, in terms of what Arjun Appadurai calls the process of commoditization (see Appadurai, 1986). This, for Appadurai, refers to the situation where a thing or person is socially and discursively 'produced' predominantly in terms of its exchange value. The children are the primary examples of this in the film. They are either kidnapped in order to be sold to Krank (that is, first their persons are commoditized, and then their dreams), or else they are used by criminal elements as thieves and pickpockets (their small size, agility and unthreatening demeanour making them invaluable in this regard).

But the commoditization of individuals is also played out in the fact that, for the most part, the characters in the movie are indistinguishable or fully exchangeable, and are dehumanized further by their various prostheses and their machine-like functions. The children, for instance, are a ragtag collection of urban orphans, of similar size, dressed similarly in ill-fitting hand-me-downs, and similarly grubby. Krank's assistants, the clones, are also identical, utterly interchangeable, and defined only in terms of the tasks they undertake to keep Krank amused or contented. This multiplicity and indistinguishability is a central feature of the film, a move which effectively challenges the notion of inalienable humanness or individuality, and leaves capitalism untrammelled.

We can trace the intervention of capitalist discourses and practices into the everyday world, from the commoditization of children and childhood to the institution of property rights in Britain in the nineteenth century. The more that things are commoditized, the more commoditization comes to seem the only way to organize a society and its property. John Frow writes:

> The history of the capitalist mode of production is, on this account, a history of the progressive extension of the commodity form to new spheres. The most succinct formulation I know of this historical logic is Wallerstein's statement that capitalism's endless drive to accumulate capital 'pushes towards the commodification of everything'. (1997: 134)

Global capital and convergence

This image of capital as a kind of tsunami that overwhelms local imperatives and traditions originated, to a large extent, with the first wave of 'global capitalism' in the period 1870–1914, a period with which contemporary manifestations of globalization are often compared. Karl Polanyi identifies it as the time when the first crucial step was taken to impose a 'market logic' on wider spheres of human society and activity. What he means by this is that society becomes 'an adjunct to the market. Instead of the economy being embedded in social relations, social relations are embedded in the economic system' (Polanyi, 1957: 57).

Many of the demonstrators at Seattle, Melbourne and Genoa would have probably been of Polanyi's opinion, and shared his notion that, as a consequence of a move to 'market dominance' during the industrial revolution, 'A blind faith in spontaneous progress had taken hold of people's minds, and with the fanaticism of sectarians the most enlightened pressed forward for boundless and unregulated change in society' (Polanyi, 1957: 76). Certainly 'important people', that is, national leaders and other people in a position to make decisions about the extent to which market logic intrudes upon and dominates society, were firmly in the 'blind faith in spontaneous progress' camp. The official response to the demonstrations during 1999, 2000 and 2001 was that the protesters were being selfish, thoughtless and inconsiderate; that they simply didn't understand that the opening up of the world to trade and capital flows, deregulation, and generally the application of market logic to human activities would have an inevitable beneficial effect, not just on their own societies, but more importantly in the developing areas of the world. The logic that these VIPs relied on, without ever specifically naming it, was based on the idea of 'convergence', which is so central to the discourses of economic globalization.

Certainly there is evidence of some form of convergence. The World Bank points out the rapid pace of economic integration during the last decades of the twentieth century, with lowered barriers to international trade and investment, and a shift from state planning to the market and the private sector

(PREM, 2000). But it doesn't begin in the 1980s or 1990s. Kevin H. O'Rourke and Jeffrey G. Williamson outline its history in their book *Globalization and History* (1999), and they identify its origins in the improved systems of transport, and hence greater international trade, during the nineteenth century. O'Rourke and Williamson set themselves the task of looking at nineteenth-century data from what we now call OECD countries, in order to come to some conclusion as to whether **convergence theory** really worked in the nineteenth century, and if so, what factors were most responsible? After studying a range of factors, including capital flows, migration, trade, technology and education, they argued that in fact it is possible to identify economic 'global integration' in the nineteenth century, and that its conditions, scope and intensity in many ways presage what we now refer to as the processes of 'global capitalism'. Both the nineteenth century and the late twentieth century were marked by patterns of globalization, with high flows of capital and labour across national borders; both were marked by high levels of commodity trade; both saw 'an impressive convergence in living standards, at least within most of what we would now call the ... OECD' (O'Rourke and Williamson, 1999: 5).

O'Rourke and Williamson take up the question of this set of parallels between the two periods because, by reading and making sense of nineteenth-century globalization, it should be possible to apply the lessons and knowledge taken from that research to the processes of late twentieth-century global capitalism:

> We want this book to speak to today's debates about the growth of trade, the impact of immigration on local labor markets, the sources of inequality, why more capital does not flow to poor countries, whether trade liberalization can lessen immigration pressures in rich countries, why globalization backlashes arose in the past, and whether we can expect it again as we enter the next century. (O'Rourke and Williamson, 1999: 3)

Of course capitalism today, because of its reliance on 'real time' technology and network culture and logic, is very different from the forms of capitalism that characterized the periods before the 1970s. But the basic question, whether the circulation of goods, labour, technology, ideas, education and capital would decrease inequalities within and/or across 'Atlantic economies', clearly can serve as the basis of comparisons with and evaluations of global capitalism in the contemporary world.

O'Rourke and Williamson's book is far too detailed in its analysis and evaluation of economic data to allow all its main approaches, methodologies, arguments and conclusions to be reproduced here. We can sum up the findings, however, in four main points. Firstly, O'Rourke and Williamson find evidence of convergence, particularly with regard to Scandinavian countries such as Sweden and Denmark, but there is no evidence of what they term 'unconditional convergence' (O'Rourke and Williamson, 1999: 283–4). Secondly, there is little or no evidence to suggest that trade itself was a major factor in convergence, while capital flows appear to be a cause of divergence. Thirdly, there appears to have been a strong positive correlation between flows of migration (and so labour) and convergence across countries and within some countries – especially 'Old World' countries such as Ireland and Italy – and a negative correlation between those flows and convergence in 'labor-scarce New World countries' (O'Rourke and Williamson, 1999: 286). Fourthly, and finally, the idea that the globalizing tendencies of the nineteenth century were cut short by exogenous forces such as World War I is incorrect, they write; rather, political reactions to the consequences of global capital, particularly in the New World, where most of the labour flows were directed, were far more important. In short:

> The evidence presented in this book suggests that . . . a political backlash developed in response to the actual or perceived distributional effects of globalization. The backlash led to the reimposition of tariffs and the adoption of immigration restrictions, even before the Great War. Far from being destroyed by unforeseen and exogenous political events, globalization, at least in part, destroyed itself. (O'Rourke and Williamson, 1999: 286–7)

The most interesting aspect of O'Rourke and Williamson's book is also the most predictable: they find that the open circulation of trade, capital and technology, and improvements in education, can be of benefit to some countries, but not all. And they find that these benefits are unevenly spread – convergence in one country often means divergence somewhere else; benefits accruing to one section or class within a country can mean a decline in the situation of a different group in the same country. Nor were the effects of global capitalism felt equally across the globe. Many of the poorest countries – in the nineteenth century, Spain and Portugal – were largely unaffected by global capitalism in the second half of the nineteenth century: capital flows were absent, there was an absence too of an educated work force and modern technology, and migration, for whatever reason, was not significant.

Putting people back into the debate

O'Rourke and Williamson found that the biggest single factor in reducing inequality between richer and poorer countries was migration, and that, concomitantly, the 'rising inequality in the rich countries ceased exactly when labor migration was choked off by quotas' (O'Rourke and Williamson, 1999: 183). This 'migration backlash', which went a considerable way to halting global capitalism at the end of the nineteenth century, is again a part of the contemporary political landscape, as the rise of xeno-phobic political groups and policies in Britain, Germany, Austria, France, Italy and Australia demonstrates. And curiously, though world leaders such as Clinton, Bush or Blair argue consistently for the deregulation of economic activity and the free movement of capital across the globe, the free movement of people is not on the agenda. In Chapter 1 we pointed to the way in which the Australian Prime Minister in 2001 played the 'race card' in an election campaign by focusing on the threat of asylum seekers, and deflecting public attention from domestic problems in health, aged care and education. This became more extreme as the campaign drew to an end, with stories circulated in the media and by government officials about boat people throwing their children in the water, or setting fire to their own boats, in order to force their way into Australia. The question the Prime Minister asked the electorate – 'Do we really want people like this in Australia?' – was rhetorical; the perception that these people would take over Australian jobs, or reduce the standard of living, meant that they had to be found wanting as human beings. Consequently the public and the media supported the building of a (metaphorical) fence around the island continent to keep out the same people they were determined to 'save' from the Taliban – if only they would stay in Afghanistan. In the middle of this deeply racist election campaign one journalist articulated what seemed to be the general attitude: 'John Howard said what everyone thinks: "This is the best country in the world." Yes, spot on – and the subtext is, it belongs to us' (Shanahan, 2001: 13).

Rather than seeing the 'unfettered circulation' and developing pervasiveness of global capitalism as a means of facilitating convergence, there is considerable evidence for the contrary position; that is, global capital has tended to operate in what we could call a colonialist or neocolonialist fashion. We noted above that while economic globalization appears to offer a level playing field for free exchange, in fact access and opportunities are reserved for wealthy nations. Rather than providing equality of income and wealth, the coming of fully blown global capitalism at the end of the twentieth century has only served to accentuate this trend of divergence. A UNDP report from 1999 presents figures that bear this out. The report notes that 'By the late 1990s the fifth of the world's people living in the highest-income countries had 86 per cent of world GDP. . . 82 per cent of the world export market . . . 68 per cent of foreign direct investment . . . 74 per cent of world telephone lines . . . and 91 per cent of all internet users'; and it goes on to point out that 'the past decade has shown increasing concentration of income, resources and wealth among people, corporations and countries' (UNDP, 2000: 343) – by which is meant people, corporations and countries associated with the OECD countries. What these figures, and many others like them, indicate is that rather than producing the 'world of opportunity' that Ohmae writes about, or even the 'trickle-down' effect championed by Margaret Thatcher, the spread of global capital has helped to produce what could be termed 'the globalization of inequality'.

There are two main reasons for this. The first is that, by and large, worldwide capitalist activity has always been 'inflected'; that is, rather than being a universalizing force or tendency, it has been closely associated in its two periods of dominance (1870–1914 and 1970 to the present) with hegemons in the shape of Great Britain and the United States, with their supporting casts of the European colonial powers and the G-8. These two countries made the activities of global capitalism possible through their military and economic power, and their technological ascendancy, reaped the greatest rewards, and have openly and at times violently promoted the opening up of the globe to capitalism in their own interests.

But of course, steps to impose a market logic on society will not necessarily be entirely successful, so it would be wrong to take the market at its own word, and accept that even Western society has been completely given over to market logic. John Frow, for instance, points to a number of areas of historical counter-evidence of a process of decommoditization – the abolition of slavery, for instance; and of limits on capitalism – for instance, the Victorian era in Britain, when, despite the apparent giving over of everything to the capitalist dream, the state invested enormously in roads, rail, libraries, schools, hospitals and just about any other sort of infrastructure we can imagine (1999: 2). Indeed, 'every extension of the commodity form', he writes, 'has been met with resistance and often with reversal' (Frow, 1997: 135). And there is considerable resistance around the globe to economic globalization and the capitalist hegemony. Pharis Harvey, of the International Labor Rights Fund, for instance, spoke on the PBS Online program *Globalization and Human Rights* (January 1998) and described a global march against child labour which she helped to organize. The march, she said:

> was born in a conversation that I had with Kailash Satyarthi –
> the very charismatic leader of the move to bring children out
> of bonded labor in India – the head of the South Asian

Coalition on Child Servitude. We have ample proof that the children are being used as slaves. They are bought and sold. They are tortured. They are confined to workplace. They are not able to leave their jobs. These are kids working in brick kilns, working in farms as a part of bonded farm labor, working in granite quarries; kids in sexual slavery, or being trafficked across national or state boundaries for sexual purposes. Those are the kinds of kids that this global march is an effort to highlight. So we decided that the global march was a way by which we could bring international pressure to country after country.

This was just one of many actions and reactions against economic globalization by an increasingly organized network of activists. Interestingly, one of the Fund's spokespersons, Naomi Klein, insists that they are themselves part of the global identity:

> there is a new internationalism at play [she states] and the new internationalism is about realizing that all of these issues that we're struggling with, these supposedly local issues, are the same issues around the world, and fundamentally the issue is an issue of self determination. (Klein, 2002)

If indeed there is, 'an integrated, global capital network, whose movements and variable logic ultimately determine economies and influence societies' (Castells, 2000c: 78), then there is also an integrated global anti-capital network whose movements and variable logic interrogate capital's network. The anti-globalization (or, more correctly, anti-economic globalization) group use the technologies and to an extent the discourses of globalization to call it to account; in a sense, they parallel, and are the obverse of, the transnational corporations and national trading blocs which are their necessary enemy.

Workers and corporations

But this is not the only story, of course; resistance to global-ization can only go so far. Frow again writes, in this respect:

> none of this seems to me to undermine the narrative of a
> continual, if uneven, extension of commodification: these
> counter-examples qualify it, they deny it any ineluctability, but
> the logic of historical tendency, however uneven, however
> checked, and however multiply determined, retains its force.
> (1997: 135)

What looks, for instance, like the (at times) relatively erratic and politically neutral global flows of capital are 'motivated'; that is, the effects and consequences of capital moved and removed at speed and in mass inevitably benefit those groups that are economically powerful and relatively autonomous. And this necessarily has a profound impact on everyone else – those who have only their labour power to sell. Manuel Castells writes of labour in the global economy, and insists that 'work is plentiful' but 'the social relationships between capital and labor are profoundly transformed. At its core, capital is global. As a rule, labor is local' (Castells, 2000c: 79). Capital moves to form networks and to integrate its own interests, and so forms a powerful collective identity; labour, on the other hand, is increasingly fractured; it 'loses its collective identity, becomes increasingly individualized in its capacities, in its working conditions, and in its interests and projects' (Castells, 2000c: 79).

Naomi Klein, the anti-globalization activist, describes this process by listing the activities of many of the giant corporations, known around the world because of their effective branding. Corporations like IBM, Nike, Eriksson and Volkswagen, she states, no longer manufacture their products; instead, they manufacture ideas and brands, and outsource those to producing factories. What this means is that they have no funds tied up in the slow and uncertain process of production and distribution, so they can enormously increase their income – but they also have no interest in providing employment or benefits to workers, or in negotiating a safe and mutually satisfying work environment. Castells writes, similarly:

> At a deeper level of the new social reality, social relationships
> of production have been disconnected in their actual existence.

> Capital tends to escape in its hyperspace of pure circulation, while labor dissolves its collective entity into an infinite variation of individual existences. (Castells, 2000c: 80)

In the interests of disconnecting from the 'social relationships of production' and at the same time achieving savings and raising income, Klein writes, corporations move entirely away from production:

> let somebody else produce your products. . . . Better yet, get lots of people, a network, a web, a global web of contractors and sub-contractors and home-workers and temps to all have a shot at getting your contract, and then you buy from the cheapest bidder. (Klein, 2002)

But it doesn't stop there; she goes on to describe this as the paradigm of 'the hollow corporation', and to compare it with the old paradigm where:

> We say, 'OK, well a factory closed in Australia,' or 'A factory closed in the United States. It moved to Indonesia. It moved to Mexico.' And we imagine that that's how it works, right? That a factory closes and then the factory opens and people who are paid less work in that factory. But that's actually not what happens. What happens is that companies make a strategic decision to no longer be in the manufacturing business, and those jobs turn into contracts to be placed with this network.

The free flow of capital does not mean that people can move about the globe to follow opportunities; it means that corporations are free to pursue their greatest profit, pretty much regardless of the human consequences and without regard to the social costs (and benefits) of production. Bauman writes that mobility is the new wealth; because shareholders are not bound by locality, they can pick up their industry and go; and aren't committed in any way to the maintenance of the community, or the needs of locals and workers: 'If the new exterritoriality of the elite feels like intoxicating freedom,' he states, 'the territoriality of the rest feels less like home ground, and ever more like prison – all the more humiliating for the obtrusive sight of the others' freedom to move' (Bauman, 1998: 23).

Still, it is important not to overemphasize the notion that capitalism is exclusively 'of and for itself', and without regard to the social, political and cultural spheres in which it operates. We have already seen that there are always counter-hegemonic actions (protests, marches, 'illegal' flows of workers across state borders). This can have effects on national policy and on the actions of corporations. The World Bank has responded to the mass of illegal migration and asylum seeking in the years around the turn of the millennium by putting human needs and labour mobility back on the agenda. It points out in a 2002 report that legal migration levels are considerably lower than they were a century earlier, and that large flows of people in the period 1870–1914 were associated with high economic growth. The globalization of people, this implies, is good for the global-ized economy. And besides, it fits with the overall discourses of globalization and neoliberalism, and critics of free-market economics can use this 'loophole' in its own discourses. Dani Rodrick from Harvard University does something like this, writing:

> If international policy-makers were really interested in
> maximising worldwide efficiency, they would spend little of
> their energies on a new trade round or on the international
> financial architecture. They would all be busy at work
> liberalising immigration restrictions. . . . the gains from
> liberalising labour movements across countries are enormous.
> (Cited Kelly, 2002: 28)

So a combination of response to protesters, self-interest (since increased migration may equal increased profits), compliance with the central premise of the neoliberal argument, and the insistence of official transnational authority could produce a change in the severe restrictions on human flows and greater access to the benefits promised by globalization. But the precedents of the late nineteenth and early twentieth-century

United States, Argentina, Canada and Australia suggest that this is highly unlikely; even if free migration is beneficial for capitalism, it tends to be opposed by citizens of affluent states determined to protect their standard of living. If governments want to stay in power and avoid popular resentment, they will resort to policies which seem antithetical to their support of globalization (as per the example, in Chapter 1, of the Australian government's attitude to refugees).

Corporations and states

Wallerstein points out that the need of the capitalist classes to promote their interests within nation-states through the creation or strengthening of what he calls the 'state-machineries' of core states such as Britain, France and Germany means they become serious players in the game of the globalized economy. In this he is echoing Michel Foucault, who argues that the spread of capitalism occurs as an adjunct to the development of 'the reason of state'. But Wallerstein does not subscribe entirely to the view, often found in writings on globalization, that what we now have is, effectively, government by corporation. He writes, rather, that the state machineries which indeed often do work in the interests of capital also work in their own interests, and in the interests of the people who staff them. Because no state machinery in a capitalist country can serve only, and overtly, the needs of corporations but must serve the needs of the government and the people as well, bureaucracy must claim a neutral position as the carrier of universal, or general, interest; but in fact, Claude Lefort writes, 'the general interest amounts to no more than the interest of the bureaucracy' (1986: 92). This means that although, as Weber suggests, bureaucracy serves government, industry and other dominant groups, it can work counter to the dominant interests. To return to Wallerstein:

> The formula of the state as 'executive committee of the ruling class' is only valid, therefore, if one bears in mind that

executive committees are never mere reflections of the wills of their constituents, as anyone who has ever participated in any organization well knows. (2000: 236)

Certainly, we do not need to argue that the acme of capitalism (in this period, the United States) is characterized by tensions between the interests of different groups – the rivalry and tensions between the institutions of capitalism and the military, bureaucracies, religious fundamentalists, regional affiliations, lobby groups and even political parties, to name just a few, are well known. The policies and activities of, say, the US government cannot be reduced, even under the 'business-friendly' presidencies of Ronald Reagan and George W. Bush, to a mere 'servicing' of capitalism. We already noted, in Chapter 1, that after the attacks of 11 September a political momentum developed in the United States which more or less forced Bush and his allies to pursue policies which were not necessarily in the interests of capital. Indeed, what happened after 11 September was that the United States was in some ways split between two – in this case mutually exclusive – 'performances' of itself. The first was 'America as business', the second 'America as superpower'. The first revolved around the notion that 'the business of America is business'; in other words, a more or less complete identification of the United States with capitalism. This had been played out over the years in the United States, particularly under Reagan and George W. Bush, in the deregulation of the few areas of the economy that had come under government intervention: aircraft maintenance and safety requirements, for instance, were 'freed up' under Reagan. It didn't just apply to internal measures, though; in global governance forums the United States inevitably argued or voted against measures that would disadvantage the free circulation of capital. When the issue of the need for cheaper medicines for developing countries was discussed at the WTO meeting in Qatar in 2001, for instance, the United States opposed (that is, effectively vetoed) the move, despite the catastrophic spread and pervasiveness of the AIDS virus in Africa and parts of Asia, because it was not in the interest of drug companies.

The second performance of US identity after 11 September was that of the 'superpower' whose authority had been challenged: to a certain extent, the refusal of the United States to give serious consideration to either the legalities or the consequences of its actions in bombing and invading Afghanistan, for instance, constituted a testimony with regard to its belief in the 'righteousness' of its actions, and the need to re-emphasize its power. What is interesting about this second performance is the way it largely undermined the first – the notion of a direct fit between the United States and capitalism. This was played out not just at the macro-level of social politics (through policies that 'hurt' capitalist institutions), but also at a micro-level, as exemplified in the backlash in the United States against too obvious attempts to profit from 11 September, such as the marketing of goods associated with the attacks in New York.

Of course, as analysts as far removed from one another as Immanuel Wallerstein and Jean Baudrillard have noted, this ultimate refusal of any state, even the United States, to identify completely with, or be subordinated to, the interests of capitalism is reciprocated by capitalist organizations and institutions. As Jean Baudrillard once suggested: 'capitalism has never believed in, or committed to, the notion of a social contract' (1983: 29). This makes it difficult to understand corporations as citizens, since the conventions of coexistence demand some adherence to social rules, and general agreement on what can and cannot be done in a particular society. And, increasingly, corporations do at least appear to be stateless, and therefore divorced from the obligations of society, particularly because of the presence of the kinds of technology-driven changes which mark global capital. Held and McGrew write that:

> In the age of the internet . . . capital – both productive and financial – has been liberated from national and territorial constraints, while markets have become globalized to the extent that the domestic economy constantly has to adapt to global competitive conditions. In a wired world, software engineers in Hyderabad can do the jobs of software engineers in London for a fraction of the cost. Inscribed in the dynamics

of this new global capitalism is a powerful imperative towards the denationalization of strategic economic activities. (2000: 25)

We need to ask, though, whether it is valid to speak of the technology/capitalist nexus as being the dominant and defining aspect of economic activity, and overdetermining social and political imperatives. Manuel Castells addresses this question cautiously. While he is quite certain about the importance of what he calls informational capitalism, he is more ambivalent about the extent to which capitalist activity is global.

We have already discussed the problems associated with labour in a global economy; and Castells points out that, while labour markets are not yet global, labour is a global resource. This is because capitalism moves to where labour is cheap and non-unionized, and it will move away again when it senses that these conditions are changing. But while labour may be inclined to move to wherever work is, there is an increasing tendency for states to close their borders to, or restrict the movement of, immigrants – which limits the extent to which the labour end of capitalist activity can be seen as global.

Another aspect of capitalist activity is the science, research and development, and technology that are constitutive of informational capitalism. This too, according to Castells, is organized in global flows (2000b: 260), but he accepts that such flows are very much confined to selected sites and nodes of the capitalist network, particularly in Europe, the United States and Japan, while they virtually bypass many other areas of the world, such as most of Africa, the South Pacific and Western Asia – another limit on globalization.

The third feature of capitalist activity Castells notes relates to markets for goods and services. These, he argues, are also increasingly showing globalized tendencies, but this tendency is countered by the continued existence of protectionist national policies which restrict trade: in March 2002, for instance, the United States raised tariffs against imported steel to protect the jobs of American steel workers; and began discussions about new tariffs on agricultural products. Another factor that militates against the globalization of markets for goods and services is the fact, Castells writes, that 'domestic markets account for the largest share of GDP in most countries' (2000b: 260). It is the production and distribution process, and its management, he argues, which are truly global, with components being produced and assembled, and goods and services distributed, via networks ranging across firms in different countries.

For Castells this process is irreversible, for three reasons. Firstly, to be outside this 'web' of production and distribution means corporations are disadvantaged cost-wise, because they are denied access to markets and the accompanying economies of scale. Secondly, it also means being restricted in access to the flow of information essential to activities such as the programming and co-ordination of production runs. And thirdly, this lack of access would also militate against the managerial and decision-making flexibility that is required if corporations are to remain competitive with regard to the 'variable geometry' of production and distribution that constitutes the global economy.

Conclusion

These arguments as to the global nature of capitalism are disputed, or strongly qualified, by a number of analysts, including Stephen Cohen, Held and McGrew or Nye and Donahue, who deny, firstly, that the world economy has achieved a significant level of integration of production, distribution or labour, and secondly, that territoriality is an irrelevant issue even to the most transnationally inclined of corporations. Castells himself accepts that:

> There is not, and there will not be in the foreseeable future, a fully integrated, open world market for labor, technology, goods and services, as long as nation states (or associations of nation states, such as the European Union) exist, and as long as governments are there to foster the interests of their citizens and of firms in the territories under their jurisdiction. (2000a: 98)

If the continued existence of the state, and the national and local politics that characterize it, constitute an insuperable barrier to the realization of a fully integrated global economy (particularly in the area of labour), it is also true that throughout the world the sovereignty of the state, and many of the characteristics associated with it, are being eroded or challenged by the technology and activities of global capitalism. In our next chapter we will look at the one of the core claims made about globalization: that, in effect, it is supplanting and rendering irrelevant the role and power of nation-states.

5

The State and Sovereignty

We suggested in the previous chapters that debates about the reality of globalization were tied up with the politics of naming, the deployment of neoliberal ideologies through that naming, and the relationship between those ideologies and the changes in everyday life enabled by the new technologies. We also suggested that this 'doxa' of globalization operates, in John Frow's terms, as a discursive grid of power which passes over and through, and in the process transforms, people and identities, institutions and cultures, places and events.

One of the important transformations is that of the nation-state. According to some of the more enduring stories of globalization, the increasing significance of a global economy and communication network has gone hand in hand with a decline in the nation-state. The argument is that the throng of trans- and multinational corporations, international bodies of jurisdiction and management, and the congeries of regional and international blocs means that the nation-state has lost its reason-to-be, and will necessarily wither away. What will replace it is not particularly clear; in the latter part of the twentieth century occasional reports pointed to the possibility of a 'one world government', but this vision no longer has much valence. An alternative might be something along the lines of the first President George Bush and his vision of a 'new world order' associated with the Gulf War of 1991 – a kind of international commonwealth led by the United States. A third, and perhaps more likely, forecast is that of global rule by big business. This is the future that the anti-globalization protesters are resisting so vocally, in concert with academics, journalists, politicians and consumer advocates such as Ralph Nader, who voiced their fears in these terms:

> The essence of globalization is a subordination of human rights, of labor rights, consumer, environmental rights, democracy rights, to the imperatives of global trade and investment. This is world government of the EXXONs, by the General Motors, for the DuPonts. (Nader, 1998)

A fourth possibility is the retraction of nation-states into multiple small ethnic and warring communities, a global version of Bosnia during the break-up of Yugoslavia in the 1990s. Benjamin Barber writes:

> Just beyond the horizon of current events lie two possible political futures – both bleak, neither democratic. The first is a retribalization of large swaths of humankind by war and bloodshed: a threatened Lebanonization of national states in which culture is pitted against culture, people against people, tribe against tribe – a Jihad in the name of a hundred narrowly conceived faiths against every kind of interdependence, every kind of artificial social cooperation and civic mutuality. The second is being borne in on us by the onrush of economic and ecological forces that demand integration and uniformity and that mesmerize the world with fast music, fast computers, and fast food – with MTV, Macintosh, and McDonald's, pressing nations into one commercially homogenous global network: one McWorld tied together by technology, ecology, communications, and commerce. The planet is falling precipitately apart AND coming reluctantly together at the very same moment. (Barber, 1992)

Between these two extremes – the McWorld/Exxon option and tribal anarchy – and moving across the other alternatives outlined above are a set of practices of global governance that have been rehearsed very visibly since 11 September. In this chapter we discuss the effects of globalization on nation-states by examining the sets of discourse and practice that have shaped contemporary international affairs. We take up particularly the question of the 'state of the state', and whether it is indeed withering away in the face of globalizing tendencies; and if so, what is likely to replace it.

Sovereignty and Empire

The argument most commonly put forward as evidence for the decline of state **sovereignty** is that the globalization of capitalism has left its institutions and organizations (trans- and multi-national corporations, media and communication networks, the IMF and the World Bank) relatively independent of the power and control of nation-states. Michael Hardt and Antonio Negri argue, however, that the decline of the nation-state does not mean that sovereignty has disappeared or even declined:

> Throughout the continuing transformations, political controls, state functions and regulatory mechanisms have continued to rule the realm of economic production and exchange. Our basic hypothesis is that sovereignty has taken a new form, comprised of a series of national and supranational organizations united under a simple logic of rule. The new global order of sovereignty is what we call Empire. (Hardt and Negri, 2000: xi–xii)

This notion of Empire, to which we referred in Chapter 2, is based on the argument that no one state has the power or authority not just to take on an imperial role, but even to regulate and control its own so-called internal economic, political or cultural affairs. Hardt and Negri suggest that these roles have now largely passed into the domain of Empire, which is understood as a pyramid-like structure with the United States at the top, organizations such as the G-8 and the United Nations occupying the second tier, and a heterogeneous set of institutions (multinational corporations, NGOs and less powerful nation-states) on the third tier.

According to Hardt and Negri, the Westphalia model of sovereignty has been in crisis since the founding of the League of Nations, and has now been rendered all but obsolete by the combination of contemporary communication technology, the pervasiveness and power of global capitalism, and the recent development of the United Nations as a *de facto* site for, and authority with regard to, what they refer to as 'global civil society' (2000: 7). With regard to this last point, they argue that first the League of Nations and then the United Nations have overseen a move from a **Westphalia model** of international relations, based on the integrity of state sovereignty and inter-national contracts and treaties, to a totalizing framework of power based on a supranational-based notion of ethical beha-viour and rights. The UN intervention in Bosnia is one example of this development. It doesn't matter that the intervention was botched, misguided or ineffective; what is important is that it demonstrated international belief in, and commitment to, the United Nation's moral, ethical and political right to overturn the sovereign rights of nation-states.

Hardt and Negri focus on, and take seriously, the develop-ment of an Enlightenment-driven notion of a universal ethics that mediates the local on a global scale. They point out, for instance, that the United Nations and other supranational bodies play a prominent role in the so-called 'new world order' in two important respects. Firstly, Empire is predicated on establishing a consensus 'that supports its own power' (Hardt and Negri, 2000: 15), and secondly, it sets itself the task of arbitrating and solving all conflicts and crises that arise around the globe. Now, these two imperatives require more than mere military or economic power; any kind of military or economic intervention must, if it is to be successful, produce itself as being grounded in an (largely) uncontestable ethics (the commitment to restore democracy, end human rights abuses and bring about peace, for example). Hardt and Negri argue that, from the Gulf War onward (and this is certainly the case with the 'war on terrorism'), Empire has produced its military interventions as 'just wars'; that is to say, military forces and technologies, and the destruction they cause, are represented, with the help of the media, as 'ethical instruments'. This would be impossible, of course, without the support, authority and credibility provided by the United Nations.

This focus on the role of the United Nations and other supranational bodies does not mean, however, that Hardt and Negri endorse the narrative of political affairs moving, in a transcendental, Hegelian way, from being dominated by local inflections (primarily played out within the parameters of state sovereignty) to being grounded in, and mediated by, a universal ethics which, Fukuyama-like, signals the end of history. On the contrary, they understand the narrative of the 'end of state sovereignty', like the story of Empire itself, as being driven by changes within capitalism and, concomitantly, by developments in communication technology. And these changes are so pervasive that Hardt and Negri insist that the decline of nation-state sovereignty is not only played out in international relations; it extends to power relations at the level, and within the boundaries, of the state.

We outlined Hardt and Negri's account of the narrative of the transformation of contemporary capitalism, and its relationship to the nation-state, in Chapter 4. It is sufficient to say here that the so-called consensus that Empire purports to bring about at both global and local levels is predicated not on any commitment to universal ethics (except at the level of the necessity of a discursive performance of commitment – something which drove, to a large extent, the eventual United Nations intervention in East Timor), but on economic imperatives, values and ideals such as free trade, economic deregulation, a positive trade balance and floating currencies. In basic terms, the imperatives that supposedly animated the nation-state, such as responsibility for and control over the production and regulation of social relations, are replaced by the notion of the state's responsibility to the market. The market then partly picks up the slack of the social through its various institutions (banks, international organizations, corporations) which, along with the non-market players such as NGOs, derive their authority from what Hardt and Negri refer to as the 'transnational level of power' (2000: 308) that is Empire.

Sovereignty and global contexts

Hardt and Negri, and most other analysts of the place of the state in the contemporary globalized world, refer to four main factors that have clearly impacted upon state sovereignty: new communication technologies; changes in economic practice; the 'end of history' thesis; and the increasingly global flows of people (including refugees and terrorists), with the related difficulty of maintaining national security. The first, new communication technologies, is considered to constitute an assault on the nation-state because they make it extremely difficult for any government to control the flow of images, information, arguments and ideas into and across its territory. In the past a state exercised a reasonable amount of control over the movement of ideas and images because these were usually disseminated in the form of objects – books, pamphlets, letters, records, films. Material objects (hard copy) can be excluded or destroyed in a way that the ephemeral forms of virtual texts (soft copy) cannot. So, for instance, Nazi Germany prohibited the ownership of books and records of which it disapproved in the 1930s and 1940s; America regulated Hollywood films, blacklisting actors, writers and directors, in the 1950s; South Africa under apartheid banned books, films and music identified as communist, obscene or otherwise unwelcome; and Russia and China censored or limited the importation of American and other Western films and books in the 1950s and 1960s. But in the contemporary world of electronic communication, restricting the flow of texts and hence of ideas is very difficult to achieve. This doesn't mean states don't attempt to control this flow. Singapore restricts internet access, China negotiated with Rupert Murdoch to exclude the BBC from its satellite service, and in Afghanistan the Taliban punished people found in unauthorized possession of Western communication technology. But these are exceptions which prove the rule that communication flows have effectively sidestepped state control.

The second reason put forward for the irrelevance of the state is tied up with changes in the economic sphere. Proponents of globalization insist that the nation is not under attack in this respect: the IMF, for instance, insists that 'globalization does not reduce national sovereignty. It does create a strong incentive for governments to pursue sound economic policies' (IMF, 2000). The reduction of national sovereignty to the pursuit of sound economic policies does not mollify those who are concerned by the supposedly growing irrelevance of the nation-state. Moreover, though states are (theoretically) in control of their own economies, and able to formulate economic policies that suit local interests, needs and conditions, there have been a number of developments that limit this control. The attempts of GATT and subsequently the WTO to reduce protectionism; the relative independence and increasing influence of transnational corporations; the move to form trading blocs such as the EU and NAFTA; the increasingly interventionist and influential role of the World Bank, the IMF and rating agencies; and the erratic and potentially destabilizing effects of capital flows and currency speculation – these factors have all contributed to vitiate, and in many cases remove, the economic sovereignty of the nation-state. This occurs overtly where states such as Indonesia, Argentina and Brazil have had their economic policies dictated to them by the IMF and the World Bank in their roles as agencies of global economic governance.

It also occurs less dramatically, but with equal impact, through what Manuel Castells terms the 'network effect'. He puts this forward as the condition of contemporary business activity for corporations, but it also applies to nation-states because the networks of trade and association between nations mean that a local (national) economic move has ramifications for many other nations. For instance, the contraction in the Japanese economy in 2000 also affected Japan's trading partners, countries normally frequented by Japanese tourists and countries which were sites for Japanese manufacturing and research and development. Such nations were faced with the choice of increasing the level of subsidies to Japanese-based locally manufacturing plants, or accepting the politically and economically unpalatable consequences of factories being closed and large numbers of workers becoming unemployed.

The third reason put forward for the irrelevance of the contemporary state is a variant of Francis Fukuyama's 'end of history' thesis. According to this thesis, the triumph of Western-style democratic capitalism, with its attendant values of individualism, human rights and liberalism, has succeeded in doing away with ideological differences and competitors in the form of, say, communism or Islam, and as a consequence has reduced states to copies of one another. That is, a Fukuyama-style argument might run, there are no fundamental political, economic, cultural, legal, technological or social differences between any of the developed states. And those states which are less developed (say, the Czech Republic, Russia, South Africa, Thailand) or underdeveloped (Nigeria, Vietnam, El Salvador, Jamaica) are simply on the way to becoming like the developed states. Given this teleological reading, it seems only a matter of time before states hand over their sovereignty in all important areas such as defence, health and education to institutions of global governance such as the United Nations, the WTO, the IMF or UNESCO.

The fourth reason, a pragmatic variation of the third, is that states are increasingly unable to maintain their sovereignty against various threats such as terrorism, international crime or illegal immigration. The security role of the nation-state is increasingly being passed over to international defence coalitions or bodies such as the United Nations: in Kosovo and East Timor, for instance, the keeping of the peace was dependent on the presence of NATO or United Nations troops. Even in areas like Western Europe, Scandinavia, Australasia or North America, where there is no obvious threat or danger of military attacks or conflicts, the sheer cost of maintaining and equipping a large military force, or dealing with the complexities of terrorism or the international drug trade, mean that it is sensible for states to pool their resources and have one organization that defends everybody – or at least to work through or with global institutions.

The end of the state?

These are all reasonable issues to take into account when considering the 'state of the state'. But a broader question that needs to be asked is, to what extent does the enmeshing of the state in global networks at cultural, political, media, economic, military and political levels actually constitute something new? Arjun Appadurai suggests that it does, and that there are a number of factors that radically differentiate the contemporary state from its predecessors. His point is that it is becoming increasingly difficult for any state to produce a sense of social/national identity because of the wide reach of the electronic media, and the increasing fragmentation of identity (Appadurai, 1997: 189). So, for instance, people might think of themselves locally as English or Welsh, and globally as part of Generation X, with their national identity of 'British' just bringing up the rear.

In order to consider Appadurai's argument that the contemporary globalized world constitutes a break from previous paradigms of the nation-state, we will revisit the reasons raised above for the argument that the state is losing relevance. We will consider the extent to which they can be read as evidence of a continuum between the ideologies and practices of globalization, on the one hand, and the interests of nation-states on the other. The arguments raised and discussed here will be deployed to outline how globalization, as a doxa and as a set of practices and technologies, has changed the condition of the state in the twenty-first century.

Technology and territoriality

The first argument regarding the growing irrelevance of the modern nation-state is that technology has made it increasingly difficult for states to regulate the flow of information, images and capital in and across their territory, and thus to control the economic sphere or the production of meanings. This is an important point, because to a large extent the economy and the sphere of meaning are the bases of state sovereignty. We tend to think of the nation-state as relatively ahistorical; after all, it is difficult for people in the contemporary world to imagine a time before America, or to recall that populations in areas that we now call Italy and Germany quite recently thought of themselves not as Italians or Germans but as members of the aristocracy or the peasantry, as Milanese or Prussians, as Catholics or Protestants. But the system of sovereign nation-states that we know today was not always there. Most analysts accept that this system emerged with the signing in 1648 of the Peace of Westphalia, which ended the Thirty Years' War in Europe. A condition of the Peace was the recognition of sovereign states with clear geographical boundaries, and recognized governments which held the monopoly of force over their territory. It changed the previous system of government and forms of identification because of this institution of territoriality and autonomy:

> Territoriality means that political authority is exercised over a definite geographic space rather than, for instance, over people, as would be the case in a tribal form of political order. Autonomy means that no external actor enjoys authority within the borders of the state. (Krasner, 2000: 124)

Not that the Westphalian model has been fully successful; it operates more as a principle than an actuality, and it has often been overturned by inequitable international power relations, or by the atrophying of the state apparatuses used to control and govern populations. Krasner continues:

> Breaches of the Westphalian model have been an enduring characteristic of the international environment because there is nothing to prevent them. Rulers have chosen or been forced to accept other principles, including human rights, minority rights, democracy, communism, and fiscal responsibility. There has never been some golden age of the Westphalian state. The Westphalian model has never been more than a reference point or a convention. (Krasner, 2000: 124)

Despite the regular instances of breaches in the Westphalia principle, it has still exercised a great deal of influence over the behaviour of states. One example can be seen in the way the

Australian government addressed the Indonesian treatment of East Timor from the 1970s to the late 1990s. Australia maintained a strong commitment, at least on paper, to human rights, but it effectively turned a blind eye to Indonesian genocidal policies in East Timor until after the fall of President Suharto, largely because of the question of sovereignty – and, importantly, because of Indonesia's ability to protect its interests. When Australia and the United Nations did finally intervene to facilitate the independence of East Timor, Australia–Indonesia relations were seriously impaired because there was a perception in Indonesia that Australia was interfering with Indonesian sovereignty.

The second issue with regard to the lineage of the nation-state is that states are neither natural nor homogeneous entities. Putting together and maintaining a nation-state is an extraordinarily time- and resource-consuming performance, in which groups of people who may be separated by many of the factors that are central to identity – such as religion, geography, dress, customs, values, language, political affiliations, history or diet – are brought together through what Benedict Anderson calls 'the imagining of community' (1983: 17), which is effected by the mass media and other cultural products. Governments are closely involved in producing the sense of a homogeneous community of 'us' by various mechanisms, such as the constant reiteration of national pride and traditions, state investment in cultural products like films and visual art that are identified as the 'face' of the nation, policies and practices like electoral rolls, visa control and a national exchequer, all designed to 'prove' the nation's existence because of the mass of material culture that goes under its name. At the same time, most governments also put considerable energy and investment into building places and technologies of discipline and surveillance of their own populations – police forces, secret services, prisons, the whole bureaucratic mechanism – designed to ensure that the people remain committed to and believing in the idea of their nation, and that they behave accordingly.

What makes this a particularly difficult task for a nation like Indonesia is its quite exceptional geographical, cultural, linguistic, racial, economic and religious diversity, coupled with the resentment brought on by widespread local perception that Indonesia is being run by and for the Javanese. When Indonesia first gained independence from the Dutch, President Sukarno attempted to overcome Indonesia's diversity and differences by developing a state ideology – Pancasila – which supposedly incorporated core Indonesian traditional values. There were two problems with this move. Firstly, it took its core values from a national tradition which the values themselves were meant to bring into being; in other words, it presumed the nation in order to justify and perpetuate the nation. Secondly, the five core values of Pancasila were so vague that they constituted an 'empty set' which any government or ruler could fill in, in order to exclude groups and exercise power. This means, as a corollary, that the nation-state is always a precarious entity.

But if nation-states such as Indonesia are such precarious entities, then surely the challenges posed by global communication technologies have dealt them a death blow? One line of argument certainly supports this position, with the notion that governments are increasingly losing control over what is perhaps the central reason of state: the management of their populations. As we pointed out above, states came into existence by first producing and then stage-managing a national or collective identity for their citizens. Now people have the option of various forms of identity which are made available to them through the electronic domain and which threaten the ability of a state to maintain its own identity, and to sustain its citizens' belief in, and adherence to, its legitimacy.

The growing independence of the media is a very important factor in this situation. The mass media have served as a tool of nation-building by such means as public broadcasting in the official language of the nation, documentaries on 'our history' or the dissemination of national ceremonies – the broadcast of the coronation of Queen Elizabeth II by the BBC in 1953, for instance. But the media are no longer as susceptible to government needs as in past decades. In *The Power of Identity* (1997: 254–60) Manuel Castells tracks the changes from the early 1980s, when virtually every television network was state-controlled and radio and print media were carefully regulated, to the 1990s, when, as an effect of the emergence of new technologies and of media mergers, most governments lost the ability to control the media of transmission, and became increasingly influenced by, and even dependent upon, the fourth estate. Instead of exerting power over the media, governments had to fall back on the lesser form of influence over the media.

This vitiation of state regulation of the media and, as a consequence, of national identity occurred across two trajectories – exterior/global and interior/local. The external trajectory is associated with the inability of governments to control or limit the pervasive reach of transnational media corporations such as AOL-Time-Warner, Bertelsmann and Viacom. Flows of images, information and ideas from across the globe offer citizens a smorgasbord of forms of identification; and of course provide reportage that may be very much at odds with the local government's interpretation of national or global events. An example of this is the South African government's refusal to develop a television network until the mid-1970s, which was associated with unwillingness to let South Africans see other ways of organizing a multicultural and multiracial nation. Ironically, prior to the collapse of apartheid, one of the most popular television shows among all the population groups was the *Cosby Show*. This African-American family sitcom presented both black and white communities with a representation of black identity that was utterly precluded by South African legislation, and that demonstrated the emptiness at the heart of apartheid's logic of separate development and the 'natural' inequality of races.

The second trajectory affects the other end of the scale – that is, local levels – and is associated with the rise of local radio, newspapers and cable television, which present local audiences with local stories and images, and local forms of identification. The media, which were so important in the construction of national identity by interpellating (or calling into being) small groups as part of the nation, here again slip away from the state's control by ignoring or downplaying national stories and images in favour of the local or ethnic. An example of this effect can be seen in the debates in the late twentieth century about the institution of, say, Welsh-language television. This allowed the people of Wales to see themselves and their own lifestyles and interests, and to hear their own language in an authorized site (the media) and so to be 'interpellated' as 'Welsh' and local-specific rather than under the collective national identity of Britain. These two trajectories of global and local media thus simultaneously attenuate the nation-building project which the state has run through the media, and strengthen local identifications.

The global economy and national identity

Globalization has thus changed the rules of the game for nation-states in the areas of the media and culture; a second reason for the supposed irrelevance of the state is to be found in the economic sphere. Castells cites a variety of examples to back up this latter contention, from the inability of states to with-stand pressure from powerful financial institutions to the dependence of states on global capital markets to finance their fiscal deficits. This is not restricted to the usual cases of, say, the IMF and developing nations, but also the *de facto* influence of the Bundesbank over European economies, and the struggles of major national economies like Germany and the United States to balance their books.

Related to this issue is the argument that, because of the increasing influence of world capital markets and transnational corporations, states now tend to function primarily in the interests of global capital, rather than functioning for their citizens and for national interests. This has had a devastating impact on the welfare state, as Pierre Bourdieu points out in his critique of an article written by Bundesbank Chairman Tietmeyer and published in the French newspaper *Le Monde*. He cites Tietmeyer as stating that 'The crucial issue today is to create the conditions favourable to lasting growth, and the confidence of investors. It is therefore necessary to restrain public spending' (1998a: 46). Bourdieu interprets this as a call to bury the welfare state so that taxation can be reduced, and investors assured that their interests – and not the interests of the poor or the working classes – are the government's priority.

In these sorts of neoliberal arguments, which have been turned into policy by many previously 'welfare'-oriented states, we can identify a shift from government 'for the people' to government 'for the economy'. Proponents of this approach do not see it as having a negative effect on the state. Rather, they argue, this overdetermination of the state by global capital will in fact benefit and strengthen the state. This is, they say, because global capital is drawn to countries that offer security, stability and continuity because transnational corporations need to know that their investments and their workers will be able to operate without interruption or threat from social and political upheaval, crime or economic crises. Thus a corporation choosing between, say, Argentina and Canada, may identify economic advantages on the Argentinian side in the form of cheaper labour or lower taxes, but the long-term stability of Canada may win out in the end.

While this appears to offer a mutually profitable outcome for corporations and countries, in fact its effect is still that the state is governing for the economy. The argument that global capital is drawn to stable states means that the states that 'win' are the ones capable of keeping order through their police forces, bureaucracies and compliant media, so that business can get on with its job of making money. This may allow a government to attract global investment, but it is likely to contribute to the growing fragmentation of its population, and to undermine its citizens' belief in its own legitimacy. We made the point earlier that nation-states are not natural or homogeneous entities; they are imagined into existence, and need to strive continuously to induce their citizens to believe in them. Such belief is, in the long term, likely to be given only if the state reciprocates; that is, if it acts as if it believes that it has a duty to care for its citizens.

Now of course states always 'perform' – through the media, bureaucracies and educational institutions – what we can call their commitment to the notion of the social contract. But once it becomes apparent that a state's primary concern is 'someone else' – say, global capital – then both the government and the idea of the nation are on thin ice. So the kinds of issues that Bourdieu refers to as being de-emphasized by states in his piece on Tietmeyer (Bourdieu, 1998a: 45–51) – broadly gathered together under the rubric of social services – are in fact crucial to a citizen's belief that the state is holding up its end of the social contract.

The failure of most nation-states to convince their citizens of this is demonstrated by the continuing trend towards the atomization or localization of social, cultural and economic functions and identities within states. Castells has argued, using examples taken from the United States, China, Latin America and Russia, that the state has been unable to deal effectively with the increasing disappearance of a single national identity in favour of local identities, and the mass of competing demands made by the many discrete groups that now so vocally make up any nation-state. He writes that the response of many nations has been to decentralize, to establish local and regional sub-governments, and thus reclaim their own legitimacy as the government of the governments. Of course, this presents new problems for the state: 'local and regional governments may seize the initiative on behalf of their populations, and may engage in developmental strategies vis a vis the global system, eventually coming into competition with their own parent states' (Castells, 1997: 271–2).

So the combination of the state's dependence on global markets, its vulnerability to capital flows, the growing independence of the media and the growing fragmentation of identity among its citizens clearly vitiate state sovereignty. But there are aspects of the so-called 'withering away' – or at the very least the transformation – of the state which need to be mentioned. Castells insists that, while the nation-state may have been radically changed by globalizing pressures, it is by no means irrelevant or likely to disappear in the near future. Zygmunt Bauman (1998: 64) provides evidence of this, pointing out that after the fall of the Soviet Union many of the now splintered groups, although small and impoverished, insisted on the right to form themselves into states along the Westphalia principles of territoriality and autonomy, and to begin negotiations to join alliances such as the European Union and NATO. In other words, having escaped the Soviet Union and their satellite status there, they were very eager to be identified first as independent states and then as co-operating members of a different sort of transnational union. This sort of instance seems to support the line of argument that state sovereignty is not necessarily incompatible with globalizing tendencies.

The nation-state and the 'end of history'

While contemporary states may have ceded or lost authority within their territories, perhaps a bigger threat to their sovereignty has come in the sphere of international relations. The two final arguments we referred to earlier in this chapter regarding the supposed irrelevance of the state in a globalized world are in a sense opposite sides of the same coin. One side is the 'end of history' thesis, the contention that states are naturally evolving into supranational or global organizations that are increasingly taking over responsibilities in wider economic, legal, cultural, technological, diplomatic, social and military spheres. The other side argues that these areas have become so complicated that states can no longer address them, and are effectively ceding their authority to inter- or transnational organizations that can, such as the United Nations, the World Trade Organization, NATO, the International Monetary Fund and the European Union.

Whichever side of the coin we subscribe to, it does seem valid to argue that states' autonomy is under threat in an age of global networks. Probably the most obvious example of this trend has occurred in the military sphere, and in what has been termed 'global governance'. The World Trade Organization and the United Nations, for instance, consistently intervene in and police their areas (respectively, trade and international relations), and neither has allowed the issue of state sovereignty to stand in its way. The WTO maintains its power by threatening to impose penalties on states that infringe the conventions of free trade, and the United Nations's military role allows it to intervene regardless of state sovereignty. A further intervention in one of the bastions of the Westphalia system, a state's legal autonomy, is also increasingly evident. The determination of Western courts to hold political leaders accountable is evidenced in such cases as the United States' kidnapping and trial of Panama's President Noriega for drug trafficking, Spain's attempted indictment of Chile's President General Pinochet for crimes against humanity, and the War Crimes Tribunal trial of Serbian leader Slobodan Milosovic for war crimes. Moreover, David Held writes, the European Convention on Human Rights and the statute of the Council of Europe both inscribe in their instruments a connection between democracy and state legitimacy. Held cites, as a significant indicator of the decline of state autonomy:

> the 1992 declaration of the Helsinki Conference on Security and Co-operation in Europe . . . involving over fifty states including the US and Canada. In its declaration the states recognize their accountability to each other and underline the rights of citizens to demand from their government respect for democratic values and standards. (Held, 2000: 168–9)

Similar trends towards transnational groupings, and away from state sovereignty, are identifiable in so-called risk or hazard areas such as ecology and international crime. The worldwide degradation of the environment, and the failure of individual states to take decisive action, has resulted in the problems and issues being taken 'elsewhere', to international accords and treaties (the United Nations, the Kyoto Accord), transnationalist political parties (the Greens), global NGOs (Greenpeace, Earthwatch) and locally based pressure groups. Similarly the size, power and pervasiveness of global criminal networks (such as the Italian and Russian Mafia, Japanese Yakuza, Chinese Triads and Colombian drug cartels), and the ease with which such networks can use technology to communicate, move money around and infiltrate state apparatuses, have made international co-operation essential in their detection. While these and other moves towards global governance and co-operation certainly constitute a break with the bipolar world of the Cold War, they fall far short of replacing or even seriously vitiating the sovereignty of powerful states.

Let's look at the examples we referred to in the areas of governance, economics, law, the environment and crime. While there has been a proliferation of organizations established to deal with a wide range of issues such as humanitarian aid, trade and economic development, health, education and peace-keeping, such organizations have rarely been able to reconcile the supposed neutrality of the organization with the interests of its members. Fred Halliday writes, apropos of the UN involvement in Yugoslavia in 1995, that despite the United Nations' active involvement in diplomacy and peacekeeping, and despite the many resolutions passed and actions taken, little was achieved. The United Nations was unable to bring about peace, unable to follow through on its threats or demands, unable to provide safety for people even within the 'safe havens' it established. It was also unable to reconcile the interests of the various nations participating in the action with the United Nations own official neutrality (Halliday, 2000: 434).

A second problem such organizations face is what Halliday refers to as the 'incompatible' types of intervention in which they become involved. Taking up again the case of the United Nations and Yugoslavia, he points out that the international peacekeeping organization took on multiple forms of intervention, with confounding effects:

> humanitarian intervention (i.e. saving lives) can conflict with the human rights approach (i.e. identifying and prosecuting war criminals) and with enforcement; diplomatic efforts may involve working with those responsible for ethnic cleansing, and may, at times, lead negotiators to accept the results of such forcible expulsions; most obviously of all, peace-keeping, with white vehicles and with a presumption of neutrality, conflicts with peace-enforcement, which involves bombing violators of cease-fires and safe havens. (Halliday, 2000: 435)

Not surprisingly, the United Nations was largely ineffective in Yugoslavia, despite its apparent power as an international body, able to make and apply international law, and drawing on powerful nations like the United States and Britain for its resources.

Globalization as neocolonialism

It can be argued that trends towards international alliances are best understood not as a teleological evolution from state to global identity brought on by the triumph of democracy and the free flow of information, ideas and capital, as neoliberal ideology and Francis Fukuyama suggest, but as a form of neocolonialism. We can see this in the practice of global organizations operating in the areas of economics, the law, the environment and crime. We have already suggested that the WTO, the World Bank and the IMF are perceived to be carrying out strongly pro-capitalist agendas, and more particularly acting on behalf, or under the influence, of the United States. And even if such organizations were to act in a neutral manner, they could not realistically exercise control over the more powerful states, and therefore cannot be fully effective. Ngaire Woods writes of the WTO that for it to uphold the international rules:

> it needs compliance from its largest and most powerful member. Yet the United States had the worst record of compliance with GATT panel judgements of any country, and further 'retreated from multilateralism' in the 1980s, adopting policies which were increasingly aggressive and bilateral. (Woods, 2000: 393)

The same story has been played out in the United Nations, with the US veto of any Security Council resolutions directed at Israel; and again in the Kyoto Treaty on measures to address climate change, where the United States under George W. Bush stepped back from its earlier quite modest commitment to limit greenhouse emissions. And in the area of international law, the idea that a powerful state such as the United States would allow one of its leaders to be arrested and tried on war crimes charges, regardless of how much evidence was available, is too absurd to contemplate. It is practically unthinkable that, for instance, Henry Kissinger would ever be tried for crimes against humanity, despite the occasional mutterings in the media about his involvement in the bombing of Cambodia; while, as noted above, the leaders of Panama or Afghanistan can easily be held accountable.

This neocolonial tendency is predicated on the relationship between power and the politics of naming that we introduced in Chapter 1, and the post-11 September world provides us a striking example of its effects, this time in the area of international law. The US treatment of captured Taliban and al-Qaeda fighters violated the Geneva Convention, one of the most important and durable international legal imperatives on the treatment of prisoners of war. Secretary of Defense Rumsfeld circumvented the Convention by refusing to allow the captured troops the status of prisoners of war, instead (re)naming them 'battlefield detainees', which in effect meant that they could be tried and executed by the American military. What this demonstrates is that, regardless of the proliferation of global agencies and organizations, or of their increasing involvement in the construction of what has been termed the 'new world order':

> there is little indication that powerful member states have any intention of altering the hierarchical basis on which order has traditionally been maintained, even though that hierarchy will not serve to meet the more complex challenges of order in a globalizing world. (Woods, 2000: 396)

There is a further way in which the performance of the politics of globalization after 11 September could be seen as something closer to neocolonialism, with a strongly nationalist inflection. Consider the following excerpt from Charles Krauthammer's article 'Unilateralism is the key to our success' (first published in the *Washington Post*), which provides a conservative, but relatively realistic, reading of Bush's apparent abandonment of unilateralism for multilateralism after 11 September:

We need friends, they [Bush's critics] said. We need allies. We need coalition partners. We cannot alienate them again and again. We cannot have a president who kills the Kyoto protocol on greenhouse gases, summarily rejects the 'enforcement provisions' of the bioweapons treaty, trashes the ABM treaty – and expect to build the coalition we need to fight the war on terrorism.

We cannot? We did. Three months is all it took to make nonsense of these multilateralist protests. Coalition? The whole idea that the Afghan war is being fought by a 'coalition' is comical. What exactly has Egypt contributed? France sent troops into Mazar-e Sharif after the fighting had stopped . . . Like the Gulf War, the Afghan war is unilateralism dressed up as multilateralism . . . everyone knows whose war it is.
(2001: 22)

Krauthammer's abrasive nationalism doesn't vitiate the accuracy of his observations about the war against terrorism being, effectively, a US war (more accurately, a US extended act of revenge) dressed up as a globally endorsed campaign to eliminate barbarism and free the women of Afghanistan from the 'tyranny' of the burkha. In other words, a war between states was represented as a mere extension of the processes of globalization-as-neocolonialism already being played out in economic and cultural spheres.

Limits on neocolonialism

One of the main arguments against the spread of globalization – made by protesters at Seattle, Melbourne and Genoa, as well as by analysts such as Bauman and Bourdieu – is that, rather than constituting a progressive move to reduce inequalities in wealth, health and education, and spread democracy and human rights, global processes and institutions serve the national interests first of the United States and then of developed states such as Japan, Germany and Britain. When we analyse and compare the ways in which the events of 11 September and their aftermath are negotiated, rationalized, represented and articulated by different world leaders using different orders of discourse two things become clear. Firstly, the state – and interests of state – at the beginning of the twenty-first century are certainly anything but irrelevant or anachronistic; America's thinly disguised unilateralism, as well as the various nationalist inflections given to the 'global war against terrorism', testify to this. At the same time the fact that the American war against Afghanistan could be pursued – and here we need to part company with the pronouncements of Charles Krauthammer – only in concert with a *performance* of multilateralism that borrowed its justification from the same neoliberal ideology that drives the doxa of globalization means that there has been a change in the international arena. *Pace* Krauthammer, the war would not have gone as it did – the Taliban routed and al-Qaeda forced to flee Afghanistan – if Bush and Blair had not emphasized the multilateralism of the campaign against terrorism. Egypt, Saudi Arabia, Pakistan, Indonesia, Iran and other Islamic states openly supported the war (at least initially); even more crucially, Pakistan effectively cut itself off from the Taliban. The support of these states made it more difficult for the Taliban and al-Qaeda to represent the war as being fought by the West against Islam – a crucial reason for the war's success.

This does not mean that the governments or leaders of states such as Pakistan or Iran (or of Western democracies, for that matter) believed in the war, or were supporters of political globalization. What it does mean is that a state's response to issues such as the war in Afghanistan or the Israel–Palestine conflict is necessarily considered and contextualized in terms of what Castells calls 'global networks'. Castells suggests that it is extremely difficult for any transnational (or even local) corporation to act unilaterally or independently because it is enmeshed in a variety of networks and relations (political, bureaucratic, technological, cultural, economic, media and communication) that delimit what it can and can't do. The same applies to states – including, to a lesser extent, the United States.

Let's consider how this works: Pakistan, like the United States under Ronald Reagan, had strongly supported and resourced the Taliban. But it was also keen to remain on good terms with the United States, and to avoid becoming the target of American military action or economic embargoes. The conflict with India over Kashmir meant that Pakistan had even more reason to placate the West. However, in allowing US and Western forces to operate from its territory, Pakistan President Musharrif brought on a political crisis in his own country: crowds rioted, Pakistanis crossed the border into Afghanistan to fight against the United States, and Afghan refugees poured into Pakistan to escape the fighting. Finally, there was quite clearly a split within the state; although Musharrif supported the war, elements within his own military and secret service organ- ization continued to support the Taliban and al-Qaeda. The government of Pakistan, like those of many other states, inflected the global war against terrorism in terms of its own interests, while being inflected, in turn, by the consequences of providing support for the war.

Even the United States found itself caught up in a kind of game which it had effectively initiated, but couldn't entirely control. Charles Krauthammer's article proposes that the United States acted unilaterally and decisively to protect its interests, but this ignores the various networks and relations which informed and constrained US and international action. Firstly, and as we have seen in Chapters 1 and 2, the performance of global unity after 11 September was expedient at best; individual nations' response to the calls to a global war on terrorism were clearly informed, if not motivated, by issues of statehood and state sovereignty. Just about every state that signed up to the global war against terrorism did so in terms of its specific national interests. Even states such as Britain and France, which seemed to be acting out of a genuine commitment to the notion of global governance, were supporting Bush partly in order to maintain influence with him regarding a solution to the Israeli–Palestinian conflict, which they saw as crucial to peace in the Middle East, where they both had economic interests.

A second aspect of the statehood issue is that, despite Bush's attempts to represent the 11 September attacks as 'senseless, barbaric evil', they were informed, if not motivated, by the issue of state sovereignty. At a time when American officials were representing the war against terrorism in terms of a global struggle between good and evil, many analysts and politicians saw the question of statehood – specifically, Palestine's statehood – as central to both the cause and the solution of terrorist activity. And, interestingly, despite the rhetoric, American officials seem to be acknowledging this too. In an article dated December 2001, *The Age* journalist Gay Alcorn makes a connection between 'America's fight against terrorism' and the 'carnage in the Middle East', and writes that:

> The US media made much of the President's statement at the United Nations . . . that America was 'working towards the day when two states, Israel and Palestine, live peacefully together within secure and recognised borders'. It was the first time Republicans had used the word 'Palestine' to describe an embryonic state, although it had long been accepted that there would never be any peace in the Middle East without it. (2001: 13)

That a Republican President should entertain, let alone endorse, the notion of Palestine demonstrated the sea change that had come over American thinking both officially (that is, politically) and in the media, since only a year earlier Hilary Clinton had been lambasted by both spheres for raising the issue in public.

But these concerns were only part of the picture; there were several other major contexts that influenced the way America responded, over time, to 11 September. One context that influenced American reactions was the media's handling of the events and aftermath of 11 September, which we describe in Chapter 1, and analyse in Chapter 7. Central to this was the media's role not in reporting, but in actually producing, the sudden upswing in patriotism among people across America. The strong 'America will not be intimidated' rhetoric emanating from the media meant that Bush would have been seriously out of step with the public mood if he hadn't done something – anything – such as bomb Afghanistan as soon as possible. In a sense what the media did to influence American foreign policy –

albeit relatively unwittingly – after 11 September comes close to duplicating William Randolph Hearst's infamous telegram to his bemused reporter in Cuba in the early twentieth century: 'Stay where you are – I'll supply the war.'

Once the war had been supplied, of course, it had to be fought, and this brings in a second context that framed America's actions. The problem was that the strategy of bombing Afghanistan back to the Stone Age (and consequently keeping American casualties to a minimum) involved considerable 'collateral damage' among Afghan civilians. Although the US, Western and to a certain extent the world media were remarkably quiet when it came to Afghan villagers being accidentally blown to pieces, protests from Northern Alliance forces and some members of the new Afghan government about the needless slaughter of civilians brought the conduct of the war into question. This, coupled with the general lawlessness of the Alliance, and America's apparent lack of interest in Tony Blair's civilizing mission in Afghanistan, meant that Western enthusiasm for America's war on terrorism, wherever it found it, waned considerably. More importantly, the greater powers given to the military and secret services, and the withdrawal of the right of public trial for foreigners held on suspicion of involvement in terrorism, signalled the beginning of a strong assault on America's supposed commitment to the ideal of freedom of speech. Newspaper columnists, cartoonists, comedians and even a fifteen-year-old schoolgirl (expelled from school for wearing an anti-war t-shirt) became the victims of censorship. The US media, which did so much to ignite the war in Afghanistan, ended up becoming, to some extent, one of the casualties of the war.

A further part of the network of relations that contextualized events in the United States after 11 September was the economy; more specifically the falling share market, and the crisis in the tourism and airline industries. There was considerable debate both within government and across the US media about the need to reconcile the need to respond decisively and strongly to the attacks with the realization that such responses were likely to exacerbate economic problems. The obvious examples were the government decisions, which we referred to in earlier chapters, to allow the US military to shoot down commercial aircraft that were considered likely to pose a danger, and the use of armed marshals aboard all large commercial flights. But even more important was the financing of the war, which was estimated to be costing the United States $1 billion a day, putting even greater pressure on US domestic economic policy.

Conclusion

What these various contexts and the practices that characterize them demonstrate is that, regardless of what may be asserted as a doxa, the practices and politics associated with globalization are undeniably inflected, if not driven, by the interests of nation-states. We have reached neither the 'one McWorld' that Barber fears nor the alternative threat, the 'Lebanonization of national states'. However, we cannot argue either that the nation-state exists in the terms of the Westphalia principle, guaranteed territoriality and autonomy. It is clear that the ability of states to control the events around them, including those occurring within their own domestic economic, social, cultural and security/military spheres, has been undermined. This has been brought about, firstly, by the advent of 'global networks', and secondly by developments in communication technology and, as a corollary, the transformation of the public sphere in terms of its commoditization, localization and internationalization.

In our next two chapters we will address the ways in which this second aspect of globalization has influenced and impacted upon societies at a micro-level. Chapter 6 will look at how everyday life and culture, and categories of identity and citizenship, are being transformed by this process, and Chapter 7 will explain how the meanings and consequences of globalization are played out and negotiated within the public sphere.

6

The Global Subject and Culture

In previous chapters we addressed the connection between globalization and neoliberalism, and discussed how globalization transforms sites such as capitalism, governments and communication technologies. The central issue that has emerged in this discussion is that globalization can be understood not simply as a process or set of institutions and practices, but as a doxa. We described doxa as the effect of something coming to seem true and necessary, so that people will accept that it is 'just the way things are'. People are the subject of this chapter, because the doxa of globalization and its effects do not exist in a vacuum, and nor do they affect only governments and corporations. Ultimately their impact is on the lives, aspirations, understandings and bodies of everyday people. And just as the grid of globalization passes over and transforms institutions and broad socioeconomic practices, so too it affects, and potentially transforms, the people who inhabit these sites.

We begin by providing an account of the idea of the subject, or 'what makes a person', and discuss the extent to which questions of identity and relation are being transformed by the doxa, institutions and practices of globalization. We outline some of the central approaches taken over history to what it means to be a human subject, and how theoretical notions such as biopower and habitus can explicate the relation between subjectivity and capitalism. Finally, we address ways in which traditional cultural formations and community identity are now mediated by technologies and discourses, and particularly the role of the medical technologies and communication technologies – the increased mobility of ideas, capital and people – in transforming **cultural fields**.

The question of the subject

Michel Foucault stated that the entire point of his work, which spanned more than twenty years, was 'to create a history of the different modes by which, in our culture, human beings are made subjects' (Foucault, 1984: 7). We will take a more modest perspective, and draft a brief history of subjectivity as a way of discussing the impact of globalization on people in their everyday lives. Our founding principle in this is the poststructural, and specifically Neomarxist, account of the subject which holds that people are not 'naturally' themselves, or 'naturally' human (in a cultural sense). Nor are individuals either the source of meaning, or free agents who make their own meanings and control their own lives. Rather, identity and meaning are produced out of social discourses and institutions, and the doxa that emerges from relations of power; people become 'themselves', human subjects, by virtue of these social forces and within cultural contexts.

This goes against the commonsense idea of what it means to be an individual, a 'me' who has certain tastes and dispositions, and who possesses certain qualities and facilities. But philosophers have never accepted a straightforward response to the question of being – or 'What does it mean to be me?' This question has been answered variously, over the centuries, initially by the ancient Greek and Roman philosophers, subsequently by the early Christians, and yet again during the shifts in understanding that came about first with the Renaissance and then with the Enlightenment. Throughout these transformations in the understanding of the subject a central idea can be traced: that being was always 'for' someone or something else. In very broad terms, we can say that the individual always had a duty. The ancient classical philosophers considered that to be truly human was to strive for perfection of the self for the good of society. The early Christians similarly believed that people needed to strive for perfection, but in their case the aim was the glory of God and the good of one's immortal soul. In each case, truth (or Truth) was the reward of effort, and the marker of privileged subjectivity, though in each case this subjectivity, or identity, was not for oneself but for society, or God, or the principle of Truth.

The notion of identity was somewhat transformed, during the medieval period, by the conceptualizing of the great Chain of Being. This concept held that all being was organized within a rigid hierarchy: God at the top, then angels, kings, feudal lords, ordinary people, and so on, right down to worms and bugs. People's identity subsisted in this chain, and in their relationship to other beings; this implied too that identity was 'for' one's God, feudal lord and family. By the seventeenth century, though, ideas about identity were beginning to change to terms that are more familiar to people in the twenty-first century: 'the subject' emerged firstly as an object of scientific investigation with the development of scientific reason and systems of classification. Relatedly, the subject also came to be identified as the discrete, self-sufficient and self-motivating source of scientific reason through Descartes's famous *Cogito, ergo sum* ('I think, therefore I am').

But the person who is this 'I', a rational and self-actualizing subject, is also of course the *subject of* social and political forces. Philosophers focused more explicitly, now, on the question of human responsibility, and the tension between whether individuals are free (and abstract) subjects, or subjected to the control or regulation of dominant groups, discourses and institutions. The emerging 'human sciences' – particularly sociology, psychology and criminology – also weighed in on the debate, and raised the question of how to classify people, and how to analyse and articulate the 'right' relations between people and people, individuals and their societies? This, in turn, led to considerable attention to what makes someone 'human': we cannot classify something unless we know the terms of classification, and the qualities of the thing being classified.

This was an important question in a period of rapidly increasing contact with peoples from beyond Europe. The explorers and settlers were coming up against peoples whose language, culture, traditions, social systems and indeed appearance were often radically different from those of their own. It was important to know what order of being they were, so that the colonists- and settlers-to-be would know the appropriate way to deal with them. So the question of what makes a human being was as much an evaluative as a taxonomical exercise; not just classifying, but comparing one with another, and making judgements about their relative value. And just as in earlier periods those who were privileged (Greek nobles, great saints, aristocrats) seemed to be more particularly human, more free and of more value than everyone else, so too now the European explorers generally considered that they were themselves more particularly human, more free and of more value than the people with whom they were coming into contact.

This has hardly changed: we pointed out in Chapter 1 the way in which the politics of naming ensured that some categories of people – Westerners – were humanized and personalized by the reportage of the 11 September disaster, while other categories of people – Somalis, Chechens, Timorese and, of course, Afghanis – were not humanized to anything like the same extent, and the deaths and disasters that they endured were therefore not tragic to the same extent. Clearly, some kinds of identity mean more, matter more, and are worth more air time, more relief funding, more empathic grief. And certainly in many cases the peoples encountered by the explorers seemed so different that they were not considered 'real' humans, and need not be treated as such. In Australia their existence was barely acknowledged, and despite the millennia of continuous occupation of the land by the Aboriginal peoples, the British settlers designated it a *terra nullius*, an empty land, belonging to no one because no one – in the sense of 'human being' understood by the British – was there. In other places the peoples were massacred, enslaved or brought into relations of subordination as the colonized; and this was possible in each case because the native peoples were not classified as truly human, and so could not be the recipients of the benefits of subject status.

The confidence in the Cartesian notion of the self as the abstract product of higher thought did not last into the twentieth century. By this period there was fairly general agreement among scholars that the subject was neither free nor natural, but a product of time and space, and the imperatives of the local context. This had several origins, of which perhaps the best known are the writings of Freud and Marx. Sigmund Freud undermined confidence in the Cartesian subject by constructing a model of subjectivity based on the notion of the unconscious. Rather than seeing humans beings as self-regulating, abstract and rational subjects, he argued that we are governed by repressed desires and the prompting of the unconscious – that which is beyond reason or conscious thought. Karl Marx and later Marxist writers developed the notion of the subject as that which is subjected: not a free, rational or indeed 'natural' entity, but that which takes up identity only when interpellated (or called up) by powerful social institutions. What is meant by this is the compulsion (or impulsion) to identify with ideas and characteristics that are promoted as good, desirable or right. Society provides us with a number of models of good subjectivity and good behaviour, and 'summons' us to identify with them, and shape our behaviour and sense of self according to those standards.

Subjectivity, biopower and Empire

The French philosopher Michel Foucault explains this through what he terms 'biopower', which can be understood as a series of technologies and techniques – hospitals, schools, prisons, nuclear families – developed in order to analyse, control, regulate and define the human being. For Foucault, biopower – or the attitude of seeing people as resources or commodities – is tied in with the development of capitalism and changes in the role of the state. He argues that prior to the seventeenth century the state was mainly seen as a means to an end – the glory of the sovereign, or the welfare of the people – but from the seventeenth century the state came to be seen as an end in itself. In other words, what mattered was the strength, wealth and power of the state. Its people were now thought of not as an end in themselves, with their own rights and duties, but as a resource which had to be used and taken care of, in their everyday activities, to ensure the viability of the state. His argument is that biopower helped in this change, and simultaneously contributed to the development of capitalism, by providing a healthy, active, disciplined population that was a commodity for the state and organized capital. The principle of biopower, then, means that people are not free, are not Cartesian subjects. Rather, the way people come to understand the world, the way they behave, the values and aspirations they develop and the way they react to events are fashioned out of the various apparatuses and technologies of biopower, and render people self-regulating subjects in the service of society and capital, rather than self-constituting individuals.

That is not the end of the story, though. Foucault also points out that biopower is in many ways antithetical to the ideas of human being, and of progress and reform, that came out of the Enlightenment movement of the late seventeenth century. So, while the technologies and institutions associated with biopower may have been designed to make people 'docile bodies' at the service of major organizations, the ideas that helped formulate the systems of biopower were associated with freedom and self-actualization. Because of this rift in its own discourses, and because society and capital are not homogeneous but made up of competing discourses and groups which produce different versions of events, biopower can never be fully successful. It does in many ways produce the sorts of people – human resources – that are useful for the state and for capital. But it also produces resistances. Foucault takes the prison system as an example of this; he notes that while the technologies of power used in prisons are supposed to produce 'docile' bodies and behaviour, in reality the opposite happens, and prisons in fact function as 'criminal factories'. Biopower may be successful in producing particular kinds of subjectivities, but the effects are not always what was intended.

Hardt and Negri pick up on this notion, pointing out that one of the distinguishing characteristics of the contemporary globalized world is the imbrication of capitalism, the '**affect industries**', and biopower. They argue that the first task of the 'grid of globalization' is not just to produce consensus among subjects, but more dramatically to ensure that all thought, every notion of morality and ethics, and the dispositions and values of subjects, are produced within, and are commensurable with, the framework of Empire. This has led to a situation where the media and communication industries now occupy a hegemonic place with regard to the social, precisely because their role is to transform the social into something else – a kind of simulation of the capitalist system of production. In other words, everything that is considered inalienable within society – sporting teams, artistic production, human body parts, children and childhood – is to be reformulated and rethought as alienable, as being subject to the market. The imperative, then, is to produce subjects disposed to see and understand the world almost exclusively through capitalist eyes and categories.

How do Hardt and Negri explain and contextualize the relationship between capitalism, the media/communication industries and the biopolitical production of subjectivity at a global level? They suggest that while capital has always been disposed towards the global, it is only in the post-World War II period, and most particularly since the 1970s, that capital has effectively replaced the nation-state as the organizing apparatus and principle of the management of populations. And as the nation-state has progressively been integrated into the networks and system of Empire, the function of biopolitical management and control formerly undertaken by public institutions has given way to apparatuses and ideologies of capital-as-Empire.

In one sense this is explicable in terms of the straightforward shift from what was largely a public communication system in the first part of the twentieth century to what is the overwhelmingly commercial system today. But Hardt and Negri push this argument on another level. They suggest that the civic sphere within which the production and negotiation of meanings (and, consequently, subjectivities) take place is now almost entirely a global civic sphere constituted by the communications equivalent of Castells's 'network society'. So, just as it is virtually impossible for corporations to compete and work outside the networks of information, technology, logistical imperatives and relationships that make up global capitalism, similarly ideas, principles and modes of subjectivity are subject to the same kind of limitations, precisely because there is nowhere else to think or be, no 'outside' the system.

Hardt and Negri's insistence on the saturation levels of biopolitical control exercised through and by the communication and media industries seems to overlook the strong anti-globalization movement which is expressed not only in demonstrations and protests, but also in local political results, movements and trends – part of what has been termed the 'turn to the local'. But, interestingly, Hardt and Negri have no time for any of these local movements, whether they involve attempts to 'reclaim' the state, or are manifested in religious revivals. Empire, for them, is a step along the way, and an important development, from modernization and the nation-state to the eventual founding of a truly (socialist) global society. The (empty) performances of politics and the erasure of difference that are played out in contemporary media under Empire in a sense presage, from their perspective, the coming of the real thing under world socialism. Hardt and Negri's theoretical orientation means that they place one of the most important aspects of the Foucauldian notion of biopower – that it can never be thought of in purely negative terms, since it creates identities that are disposed to oppose it – at the service of a kind of Marxist teleology. But there are other, non-Marxist, ways of making sense of the relationship between globalization, capitalism, biopower and subjectivity.

Individuals and the habitus

One of the central factors involved in this shaping of behaviour and ensuring a connection between the individual's sense of self and the wider socioeconomic framework is what Pierre Bourdieu terms 'the habitus'. This refers to those:

> systems of durable, transposable dispositions, structured structures predisposed to function as structuring structures, that is, as principles which generate and organize practices and representations that can be objectively adapted to their outcomes without presupposing a conscious aiming at ends or an express mastery of the operations necessary in order to attain them. (Bourdieu, 1990: 53)

That is, a subject's personal history, embedded within a social context, produces tendencies to act in particular ways, in a variety of situations. Practices – including our sense of self, and what we understand by 'human' – are strongly informed by past conditions. These past conditions – or rather their effect on our identity – are immediately forgotten. So, as Bourdieu writes, habitus is 'history turned into nature, i.e. denied as such' (Bourdieu, 1977: 78). This is most easily observed in the conversation of children, who prefer not to be reminded of the time before they knew how to behave 'appropriately' in public. Children will often hotly deny that they ever wailed loudly during a church service, or threw a tantrum in a supermarket, insisting that they have always been model citizens. Their history, which has produced the person they now are, must be forgotten so that their identity can seem secure and permanent.

The habitus develops, then, out of a particular combination of social contexts, personal experiences, and one's relation to objective structures; and these past conditions, or 'history', are forgotten in the interests of producing the fantasy of the subject as self-constituted and autonomous. This has a Freudian inflection, recalling the centrality Freud accorded to the unconscious in the constitution of the self. After all, what is forgotten is also, arguably, repressed, as is the matter which Freud insisted was the stuff of the unconscious. So, if we are motivated by forgotten history, then we are motivated in fact by the unconscious.

Where does habitus come from? It is a product of individual tastes, tendencies and dispositions which are developed by, and must be contextualized in terms of, its relation to the objective structures of a culture. For Bourdieu the relationship between these objective structures (which he refers to as '**cultural fields**') and habitus doesn't completely determine people's actions and thoughts, but no practice is explicable without reference to them. As agents move through and across different fields, they incorporate into their habitus the values and imperatives of those fields, and this shapes their own dispositions. We are who and what we are largely because of where we have been, and how this has informed our sense of self and our sense of choice. We have thus moved a long way from Descartes's autonomous, abstract individual and also from the earlier understandings of the subject as one who was potentially self-actualizing, and able to decide freely to be ethical for the good of all. Bourdieu's subject – the subject of the twentieth-century world – is not precisely flotsam, to be tossed about by the winds of time and place, but is certainly a product of time and place.

The habitus, and hence our sense of self and of human identity, is also intimately bound up with how the physical body is understood. This is one of the apparently solid aspects of identity, and central to our understanding of the self because the body encompasses us, and provides our individual boundaries. The nineteenth-century philosopher William James wrote that the body is 'the storm centre, the origin of co-ordinates, the constant place of stress in all that experience-train. Everything circles around it and is felt from its point of view' (James, 1967: 284). For James, then, we are because we are embodied – which again takes us a long way from Descartes's purely cerebral subject. Bourdieu provides a way of thinking across these two positions, writing that 'The body is in the social world, but the social world is in the body' (2000: 152); in other words, we become who and what we are because our world – the contexts in which we live, and through which we move – insinuates itself into our being. This 'being' includes the body, its characteristics, and ways of seeing and recognizing the world; and how we look, how we feel, and what we do with our bodies thus 'proves' who and what we are.

Robert Altman's 2001 film *Gosford Park* makes much of this notion of the socialized body and being. The film is set in

England in the period between World Wars I and II, when the strict social division between classes was beginning to break down. It moves between and across two general 'communities', or types of subject: the servant and the upper class. In the process it traces the effect of being on the body, and perhaps of the body on being. In general terms, the 'maids' are either over- or underweight and of course poorly dressed; their bodies do not fit with the norms of the leisure class. The 'ladies', by contrast, are slender and toned, and always beautifully dressed. But the below-stairs people for the most part move briskly and purposefully through the great country house, while the above-stairs people – particularly the women – are languid and slow in their movements: they have no purpose, and no tasks to perform, and so their bodies are not functional units. In fact, their bodies, however slight, often seem a burden – they slump on to furniture, rest their chin wearily on their hands, or lean against a wall. But class and gender are not the only determinants of embodied subjectivity. The daughter of the house, Isobel (played by Camilla Rutherford), embodies anguish and uncertainty; her shoulders are hunched, her head droops, and her every move is awkward, as though she is expecting to fall, or to be struck. The housemaid Elsie (played by Emily Watson), on the other hand, is statuesque and confident; and though she loses her job when she moves outside her formal role as 'servant', her body never loses assurance, and her identity remains secure.

This is what we could call the 'materialist' dimension of the habitus; in Bourdieu's terms, 'Social reality exists, so to speak, twice, in things and in minds, in fields and in habitus, outside and inside of agents' (Bourdieu and Wacquant, 1992: 127–8); we always embody both physical and social identity. And though we may think of the body as something individual – as subject to, belonging to, and characteristic of the self – this notion of the individual, self-contained body is itself a product of the habitus:

> this body which indisputably functions as the principle of individuation . . . ratified and reinforced by the legal definition of the individual as an abstract, interchangeable being . . . [is]

open to the world, and therefore exposed to the world, and so capable of being conditioned by the world, shaped by the material and cultural conditions of existence in which it is placed from the beginning . . . (Bourdieu, 2000: 133–4)

What this means is that the body is no more 'natural' or inevitable than other aspects of identity and classification. How bodies are viewed, understood and evaluated changes from period to period, place to place. Moreover, the body is the grounds too not only for the exercise of biopower we discussed above, but also for that process of classification – the politics of naming – to which we referred in Chapter 1. So people are identified and produced in evaluative as well as taxonomic terms: as men/women, Euramericans/people of colour, Anglos/Asians, old/young, rich/poor and so on. Consequently, the relation between the body and the self is central to the relation between the body and the wider community. Individuals are 'themselves' because they are simultaneously members of class, age, profession, race, ethnicity and family sets, among others. And our wider social (political) identity is also tied to the body: under both kinship and ethnicity social formations the individual's identity is firstly that of a 'natural' connection with the group, predicated on 'blood ties', family relationships, or having similar physical characteristics.

Technology and the subject

Globalization changes this, and changes the connection between habitus and context, because it transforms social understandings of time and place, the limitations on the body, and the wider question of being. In a period when we can claim any identity in an internet chat room, when medical technology has made so wide a range of prosthetics available that any of us could potentially be the Six Million Dollar Man, and when scientists are on the verge of cloning humans, we seem to be standing on the brink of a Brave New World where the interface between human and machine has fallen away. The very idea of human being begins to take on shades of Foucault's famous declaration of the 'death of the subject':

> As the archaeology of our thought easily shows, man is an invention of recent date. And one perhaps nearing its end. If those arrangements were to disappear as they appeared, if some event of which we can at the moment do no more than sense the possibility . . . were to cause them to crumble, as the ground of Classical thought did . . . then one can certainly wager that man would be erased, like a face drawn in sand at the edge of the sea. (Foucault, 1973: 387)

This Huxleyan world doesn't, then, necessarily deliver freedom or infinite possibility; rather, the intrusion of new ways of thinking and being may actually foreclose what we are and can be. The permeability of the boundary between human and machine is one of the central issues at stake here, and it is propelled by the new technologies that seem to be rendering the everyday material world less accessible.

Technology is, arguably, one of the most significant factors influencing the nature of subjectivity, because it radically calls into question the definition of human being. Advocates of the technological turn may argue that we are all, in fact, already cyborg, at some level. If we have fillings in our teeth, if we have had inoculations against disease, if we use computers and telephones, then we are already intimately, physically, interfacing with machinery. In fact, simply using a basic tool can take on a cyborgish quality, if we consider the process of perception involved. Michael Polanyi reminds us that any use of a tool – using a hammer, probing something with a stick – involves the interface of the body with that tool:

> The way we use a hammer or a blind man uses a stick shows that in both cases we shift outward the points at which we make contact with things outside ourselves. While we rely on a tool or a probe, these instruments are not handled or scrutinized as external objects. Instead, we pour ourselves into them and assimilate them as part of ourselves. (Polanyi and Prosch, 1975: 36)

Thus we always have a very permeable boundary between ourselves and the technologized world we inhabit, and this has always been a disturbing concept, explored over and over in films and books. The almost-human is far more frightening than the obvious machine, or indeed the savage. Think of the deeply unsettling quality of the cyborgs in *Alien* or *Terminator*; their machinic power, both physical and 'intellectual', is unsurpassable by 'mere' humans; their implacability due to the absence of human affect makes them terrifying; and the fact that they look like people means that we can never be certain of who is what.

Of course these are films of the late twentieth century; the twenty-first century may well take a different reading of beings, and has already introduced alternative forms of quasi-human identity in the form of vactors (virtual actors): Lara Croft, for instance, is not really human, not really machine, and not just cartoon either, but is capable of straddling all those formations. What we may identify increasingly is the category of the quasi-human. One of the more surprising instances of this category, relevant here because it was produced by and through technology, was the case of little Leo, a pet dog who was flung into the traffic near the San Jose International Airport in California in a road rage incident in February 2000. The story of his death was run on CBS News, and touched a nerve among the public around the world. A web site was set up, and a photo of Leo published there along with a photofit of the killer. The language throughout the incident, both on news reports and on the web site, seems more pertinent to that of a child killing than the death of a dog. For instance, the web site included a letter from 'Leo's mom', written in the language of grieving with which we are familiar in human circles; the writer even referred to 'my precious little boy who I loved with all my heart' (Burnett, 2001). Frustrated by the slow progress made by the police, she hired a private investigator, and finally Leo's killer was arrested, found guilty and sentenced to three years in prison.

While it is not unusual, perhaps, for pet owners to invest the relationship with a parent/child quality, the extent of this case, and the outrage expressed in the (virtual) community makes it significant. What does it mean if a considerable portion of the community can evince such a reaction to the death of an animal, while (human) children are routinely killed by parents and strangers with only very occasional comparable community action? We can suggest that it is the effect of media technology; we have already seen its ability to personalize and humanize, and in this case it has allowed even an animal to become part of 'us', while simultaneously dehumanizing, say, children in Iraq. When it comes to the question of human being, it seems, technology is never neutral.

This goes against the perspective on technology posited by the German philosopher Martin Heidegger. Heidegger's central point is that technology is related to truth (or, rather, to Truth) because it is committed to what he calls 'revealing'. He pins this argument on the original Greek term, *technē*: 'the name not only for the activities and skills of the craftsman but also for the arts of the mind and the fine arts. *Technē* belongs to bringing-forth, to *poiesis*; it is something poetic' (1977/1993: 318). When he shifts his attention to the modern era (the mid twentieth century), he identifies technology's threatening quality, and locates this in its 'challenging' aspect, its ability to unlock natural resources and natural power sources, and so to 'unconceal' the actual. Human beings cannot 'unconceal', according to Heidegger; they can only notice and respond to the possibilities so exposed. This means that human beings are not autonomous, but rather are resources themselves – what he calls a '**standing reserve**'. He is not clear for whom or what we are resources, or who or what orders our use, falling back into a kind of Platonic transcendent realm which 'calls' us into action, and into being. Technology is a problem to us, then, in so far as it makes our lack of autonomy apparent to us. And he ends his essay on technology with a call to arms – or rather, to art:

> Because the essence of technology is nothing technological, essential reflection upon technology and decisive
> confrontation with it must happen in a realm that is, on the one hand, akin to the essence of technology and, on the other, fundamentally different from it. Such a realm is art. (1977/ 1993: 340)

We would agree with Heidegger's notion that technology is not just a thing, or a way of getting something done; but argue that it has nothing to do with transcendence, and everything to do with people and institutions. That is, technology is neither neutral, nor committed to the Truth, but is deployed in a way that is always interested, because it is always made available for someone's profit or power or pleasure. Because of this it is important to reject the notion of technological determinism; as Slavoj Zizek writes:

> the way computerization affects our lives does not depend directly on technology, it results from the way the impact of new technology is refracted by the social relations which, in their turn, co-determine the very direction of technological development. (Zizek, 1996: 198)

Paul Virilio too locates technological developments as entirely caught up in social relations, particularly in a kind of personal neocolonialism. He suggests that with the end of World War I the possibility of a total war against human beings was opened up because of the deployment in that war of weapons of mass destruction. The human body, he argues, became the next 'territory' to be invaded, explored and transformed (Virilio, 2000: 55). He raises such topical issues as cryogenics, human cloning and the mapping of the human genome in this respect. These are not, he argues, neutral, scientific or objective moves, but have the potential to be put to work against individuals, and in the service of dominant groups, institutions and discourses. The genome project, for instance, is ideally suited to a new kind of eugenics, one which would promote the production of 'new model' people 'built on the lines of transgenic crops, which are so much better adapted to their environment than the natural products' (Virilio, 2000: 136). This has obvious ramifications for those kinds of people who are not well suited to the neoliberal doxa. Indeed, the potential for inequity is evident in almost every technological move we can imagine. Cloning or cryogenics will hardly be available to the poor, for instance, and taken to its extreme it is possible to imagine a world inhabited by Dr Strangeloves, those with the resources to support their own inexhaustible life, while the poor, the indigent, the merely 'difficult' or noncompliant are technologized off the face of the earth.

Identity, collectivity and territoriality

For the most part, of course, we still live in material bodies in the material world, and this means for most of us that we live as members of national communities. Nationalism indeed appears to have been the primary form of identity during the twentieth century, and is the type of formation most directed to the individual; as Craig Calhoun writes:

> In the discourse of nationalism, one is simply Chinese, French or Eritrean. The individual does not require the mediations of family, community, region or class to be a member of the nation. Nationality is understood precisely as an attribute of the individual, not of the intermediate associations. (Calhoun, 1997: 46)

But nationalism has never existed in isolation from the other two formations, kinship and ethnicity. Looking back to the Peace of Westphalia, we remember that one of the bases of the nation-state was the principle of territoriality, and this is raised consistently with respect to the ethnic foundations of nation-states. Calhoun again writes:

> historical research shows noteworthy continuities between modern national cultures and their antecedents and in patterns of geopolitical regions and relations. We can also see that nationalism derives much of its force from the phenomenological experience of ordinary people that, in general, their nations are always already there. (Calhoun, 1997: 30)

To a very large extent, then, the subject has always been a territorial identity: *in place* as a member of a kinship group; *in place* as part of an ethnic collectivity; and definitely *in place* under the national principle of territoriality. We can identity this 'always already there' in the discourse of national leaders and activists for social change, particularly at times of great social flux. The former Yugoslavia is an example of territoriality and its antecedents taken to a violent extreme; the state of Israel is another, because the idea that Jerusalem was always 'ours' (whoever may be represented by the 'our') is central to the fifty-year struggle between the people of Israel and the people of Palestine. Clearly, then, though collective identity may be in fact a bureaucratic formation, produced rather than necessary or natural, it is also mobilized to classify and divide. And, like all principles of vision and categorization, collective identities divide at the same time as they unify. Within the religious/ethnic formation we can identify, for instance, 'Jews' as a distinct category of people, possessing a shared set of values, traditions, beliefs and sense of identity, and radically separated from Gentiles as well as from other Semitic peoples. But this collective identity of 'Jews' is not just a unifying force against the outside; it is also marked by internal divisions and 'racisms'. Think of the categorical and evaluative difference between Ethiopian and Israeli Jews, for instance, or between reform and orthodox Jewish congregations. Another example, one which shows up the internal 'racisms' of a modern state rather than an ancient religion, can be seen in the history of California. Virilio writes that this state actually organized itself to include only those people selected as worth having:

> in the early 1930s California had to cut itself off from the rest of the Union to avoid being submerged by the tide of humanity. It was ringed by the 'blockade' . . . Indigents, tramps, people of colour, lone women, abandoned children, the sick and the infected were pushed back, or pitilessly interned in camps in the desert, health criteria here becoming mingled with social and racial prejudices. (Virilio, 2000: 25)

In other words, the 'us' that was California was a product of elitism driven by economic and social pressures. And indeed, the process of collective or community formation is never pure, straightforward or 'natural', but is always 'interested', always changing, and always productive of identity and understandings of who and what the subject is.

We have argued that the question of subjectivity is intimately connected with the body and the way particular bodies are classified, assessed and valued through notions such as Foucault's biopower, Bourdieu's habitus and James's 'storm centre'. The body is also connected with our relations and associations with others, whether we are considering categorical forms of identity like age groups, gender and race, or specific formations like kinship, ethnicity and nationalism. We can trace in this a parallel between individual identity and group identity: they go through similar patterns of formation and constitution. Bourdieu writes that there is a collective or shared habitus, predicated on what comes to seem, for any community, 'a commonsense world endowed with the objectivity secured by consensus on the meaning (*sens*) of practices and world' (Bourdieu, 1977: 80). These meanings are generated by a society's dominant stories about tradition and the present, about the norms which circumscribe practice; and they produce in community members a sense of a common history, a common relation to objective structures, common beliefs and dispositions to practice. Like the habitus, this historical process of becoming is forgotten; as Craig Calhoun writes, 'Clearly people experience their social worlds as always in some part given to them prior to their own actions' (Calhoun, 1997: 31). It is 'their own actions' that produce the systems and structures in which we live as communities, and the narratives of the community that come to seem the 'truth' of the community.

Culture is central to this notion of collective habitus, and the field of cultural production can be understood as being every bit as significant to, and inflected by, globalization as the media, the economy or technology. And certainly it has long been a significant part of community identity: one of the important indicators of nationhood is the identification of a body of art and cultural heritage which is distinctively 'national', located in sites with are identified with the nation (the *British* Museum, the

Australian National Gallery). But culture itself is always subject to change, as Raymond Williams writes, though defining culture as 'the whole life of a people', rather than the restrictive 'art and heritage' definition.

Williams argues that there are three levels of cultural meaning which organize our collective lives, and our understandings of ourselves and our society. These he terms dominant, residual and emergent cultures (Williams, 1980: 40). Dominant culture is the norm of current practice, being the contemporary doxa that structures identities and actions. An example of this is the process of nationalism in a globalizing world, and the way the doxa of neoliberalism shapes social structures and practices. Residual culture is that which forms the basis of traditional beliefs and practices, and may be very much at odds with dominant culture. Although the earlier modes or residual forms may have been forgotten, and have lost their power, our sense of self is still influenced by old belief systems; as Gilles Deleuze writes, 'we continue to produce ourselves as a subject on the basis of old modes which do not correspond to our problems' (1988: 107). We can see ongoing examples of this in the protracted struggles between Catholic and Protestant people in Northern Ireland, or between Jews and Palestinians in the Middle East; their founding principles of difference are based on a set of religious ideas that have little relation to the problems that in fact are being engaged.

There is always a point of conflict between dominant and residual culture, because the latter constitutes a threat to the present, a way of undermining its legitimacy by reference to the authority of antiquity ('We've always done things this way,' which carries the subtext of 'So the old ways must be right'). The third form, emergent culture, influences both dominant and residual culture. It includes those meanings, values, ways of being and ways of understanding that are in the process of being constructed, that have not yet been fully incorporated into the social, or defined as part of effective contemporary practice. Again, aspects of globalization are part of this notion of emergent culture, particularly the possibility of being fully connected through the global technological networks, or the possibility of cyborgism that continues to seduce and threaten human 'being'.

For any social formation, the past continually inflects the present, while the future continually beckons, offering new formations and new possibilities. This means, by extension, that subjectivity or a sense of identity, whether individual or collective, is also constantly facing change. How can we explain this with reference to what we have insisted is the durable and transposable nature of the habitus? We have argued that a person's habitus can tolerate social upheavals, and moving from one field to another, because there is a 'continuity of meaning' throughout most national cultures (usually promoted by governments, in concert with major institutions). Globalization affects this, Arjun Appadurai has suggested, through the more or less unregulated flow of cultural texts, in concert with the continuous 'flowing of peoples' and ideas that characterizes the contemporary world. These continually and rapidly changing circumstances and contexts work on the habitus, and 'move the glacial forces of the habitus into the quickened beat of improvisations for large groups of people' (Appadurai, 1997: 6). We have to improvise more often, he argues, because in the contemporary world we are continuously confronted with images, narratives, information, voices and perspectives from all corners of the globe that don't equate with the 'received ideas' of our habitus, or the terms of residual or (local) dominant culture. So, rather than having stable identities, people have to 'make do' with whatever is at hand – to borrow identities from various (usually media entertainment) sources. This means that people are necessarily distanced not just from 'official' cultural texts and their meanings, but from any institution or text which claims to have a monopoly of meaning, simply because, in a globalized world, what is understood as normal is always subject to (very rapid) challenge and change.

Mobile identities

Globalization thus transforms the habitus, the idea of the subject, and the constituents of collective identity because it breaks down the 'natural' connection being identity and the physical body, identity and place, identity and tradition. Nicholas Negroponte writes:

> The post-information age will remove the limitations of geography. Digital living will include less and less dependence upon being in a specific place at a specific time, and the transmission of place itself will start to become possible . . . In the post-information age, since you may live and work at one or many locations, the concept of an 'address' now takes on new meaning. (Negroponte, 1996: 238)

This notion that distance and physical limitations have become irrelevant is becoming a doxa of the globalizing era. We discussed in Chapter 3 the tendency of time and space to collapse, or be truncated, through the effects of technological networking and the almost instantaneous flows of investment and ideas. But the notion that this transfers directly to the freedom of individuals to move is rather specious. Boundaries are indeed collapsing, or at least becoming permeable, but not everyone can move, or move freely. There is a profound difference between the 'nomadic chic' available to globetrotters and the enforced nomadism of the refugee, for instance. In other words, class has a considerable effect upon who moves, how often they move, and under what conditions.

Zygmunt Bauman points out that only the wealthy, the 'high up', actually travel freely and by choice around the world. The poor, the undesirable, the 'low down' are either trapped in place, or driven out of their homes. He writes that 'In 1975 there were 2 million forced emigrants – refugees – under the care of the High Commission set up by the UN for that purpose. In 1995 there were 27 million of them' (Bauman, 1998: 86–7). So while people flows are high and increasing, as are the flows of ideas and capital, for the most part people are moving unwillingly, and arriving unwelcomed. The global networking of which Castells writes does not equate to access for all. Rather, it reinscribes differences and inequities: the old patterns of us and them, core and periphery. It also renders the question of identity highly problematic: our identity is very much tied back to our national identity, and so 'A person without country must therefore be understood to lack not only a place in the external world but a proper self' (Calhoun, 1997: 46). Thus it is possible to treat refugees, asylum seekers and illegal immigrants as subhuman, not-quite-subjects.

The example of the Australian detainee camps is a case in point, where people who arrive without papers, and without a clear warrant of identity, can be incarcerated and denied access to normal channels of communication, in remote, inhospitable and inaccessible parts of the country. Denied freedom of movement, only barely accorded the status of human beings, they have become not subjects but objects of national policy, tools for the winning or losing of elections, absences around which discourses can circulate. That this is not accidental is demonstrated by the fact that the Howard government in Australia forbade the navy and the press to photograph asylum seekers prior to the hotly contested 2001 federal election 'because it would humanize and personalize the people' (ABC News, 17 April 2002). The asylum seekers subsequently protested at their treatment with tactics that included hunger strikes and, in some cases, the stitching together of their lips. These were met with scorn and outrage by government spokespeople, who said that it was proof that they were 'not the kind of people we want here' – not 'like us'.

The farcical nature of this government attitude can be seen in (at least) two respects. Firstly the asylum seekers had, in the opinion of numerous medical officers, been driven to distraction and despair by their treatment, and a number had attempted suicide and been committed to psychiatric care. In other words, first we drive them mad, then we use their madness to prove that they don't belong among us. Secondly, it is not rare to starve oneself or pierce one's flesh in Australia; many people are continually dieting, or coping with eating disorders like anorexia or bulimia; many people have pierced lips, tongues, noses, brows and genitals; but in neither instance is this used to insist that they are not properly human, not 'part of us'. And while all this was happening, Australia was still welcoming business migrants, tourists and foreign investment. It was possible for the Australian government to exclude the asylum seekers despite the fact that were are in no way different from other Australians (many of whom in fact have the same ethnic and linguistic background as the detainees) because they had first been dehumanized.

To what extent is it possible, then, to talk of a global culture, or a global subject? Clearly, some subjects are indeed global – Bauman's 'high up' being that instance. But, for most, identity is always being negotiated across and between local, regional, national and global spheres. As Bauman again points out:

> Progressively, entry visas are being phased out all over the globe. But not passport control. The latter is still needed – perhaps more than ever before – to sort out the confusion which the abolition of the visas might have created: to set apart those for whose convenience and whose ease of travel the visas have been abolished, from those who should have stayed put. (Bauman, 1998: 87)

And of course for those who possess the capital and the literacies, it is possible to travel while staying in place, and to participate in a community that is truly global and free, because virtual – the cyberculture community of MUDs and chat rooms, web sites and e-zines, multimedia entertainment and digital cultural production. Other global cultural moments might include the experience of being part of a fan community, for instance, whose members across the world have posters of Will Smith on their walls, or listen to classical music; or being among the audiences gathered for media events like Live Aid or the funeral of Princess Diana.

Global culture?

This does not necessarily mean that what they are experiencing is global culture. In fact, some theorists argue that there can be no such thing as truly global culture because identity and

cultural attachment rely on emotional and traditional reso-
nances. The Coca-Colonization of the world can't hope to
achieve this because it is comparatively recent, manifestly commercial, and lacks the specific signifiers of cultural identity to
which people can relate. Held and McGrew write in this respect
that 'there is no common global pool of memories; no common
global way of thinking; and no "universal history" in and
through which people can unite' (2000: 16). This means global
culture is limited in its capacity to mobilize identity and affect.
Indeed, being necessarily premised on capitalism and the
dissemination of narratives through the electronic media, it can
exist only in so far as corporations find it profitable to construct
and market new memories and new shared experiences. Rather
than an actual culture, they might argue, it is a fiction conjured
up and disseminated by the global media.

Most theorists, though, fall into one of two camps with
respect to the question of a global culture. One is the cultural
homogenization camp, the other the cultural hybridization
camp. The former equate globalization generally with the
homogenizing of culture, the resultant retraction or dismissal of
local cultures, and the Westernization of the globe. Though
cultural products of course flow across and around the globe,
most of the flow is from the West out. And because of the power
of the media to mobilize identity and affect, it is argued, the
effect is of a single commodity/identity world, the destruction
of the local and the authentic, and the reimagining or renarra-
tivizing of traditions as commodities. In this perspective, global
culture means Western culture writ large. For those without the
resources to resist this cultural neocolonialism, the future is
Western. Those with some resources, though, can resist and turn
the homogenizing process back on itself. Curator and critic Hou
Hanru makes this point in discussing the interaction between
Western and Chinese art, writing:

> After some initial moments of excitement and hope, Chinese
> contemporary artists' contact with western-dominated global
> art has been disappointing and frustrating, which has pushed
> many artists to reconsider their relationship with the

international art world. On the one hand, they confirm the
necessity to search for a space for expressions which are both
personal and universally significant. On the other hand, they
recognise that it is now time to restructure the art world and
create a genuinely global scene. (Hou Hanru, 1999: 191)

It is unlikely that everyday people in their everyday worlds
would have the capital, the literacies or the contacts to be able
even to dream of restructuring any part of their world, but the
art world is of course a somewhat privileged sphere, and one
that is able to claim some of the benefits offered by globalization.

Hou Hanru doesn't, though, suggest an inversion of the
West-out flow of cultural forms. Rather, he takes up a concept
previously applied to the economic sphere: 'the *glocal*'. This
unlovely word was coined by Roland Robertson to describe the
selling of goods and services on a global scale, but targeted
appropriately to particular local markets. For Hou Hanru, it can
also describe the possibility of producing art in a dynamic tension between global and local tastes, traditions, narratives and
imperatives. This is an expression of the second strand of the
cultural globalization debate: the idea of cultural hybridization,
or the blending of foreign and local to make a new form.

According to Beynon and Dunkerley (2000: 18–19), this flow
(what Hou Hanru calls the glocal) is two-way. While global
culture obviously impacts upon the local in the massive
production and distribution of global consumer goods and
images, the local impacts on the global too. There is a practically
limitless pool of examples of these practices. We can think, for
instance, of popular music, where gamelan instruments and
sitars interface with rock guitars, where African-informed rap
music is picked up and reworked by Japanese or Australian
Aboriginal musicians. We can look to Fiji, where politicians and
businessmen wear traditional *sulu* wraps with Western suit
jackets and ties, or Papua New Guinea, where the traditional
woven bags, the *bilum*, are increasingly being made with
Western products, and incorporate Western designs. With
globalization, clearly, things change; old cultural forms may be
swept away, or replaced, or they may absorb and re-form the

new cultural products that impinge on their space and sell them back to the centre.

Commentators who align themselves with the hybridization argument sometimes suggest that the networking of the globe does not necessarily lead to the extinction of local culture and local forms. Rather, they argue, it may regenerate traditional practices, languages and forms of cultural production. A.D. Smith, for instance, argues that the new communication technologies 'make possible a denser, more intense interaction between members of communities who share common cultural characteristics, notably language' which can re-energize 'ethnic communities and their nationalisms' (Smith, 1990: 175). Examples of this can be seen in the Zapatista movement, whose struggle for independence and dignity is mobilized via the internet, as is the Electronic Intifada associated with Palestinian resistance. And the 'dense interaction' Smith observes is evident among many diasporic communities. We can think of, say, expatriate German associations which keep alive traditional music, dancing and stories, or Chinese Associations which ensure that second and third-generation children learn their languages, and Chinese history and culture. Such groups operate not just in town halls and community centres, but also via web sites, newspapers, radio stations and films produced in their languages and about their cultures.

The counter-argument is that such practices do not demonstrate 'authentic' cultural practice. As often as not, the traditions maintained by diasporic communities bear little resemblance to what can be found in the original country, which is often known only in an idealized version, and is transformed anyway by the new context. The Chinese dish *chop suey*, for instance, served in restaurants across the West, is never found in China; the name of the dish comes from the Cantonese for 'odds and ends', and it is an invention of Chinese in America. Gregory Lee notes that 'Non-Chinese think it's Chinese. The Chinese outside America think it's American. It is neither one thing nor the other: it is hybrid' (Lee, 1996: 219). The films used by diasporic communities, and the advertisements and other products designed to inform others about a local culture and its traditions, are often no more than the work of global capital in packaging something that signifies the 'exotic' to sell it to a global market. Wrenched from its local place, decontextualized and repackaged, there is arguably little connection between the globally distributed form and the original to which it refers. As Beynon and Dunkerley point out (2000: 20), many of the 'traditional' arts and craft on display in tourist centres are highly dubious in their origins, and their function is not the revival of a local culture but the production of tourist goods. Difference is deployed, then, as part of the global market trajectory, and not because of any inherent appreciation of other cultures and their values. As Baudrillard writes:

> For 'We respect the fact that you are different' read: 'You people who are underdeveloped would do well to hang on to this distinction because it is all that you have left'. Nothing could be more contemptuous – or more contemptible – than this attitude, which exemplifies the most radical form of incomprehension that exists. (Baudrillard, 1993: 132)

Of course it isn't only the West that decontextualizes or appropriates other cultural forms. Masato Nakamura, a contemporary Japanese artist, directly addresses and plays with this issue. One of his more famous series of works constitutes displays of multiple McDonald's 'golden arches' signs, obvious markers of multinational corporate, market-driven value. In these installations he produces visually stunning works that also decontextualize these markers of global capital from their function and their identity, repositioning them as art objects whose value is firstly in the aesthetic, and secondly in the pleasure of poking fun at a major transnational corporation.

The second counter is that fears about inauthenticity depend on the belief that there is, or ever was, a truly authentic form. Few poststructural theorists would argue this. Jean Baudrillard discusses this concept with relation to the thesis of the relation between reality and representation. He argues that rather than an original object or form – the real – producing its referent or cultural variants, in fact the real is preceded and produced by its representation. He terms this 'the simulacrum' (1983: 3), which points to the extent to which reality can exist for us only as and where we have cultural referents to give us frameworks in which to think and see. Photographs, video recordings and other memory banks, for instance, not only record the important moments of our lives, but can even become more important than the original moments, as Susan Sontag pointed out. Of course, although 'the real' has effectively disappeared, communities behave as though it exists and still provides an epistemological basis and a teleological focus to everyday practices. So the real does not have a material history or ontological status, but it is a constitutive fiction around and upon which social practices are organized, evaluated and explained.

Conclusion

Why should we be interested in this insertion into national and local cultures of a homogenizing, globalized culture? One answer, offered by Arjun Appadurai, is that culture is that which expresses, or sets the groundwork for, 'the mobilization of group identities' (Appadurai, 1997: 13). So the effect of flows of texts that offer new or different ideas of how to understand ourselves as members of a collective is that the terms of membership of the national group are open to being redefined, and the hegemony of so-called 'national cultures' can be challenged. This does not mean that identity is entirely up for grabs; there is little evidence of any genuine global culture. Rather, what we see in the realm of cultural identity is what we have seen in the other fields passed over by the grid of globalization: those with capital are able to exploit the vast opportunities made available by the doxa of globalization, and its practices as undertaken through the economy or the realm of technology and the media. Their identity may be transformed in terms of what Appadurai calls 'elements of a postnational imaginary' (1997: 428): transnationally oriented social and cultural forms that resonate with the possibility of reworking neocolonialist cultural flows and renegotiating the imposed homogeneity of the nation-state or the ethnic tradition. But those without capital and specific literacies are likely to be appropriated, disadvantaged and disturbed by globalizing tendencies. This doesn't mean they will necessarily sink into invisibility. The 11 September attacks in the United States; the anti-globalization protests in Seattle, Melbourne and Genoa; the popular uprising against IMF-driven economic policies in Argentina; and the success of extreme right-wing political parties in Austria, France and Italy; all these constitute, in their different ways, a 'biting back' of the social and the local against the institutions, policies and practices associated with globalization. In our next chapter we will look at how the processes and doxa of globalization, and its meanings and consequences, are disseminated, reproduced, played out and negotiated within the public sphere.

7

The Public Sphere and the Media

The relationship between the **public sphere**, on the one hand, and capitalism and the (global) media, on the other, is central to debates about the politics of globalization. The traditions, values and imperatives that characterize the former are clearly being negotiated, stretched and transformed by the power and ubiquity of the latter. In this chapter we will explore this question and evaluate the arguments about the effects of globalization on the public sphere. We will focus on the media, and look at the ways in which it is complicit in what anti-globalization activist Naomi Klein calls 'the theft of the commons'.

It is important to distinguish here between public sphere and national government. Chapter 5 addressed the question of what has happened to the nation-state in a globalizing era. Clearly the advent of global networks and international governing bodies has undermined the ability of nation-states to make effective claims to the principles of territoriality and autonomy which were established by the seventeenth-century Peace of Westphalia. But the state's control over its territory, policies and economy is not the only issue that affects how people understand themselves as members of communities, or how corporations and other institutions engage in practice. The public sphere is associated with, but quite distinct from, the national government, though both are what Claude Lefort would call 'capitalized ideas' (Lefort, 1986: 205). Capitalized ideas can be understood as those values or elements (he cites Property,

Family, Order, Society, Nation) that take on a foundational identity, and 'bear the constant signs of a truth which establishes the origins of facts' (Lefort, 1986: 205) – in other words, that seem natural, ahistorical and entirely necessary to social life.

The public sphere operates as a capitalized idea, in this definition, because of the importance attributed to it in various discourses (including such otherwise contradictory discourses as nationalism, capitalism and activism), and because it is within the public sphere that 'we' see 'ourselves'. The public sphere exceeds government, because it appears at least to be a site that is beyond partisan concerns and in which the interests of 'the people' take precedence over the interests of power. There is a history to the development of the idea of the public sphere, of course, and it is related to the history of the development of the national government. We will trace this history briefly here, and then move on to discuss the role of the media in the public sphere.

The state and the public sphere

We pointed out in the previous chapter that the idea of the state is a kind of fiction, a story about how heterogeneous groups of people were joined together by narratives and performances of a common culture, history, beliefs, values and ideals. The various ethnic, religious, class and gender-differentiated groups were transformed, at least discursively, from a mass of heterogeneous elements into a homogeneous entity called 'the state'. We also suggested that this performance of statehood is an ongoing, continuous process that relies on various state apparatuses, such as schools, bureaucracies, cultural institutions and the media, in order to reproduce the meaning of, and belief in, the 'truth' of the state.

This production of the modern nation-state was predicated on what the French theorist Michel Foucault refers to as the development of modern notions of governmentality and the 'reason of state'. There are two main aspects to governmentality and reason of state. The first involves the institutionalizing of different aspects of responsibility for the 'common good' – say, looking after the sick and the needy, or managing people's morals. Where these were once the responsibility of, say, the church, as the modern concept of nation-states and govern-mentality developed they increasingly became state concerns. The second issue is related to the first – that is, this change in the idea of what constituted government and governmental respon-sibility was not explicable in terms of the hegemony of one social group. Where previously, it could be argued, princes and popes ruled in the interests of the aristocracy or (later) the bourgeoisie, now the 'reason of state' reflected the interests of all in the state. It was no longer (overtly) concerned with questions of how power can be maintained – for instance, 'how can merchants or bankers keep power?' – but set itself up as having answers to questions of government, and the well-being and prosperity of the state *in toto*.

This did not mean that the new principles of governmentality were committed to equity and equality. Rather, the population constituted a resource, which meant that the proper role of the state was population management. The government's concern now became the development of policies that regulated behaviour – for 'the good of the individual', of course; which meant, at the same time, the good of the state, with the main-tenance of a happy, healthy and therefore productive population. One of the most important points about this change is that while it produced unparalleled state intervention in people's everyday lives, the state recognized that coercive government was not the most effective way of managing its human resources. People were likely to be more productive, it seemed, if they were treated as belonging to and working for a state which reciprocated by 'looking after them'. The state thus needed to achieve a balance between intervening in and regulating people's affairs and ensuring 'the free enterprise of individuals' (Foucault, 1997: 73) – then (and still) considered the best principle for producing wealth and prosperity.

Foucault writes that this problem of balance was dealt with in Britain through the development of a particular kind of relationship between the state, the people and the 'attitude' of liberalism. It can be identified in the growing importance of economics to the state, and the state's inclination to draw back from intervening in order to promote the free enterprise of individuals. Out of this process there develops the attitude of liberalism, with the notion of 'civil society' as something more or less opposed to, critical of, and a check upon, government intervention in the lives of its citizens.

These two spheres, the interventionist, regulatory state and the civil society, developed in parallel because the 'reason of state' simultaneously promoted the existence, security and prosperity of the state, and the need for a civil society which would criticize the effectiveness and necessity of the development of state policies of intervention and regulation. Questions of what constituted moral or ethical behaviour, for instance, were sometimes removed from the control of government and became matters of 'public concern'. But governments still had a responsibility to serve and provide for the 'public good'. This usually took the form of the provision of public services, usually provided through bureaucracies, institutions and utilities in areas such as health, education, transport, security, social welfare, water, electricity, insurance and banking.

This government responsibility for its citizens is central to the question of 'civil society', which in liberal democracies forms the basis of the social contract. Claude Lefort writes, in this respect, that the development of civic society went hand in hand with the advent of democracy, where government and people share a mutual obligation, and a mutual commitment to the good of all. He characterizes democracy as a 'radical break' with the past, because in liberal democracies the stability of previous social formations (the prince, the church) was replaced by uncertainty and constant change. In a monarchy, for instance, there was an actual person in whom power was located, and both prince and subjects/citizens could actually relate to one another, and understand what one meant for the other. Identification with the prince was the basis of social identity. But in democracy the prince disappears or at least becomes irrelevant in terms of power, and the governments that replace the prince cannot govern for themselves, but must be seen, at least, to govern contingently. Every three or four years government is again up for grabs, and so no one government can exist – as did princes – as the incorporation of power. Instead of stability and continuity of government in the person of the prince, government is a constant conflict, or competition, and so power is not localized, but is what Lefort terms an 'empty place' (Lefort, 1988: 17) which can never be identified with, or occupied by, one person or one class. He describes it in these terms:

> Modern democratic society seems to me, in fact, like a society in which power, law and knowledge are exposed to a radical indetermination, a society that has become the theatre of an uncontrollable adventure, so that what is instituted never becomes established. (1986: 305)

Democracy, liberalism and the public sphere

Power, law and knowledge 'never become established', of course, because power no longer has a locus in the body of the prince or the church, and so is always liable to go 'somewhere else'. What this means for citizens is a greater degree of freedom and openness about who we are, and what we can be. But it also means a greater degree of responsibility, because in this sort of civil society power moves through and across us all. This notion constitutes the basis of the ideology of the 'independent, free-thinking subject' that characterizes Western culture. It is frequently represented in texts such as advertisements (where ironically, discourses of 'right of choice' are used to interpellate mass audiences and concomitant patterns of consumption), films (where Arnold Schwartzenegger, Sylvester Stallone or Harrison Ford fight against all forms of control, including those imposed by governments) and high cultural texts such as paintings (produced by 'geniuses' who think and work 'outside' social mores and conventions).

Despite this notion of individual freedom and responsibility, and the letting loose of power to circulate in society, the public sphere and civil society are in fact inflected with group interests.

We pointed out in Chapter 3 that though the discourses of neoliberalism insist on universal good and fairness, in practice most people are disadvantaged while a very few individuals and institutions are highly privileged. Similarly, despite the notion of the public sphere being a space that is 'empty' with regard to power and interest, both the state and capitalist institutions – not to mention every pressure or interest group in a culture – attempt to use the public sphere for their own purposes. The state's concern is to maintain its power and authority; capitalism's is to extend its interests by selling commodities, and by creating desires, demands, trends and fashions; the various lobby groups aim to influence government and the public, and to advance their causes. The public sphere thus can be seen as an arena in which any and all can compete for their own interests.

But although the public sphere is not, at least theoretically, co-substantial with any one interest group, it is not free for all. Claude Lefort insists that the game of democracy is always, first and foremost, a kind of set-up, played under specific rules and regulations, and dominated by two specific ideological typologies which he calls 'bourgeois' and 'invisible' ideology. The main usefulness of this distinction is that it attempts to account for and make sense of activities in the public sphere, both before and after the advent of the mass media and modern communication technology associated with globalization.

Bourgeois ideology, for Lefort, functions in terms of a specific pedagogical imperative to regulate society through the institution of what he calls 'capitalized ideas', which we described above. John Thompson describes Lefort's proposition that, in the nineteenth century, bourgeois ideology broke away from the church and its guarantee of authority in the spiritual realm, and substituted for this authority 'general, abstract ideas; the text of bourgeois ideology': in short, capitalized ideas, which 'imply a certain way of acting which is consistent with the idea' (in Lefort, 1986: 17). The regulation of social practice through the deployment of these capitalized ideas is one obvious way of loading the dice of the democratic game. Firstly, it acts to exclude certain groups, particularly women, children and people of colour, from the game itself by designating them as non-human

166

or of lesser social value. So, until the twentieth century, women and people of colour were routinely excluded from democratic participation, and children still have no real social identity, being only potential members of the civil society, existing as full members only after they have attained their majority. Secondly, even when marginalized groups are included in the game, the pedagogical and regulatory effects of bourgeois ideology often predispose those groups to carry out the work of the dominant classes. Donzelot's 1979 study of the ways in which women were enlisted to scrutinize and regulate the domestic sphere is a case in point here.

Lefort's second typology – invisible ideology – is predicated on an identification of the increasingly important ideological function taken by the mass media. Lefort's point is not that the mass media simply take on the task of circulating and reinforcing the capitalized ideas of bourgeois ideology. On the contrary, for Lefort the advent of the mass media ushers in a new type of ideology that gives up any claim to a totalizing discourse on the social:

> Whereas bourgeois ideology presented itself as discourse on the social, distinct from the social discourse which is constitutive of everyday life, the new ideology seeks to merge with social discourse. It provides an excellent means of diffusion in the mass media . . . Therein lies the imaginary, ideological dimension of mass media: it provides the constant awareness of the social bond, attests to the permanent presence of the 'between-us', the *entre nous*. (Lefort, 1986: 19)

What this means is that the capitalized ideas of bourgeois ideology are replaced by an endless performance of communication; and the imperative to communicate is carried out through the media. Where bourgeois ideology insists on Truths that work to divide the human community up into us and them, invisible ideology makes room for every group, regardless of social standing. In fact, the less social standing the better, in one sense, because this demonstrates the openness of the system, a process of unending reciprocity that is also a process of unending communication. Invisible ideology loads the game of democracy in a different way from bourgeois ideology: whereas with bourgeois ideology the ploy was to exclude or regulate or predispose, with invisible ideology the performance of communication and community (the two terms are virtually synonymous here) takes the place of, and makes irrelevant, the kinds of political antagonisms that Lefort identifies as the defining characteristics of the democratic state.

How then do we understand Lefort's notion of democracy, and as a corollary the role of the public sphere, in the light of these two ideologies? Both ideologies are predicated on the indeterminate and agonistic nature of democratic society: bourgeois ideology fills in its empty capitalized ideas with whatever content is appropriate to the context, while invisible ideology takes every division and antagonism as the opportunity for a performance of communication as community, thereby erasing difference. Invisible ideology clearly renounces any right to speak 'on the social', because the inclination towards some kind of totalizing discourse is replaced by a performance of totality: everything is available, everything can be called up, everything can be known.

But, despite this, the public sphere is still available, in some shape or form, as a site of dissent or opposition, however subtly conveyed. In Communist China, for instance, criticism of government policies and actions is often presented through films which locate the 'problem' in the safety of history, but in fact address a contemporary issue – films such as *Raise the Red Lantern, Farewell, my Concubine* or *To Live* can be seen as allegories of the ruthless intervention of the state into private lives, and the smothering effect of government controls. In contemporary Northern Ireland, too, protest takes place 'under cover': though the government has to interdict public articulations of bigotry, Protestant shopkeepers can get around this by covering their shopfronts with advertisements for 'Orange crush' soft drink. And in the transnational domain the internet is becoming an important site of public sphere activity and perhaps the most effective foil to state control.

An example of how people make use of the net to access and communicate information despite state regulation occurred in

Malaysia in 1998, when Prime Minister Mahathir attempted to control debate and the circulation of information and opinion about the prosecution of his former deputy, Anwar Ibrahim, for various crimes, including sodomy. Clearly many of Anwar's supporters thought the charges were politically motivated, but Mahathir attempted to stifle opposition by regulating media coverage of the events and issues. However, Malaysians who logged on to the internet could (and did) access international reports, and then produce hard copies for general dissemination. Malaysia is not alone in its frustration with the internet's ungovernability: Singapore and China have attempted to limit the use of the net for political purposes by restricting access to approved users; the British government's attempts to block the hard-copy publication of politically sensitive material has been thwarted by publication on the net; and the US government has been trying to regulate the on-line availability of pornography. But generally speaking as long as the technology is available, there is no way of closing off the opportunities for communication and information retrieval available through computer networks.

The media and the public sphere

The media, including the internet, have thus become by far the most important site of public sphere debate and dissent, because they allow people and groups to reach and influence national and global audiences, including governments. Think, for instance, of the role of the media with respect to the events of 11 September. They provided information on what was going on and how we ought to feel about it, and they made a claim to manage what is normally a state matter – security. Douglas Kellner writes:

> While the Bush administration [on 11 September] obviously had no idea what was happening to the U.S. as Bush's presidential plane frantically flew around the country and Vice-President Dick Cheney was carried off to the mountains

to hide, the TV networks were fully in control with frames, discourses, and explanations of the momentous events. . . .

Media frames shifted from 'America Under Attack' to 'America Strikes Back' and 'America's New War' – even before any military action was undertaken, as if the media frames were to conjure the military response that eventually followed. (Kellner, 2002)

The media acted here as the *de facto* public sphere, the site of intercommunication and the voice of the people. In short, they humanized and personalized the events, and at the same time became the site of meaning and information for the community. But the other side of this close relationship between the public sphere and the media is that so much of what audiences are fed as news comes from a small number of corporations (News Corp, Disney/Cap Cities, Time Warner, Viacom and TCI) and associated press agencies (CNN, BBC, Reuters, AP, UPI, Bloomberg), which invariably universalize Western interests, even in the non-Western world. (Four of the five media giants are located in the United States, and the fifth, News Corp, in Australia.) A perhaps inevitable effect of this structure is that news is standardized across the world; as Mark Alleyne notes:

The quantity of news flowing from the rich countries of the North to the South greatly exceeds the quantity going in the other direction. The quality of news from South to North is lower than the reverse flow. . . . Unless there is a major natural or man-made catastrophe the average consumer of news in, say, New Delhi will hardly have available to him or her as wide a choice of news about, say, Latin America, Africa or even other Asian countries, as he or she has about Western Europe or the United States. And even when the consumer of news in New Delhi gets news from other countries of the South the quality of the news is often low . . . news about a hurricane in the Caribbean . . . might come only in words, without still or moving pictures. (1997: 13)

There are two important aspects to this news and information disjunction. Images can be used to draw people's attention to events, and to humanize them. A particularly striking example of this was the 'Tiananmen Square' photograph of the protester blocking the path of a tank during the 1989 student protests in China. The circulation of that image became an instant icon of the 'universal' struggle for human rights and democracy. Another example of the humanizing effect of broadcast images was the Vietnam War photograph of a small girl, napalmed and burning, running down a road, which became an icon of the anti-war movement, and is still reproduced from time to time as a reminder of the close-up effect of long-distance military intervention. Each of these images was used to inform and to mobilize opinion in what is effectively a global public sphere.

But more often than not the plethora of images from and about the West, and the absence of similar images from and about the South, mean that events and even lives in the two spheres take on different values. Images of the events of 11 September, for instance, were covered in such detail, and disseminated so widely, that the tragedy of what had happened to America had an effect on how people throughout the world made sense of, and responded to, America's subsequent bombing of Afghanistan. Consider, by contrast, the lack of coverage of the bombing of Afghani civilians and the deaths that ensued. There were images of rubble and destroyed villages, but few detailed or repeated shots of victims; the deaths were predominantly represented in written reports, and even these were invariably qualified by being described as 'unverified'. This meant that the events, and the lives of those affected, were depersonalized.

The second aspect of this 'news disjunction' is that when events in the developing world are deemed newsworthy, they usually come under the 'disaster, corruption and *coups*' category. In other words, when events are represented, they tend to naturalize the developing world as a place where disasters happen, where corruption and violence are endemic, where 'life is cheap', and where people behave in an erratic, barbarous and irrational manner. This has two consequences. Firstly, when lives are lost, or when violence occurs, it is easy for Western audiences to distance themselves from the events, or ignore what is happening. It seems that, to Western audiences, it is just the way things are, it is natural, it is what has always happened, and what will continue to happen until the rest of the world's people become Westernized. Secondly, the naturalization of the developing world as a place of violence, barbarism and irrationality means that nobody is to blame for what is happening. The food riots that occurred in Indonesia in 1998 under the IMF economic policies imposed on the government, for instance, could easily be located within the wider narrative of Asian or Oriental 'barbarism' and endemic poverty; therefore the question of colonialist or neocolonialist involvement in producing these effects never has to be addressed. The media produce the site for a public sphere that is inflected by, and inhabited by, powerful people and institutions. Those without power are only occasionally invited in, and then only when it is deemed to be in the interests of its inhabitants.

The media as public sphere

This universalizing of the public sphere comes about, and is facilitated by, the advent of a virtual identification between the media and the civil society; and the new communication technologies, which enable interactivity, suggest an even greater role for the media as the new public sphere. In the traditional form, after all, people could actually speak to one another, rather than simply be the objects of a lecture or one-way information flow. Interactive media such as the internet, and promised developments such as interactive television, should provide the site for a genuine, if virtual, public sphere. We suggested above, though, that this has always been the case in the public sphere; that, despite the discourses, the public sphere was always the arena of power and interest. Still, in a globalized world the media do seem to have taken the place of the old public sphere meeting places where citizens would gather to hear information, debate ideas or courses of action, or voice their dissent. The differences between the two forms of public sphere – the media and the traditional meeting place –

are exemplified in the Coen Brothers' film *O Brother, Where Art Thou?* which we discussed in Chapter 3.

The film is set in the American south during the Great Depression, and revolves around three escaped convicts trying to get to a town where a battle is going on for governorship of the state. In one scene we are shown a classic example of the old-style public sphere in action. A stage has been erected in a town square, on which the reform candidate for the governorship puts on show for, and addresses issues central to, the community. A dwarf tells jokes about the candidate working for 'the little man', a local group sings, and the would-be governor rants, accuses, cajoles and generally commandeers the (actual, physical) public sphere. The incumbent is in despair over this; he understands that the reform candidate's performance has made his defeat an inevitability. But then the new public sphere intervenes in the form of the radio, playing an old-time song recorded by the escapees under the name of the 'Soggy Bottom Boys'. The record has become a huge hit, and turned the group into celebrities without their knowing it. When the reform candidate denounces them at a dance, the incumbent quickly seizes the opportunity to turn the occasion into another 'public sphere show' via the Boys and their popularity. The reform candidate is branded as 'not of the people', and the incumbent identifies with the group's 'rough and ready ways', ensuring that he wins the election. The group's recording, and the airplay it achieves, transform the election simply because the new medium has created its own public sphere. The film points to a time when television, film, recordings and radio will be used to spread information, represent points of view, exchange ideas, criticize policies, 'call up' groups (citizens, taxpayers, patriots) and vent popular frustration or anger. It also points to a time – our time – marked by the phenomenon of 'media celebrities' being used to sway or command popular opinion.

But there are limitations on this. Zygmunt Bauman writes that the role of the media as an effective public sphere is hugely exaggerated: all that is in fact available, he says, is 'an interactive one-way medium' because so few people have access to the media: 'As for the rest, left with the network of satellite or cable television with not as much as a pretension to symmetry between the two sides of the screen – pure and unalloyed watching is their lot' (Bauman, 1998: 53). And even if there really were general public access to interactive media, members of the public (sphere) would still be constrained by the available information, their ability to process it and communicate about it, and the frames provided by the media for interaction. We know that available information seems practically limitless – you can get anything you want, it seems, on the internet – provided you can find it, and the more easily available information is likely to be that provided by mainstream corporations, because they have the saturation ability, and the funds to corner the market. As for the ability to process information: the flood of information means no one is able to consume and process everything; and besides, the information tends to be unsystematic (emerging in response to media events and fads, rather than careful analysis), fragmented in time and space (because of the means of dissemination) and typically ahistorical (because insufficient background information is provided about a media story to allow a contextualized understanding of it). Jean Baudrillard writes:

> We forget a little too easily that the whole of our reality is filtered through the media, including tragic events of the past. This means that it is too late to verify and understand these events historically, for the characteristic thing about the present period . . . is the fact that the tools required for such intelligibility have been lost. (Baudrillard, 1993: 90–1)

What these factors suggest is that rather than the media providing an interactive participatory public sphere, the public sphere operates according to business as usual: those groups and individuals able to seize the public ear and influence government can put their issues on the agenda; those variously disenfranchised cannot. But a sideline to this is what it means to the media themselves: it is important to remember that the media are business, and that the business of business is to make money. The media make money by selling audiences to advertisers; and this inevitably limits what will be up for discussion, and the extent of the discussion, within the media-as-public sphere. As Noam Chomsky insisted, 'advertisers pay for certain things. They're not going to pay for a discussion that encourages people to participate democratically and undermine corporate power' (Chomsky, 1996).

A counter-argument to this is that the role of substitute 'public sphere' has largely been taken on, in the West, by non-commercial and non-aligned institutions such as the United Kingdom public broadcaster, the BBC. But increasingly it has come to include all the media, especially the internet. As we pointed out, the state has attempted to use and control the media to further its own ends – both to enhance the public good, say, through education, and to 'ideologize' and naturalize the narratives and values that supposedly function as the foundation of the state itself. By and large the media have been inflected by, and identifiable with, the state and its interests, either because they were owned, operated and funded by the state, or because commercial operators were subject to the intervention of the state.

Globalization has radically changed this relationship between the state, the media and the public sphere. The IMF, in its self-appointed role of detecting and dismantling any mechanisms that interfere with the free circulation of goods, services, ideas and information (but not, interestingly, people), has attempted to force states to open up media markets to worldwide (that is to say, usually American) competition. This move has been resisted by underdeveloped countries (for example, India) and affluent Western states (particularly France and other EU countries). They express concern about the possible saturation effect of the American media on national culture; the inability of state-based media institutions to compete with transnational mega-corporations such as Time-Warner and News Corporation; and the threat posed to the security of the state by having 'local' communication networks owned and operated by non-national groups. This situation has been dressed up as a straightforward globalization versus localization debate in which every state has equal status, but as Mattelart points out, it is really a quintessential example of the United

States and transnational corporations using neoliberal ideology as a means of naturalizing, justifying and furthering their own interests:

> Since 1970, the American state administration and American business circles have not ceased to proclaim that if there is one rule that must govern relations among nations, it is that of the 'free flow of information' . . . This doctrine, born at the end of World War II, accompanied the international expansion of American power [and] complemented the related doctrine of the free flow of capital, commodities, and resources. (Mattelart and Mattelart, 1992: 156–7)

While developing nations sought to resist this move (the Mattelarts go on to cite an Indian delegate who said, 'Free flow is like a free fox among free chickens'), they were unable to shift the position of the United States, which simply refused to comply with UNESCO principles which opposed this effectively neocolonial action.

This 'American push' has been accompanied by the concentration, privatization and deregulation of the global media and communications market, accompanied and aided by the new communication technologies, especially satellite broadcasting, which ensure global access for the mass media corporations. Media firms are now in fewer hands, and from an increasingly smaller number of countries, predominantly in North America and Europe. Symbiotic corporate mergers or arrangements have brought together different resources and technologies, merging to form super-corporations such as Time-Warner, Disney, Viacom and News Corporation. And the various sectors of the global media market are now virtually oligopolies, dominated by a few players such as CNN, ESPN, the BBC and Star (in satellite- or cable-transmitted news, sports and documentary programs); AP, UPI, Reuters and AFP (print news services); Disney, Universal, MGM, Time-Warner, News (in the film industry); and Bertelsmann, Time-Warner and Viacom (in book publishing). The media are not just big, but huge, business: 'in 1993-95,' Castells writes, 'about US$80 billion were spent in television programming worldwide, and spending was rising by

10% a year' (Castells, 1996: 341). And this has important impli-cations for the role of the media, as Hemant Shah writes:

> First, concentration of ownership and privatization of mass media has been accompanied by commercialization of news and other cultural products, a trend that is characterized by aesthetic, technical, and professional standardization at the global level. And second, alliances between the international 'media moguls' such as Rupert Murdoch and forces of political conservatism have led to increasingly 'soft' media content. These phenomena are part of the process of globalization. (Shah, 2000)

What this indicates is that the media may indeed be the *de facto* new public sphere, but it is a public sphere that is committed to the market imperative, and not to criticism of the state, or to facilitating information and communication among the people.

Commoditizing the public sphere

The significant change in the ways in which the public sphere is constituted and functions is partly an effect of the proliferation of global media networks, and partly a simple case of the doxa of globalization and neoliberalism ensuring a 'retreat of the state' from its roles and responsibilities. Now, instead of the notion of public service, governments increasingly rely on the market-driven 'user pays' approach. This is generally articulated in terms of the government's role in promoting the free enterprise of individuals, and the importance of capitalism in ensuring wealth and prosperity. It does, however, raise particular prob-lems for the notion of the public sphere, and the public good. Even in a thoroughgoing capitalism system there have always been areas and objects that have not been reducible to market value: those things that are literally priceless, because they cannot be for sale (faith, personal identity, family love), and those things that are only obliquely related to the market (major art works, heritage objects, scientific research). As John Frow writes: 'The political sphere, the sphere of public service, that of art and of some kinds of writing may conform, or may be presumed to conform, to a different logic from that of strict profit maximization' (1997: 131).

But with the substitution of the media sphere for the public sphere we run into the problem of the divided loyalties of the media. On the one hand, and according to their own principles (which are usually articulated in a professional code of ethics), the media are committed to notions such as truth, accuracy and freedom of speech, the public's right to know, unbiased reporting and independence. These principles supposedly inform all aspects of the journalist's work, including what should constitute news, how it is reported and gathered, and whose opinions are sought and authorized. But, on the other hand, they are a business, operating under a model of capitalism that effectively advocates the rejection of the public good in favour of private enterprise. That is, alongside the establishment of the principles of journalistic ethics and practice is the increasing importance of the business of the news. The 'industrial' model of journalism is a quick-turnaround model, a jump-on-the-bandwagon model, one that relies on soundbites and media panics, and that glosses over alternative points of view in favour of the fashionable one (or the one run by all the other networks). It produces, Shah writes:

> journalism that describes events with little analysis, relies upon polls and statistics to show social trends but without providing historical context, and provides no vehicle of expression for ordinary people at the grass roots level. It is precisely the type of journalism that serves the interests of the owners of the global mass media firms because it avoids asking deeper questions about the exercise of power, the dispensation of social justice, and the prospects for cultural survival. (Shah, 2000)

This argument that journalism and the media are dominated by the market ties in with two notions, both taken from Claude Lefort, that we introduced earlier in this chapter. The first of these is that democracy (theoretically) functions by refusing an identification with one group, but at the same time 'the game of democracy' is loaded in favour of bourgeois capitalism. Secondly, and relatedly, bourgeois capitalist 'invisible ideology' makes use of the media's lack of sustained attention to any one issue in order to erase potential antagonisms or opposition within a democratic state, and thus maintain and perpetuate their own hegemony while apparently remaining committed to 'universal communication'.

How can these notions inform our understanding of what is happening in the contemporary, media-dominated public sphere? Pierre Bourdieu argues, in his *On Television* (1998b), that the media and journalism no longer seriously commit to or perform 'in the public interest' because they are dominated by the logic of the market, and that, consequently, there is no time to consider or analyse public issues. This fits in perfectly with the logic of 'invisible ideology' raised by Lefort. In the aftermath of the events of 11 September, for instance, 'experts' were called in by the media to provide explanations of, opinions about, and background regarding, what had happened. Now of course this 'selection process' was strictly limited or subject to censorship; it would have been impossible for a representative of, say, al-Qaeda or Hamas to be interviewed about the reasons behind the attacks. The various networks did find some 'representative' (Arabic) spokespersons, but this alternative was closed in advance, largely because they tended to interview 'reasonable' figures such as Arab academics or journalists who more or less accepted, and spoke within, the binary logics of terrorist/free world, evil/good or barbarism/civilization. Some interviewees did (momentarily) venture outside these binary parameters, say, by suggesting that America's refusal to take an evenhanded approach to the Israeli–Palestinian conflict contributed to the attacks. But then they were sure to move back within the boundaries by refraining from suggesting that American activities, practices and politics (say, in bombing Iraq, carpet-bombing Cambodia, slaughtering villagers in Vietnam, conspiring to overthrow the Chilean government, supporting the atrocities of the Pinochet regime, supporting the 'terrorist activities' of the Contras in Nicaragua or facilitating Israel's massacre of Palestinians in Lebanese refugee camps) disturbed the distinction implied by the American designation of the 'war against terrorism'.

This performance of communication as community was accompanied and informed by recourse to what we could call 'the politics of affect', or the production and reduction of events in terms of an immediate, unconsidered emotional reaction. Bourdieu makes the point that the restrictions of time under which the media operate ensure that issues can be explicated only in terms of, or reduced to, sensationalist or dramatic explanations. The quintessential example of this, of course, is the term 'war against terror'. Everything that happened in the war in Afghanistan and afterwards (the bombing and slaughter of civilians, the destruction of infrastructure, the millions of refugees) was contextualized within, and thus legitimated by, this designation. It worked as a kind of shorthand by which events could be understood and within which they could be framed. The logic behind this practice was simple; since the 'war against terror' was unambiguously and unquestioningly good (who, after all, could be against a war against terror; or who, by extension, could be in favour of terrorism?), any acts committed in its name didn't bear or require analysis; they were merely to be applauded or supported.

What this means is that the *de facto* public sphere of the media did not offer a genuine meeting place or site for discussion, but operated precisely as did the traditional meeting place, as a site for the practice of invisible ideologies in silencing those who do not constitute part of the hegemony. Bourgeois capitalism thus made use of invisible ideology and an attachment to the performance of communication to 'tip the democratic game' in its favour. Let's look at how this applies to the discursive grid of globalization after the events of 11 September, with particular reference to the politics of affect.

One striking example of the politics of affect concerned media reporting and representation of the position of Afghani women, and in particular the issue of the burkha. Stories and events that are processed through the 'machine' of the media are often encapsulated in a single, highly emotive image. Much the same happened in this case. Numerous articles and television reports were devoted to the West's 'duty to Afghan woman', which involved giving them access to education and beauty parlours, employment and television; but most of all it meant ridding them of the tyranny of having to wear the burkha. Consider this excerpt from an article written by Nicholas Kristof that first appeared in the *New York Times*, and was entitled, appropriately, 'Our duty now is to Afghan women':

> I was in a burka shop the other day, chatting with the male proprietor, when two women walked in to browse the latest fashions (powder blue, gold embroidery). They observed silently as the two of us men discussed whether women want to wear burkas. It seemed a bit ridiculous, so I asked the women: 'What do you think?' Scandalised, they raced out of the shop. Over the past weeks I've been rebuffed by dozens of Afghan women. To find out how much of the repression of women in Afghanistan was a result of the Taliban and how much was culture, I thought I should consult the real experts: ordinary women. But men are not supposed to talk to women here except when absolutely necessary, and accosting a female stranger to interview her is a shocking breach of protocol.
> (Kristof, 2001: 15)

Leaving aside the combination of arrogance and cultural insensitivity contained here, the most obvious point about this article is that it has already foreclosed what it purports to question; that is, the answer has to be 'No, women don't want to wear the burkha', because even if women said they did want to wear it, all that would mean was that they were acculturated dupes of Islam. The culture itself is, in this telling of it, clearly as 'ridiculous' as the protocols that Kristof doesn't observe or take seriously.

As well as the cultural insensitivity registered in this example, we can also identify an instance of the politics of affect. The international circulation of texts through the Western media, and the resultant store of intertextual references that it produced among its readers, actually draw up a set of narratives that readers apply to images without knowing they are doing it. Bourdieu and Wacquant refer to this as cultural imperialism, which 'rests on the power to universalize particularisms linked to a singular historical tradition' (1999: 41). It was this kind of universalizing that provided the context in which Western audiences read the photographs and articles about women wearing the burkha. The proliferation of media photographs and stories about Western dress naturalizes and hence universalizes Western garments; more to the point, they become markers of civilization and modernity. This means that articles about and images of the burkha are doubly negative; they are endowed with associations of primitivism, barbarism and exploitation, but they are also 'unnatural' precisely because they are 'not Western' and therefore 'non-universal'.

The globalized media, acting again as public sphere, are central to this production of 'us versus them', in keeping with Lefort's notion that invisible ideology is designed to foreclose differences partly by keeping difference out. During the 2001-02 war against Afghanistan, media representatives like Nicholas Kristof continued to pursue Afghani women about the burkha, and like Kristof generally met with the same kind of responses, either because of their insensitivity, or because of the fact that gender politics in Afghanistan has hardly undergone a sea change under the Northern Alliance. It would be difficult and even dangerous for Afghani women to start acting like Western women, which is what the Western media clearly expected them to do. But while Western media reports were celebrating the fact that Afghani women could now wear make-up and visit beauty parlours, an article on Simi Samara, the Minister of Women's Affairs in the new Afghani government, demonstrated how little things have changed for women in Afghanistan:

When the interim Afghan administration was installed,
Samara, 45, was so overcome by the accounts of women's
suffering under the Taliban that she spent her first days on the
job in tears. Here weeks later, as she receives guests in the
living room of her rented home in an over-sized grey
sweatshirt and with no veil over her close-cropped brown hair,

she is merely angry; at cabinet colleagues who are suspicious of her mission, at the delays in getting her ministry off the ground, and at the international community for making a cause celebre of Afghan women and then failing to stump up the cash as quickly as she would like. (Goldenberg, 2002: 13)

This kind of article was a rarity, but it still presumes and implies that an 'educated' woman (she is both a doctor and dresses in Western clothes) can speak for, and has the right and duty to 'free', Afghani women from their obvious and unfortunate 'enmeshment' in (at least certain aspects of) Islamic culture. Again the role of the burkha in this narrative is pivotal:

Samara's task is a daunting one. Five years of Taliban rule left women encased in the all-concealing shroud of the burkha and trapped in their homes, denied education or the right to work. A society where women accounted for 60 per cent of civil servants – and more than half of them university students – shuddered to a halt. (Goldenberg, 2002: 13).

The move here is to set up relatively unquestionable violations of human rights, including the denials of education, access to the public sphere, freedom of movement, and the right to paid work, as being coterminous with 'the shroud of the burkha'. This is Bourdieu and Wacquant's notion that 'cultural imperialism rests on the power to universalize particularisms' at work; the reader slides from the burkha as a marker of Islam to the naturalized assumption that wearing it is (universally) regarded as an imposition, and swiftly on to its association or identification with abuses of 'universal human rights'. And this process was repeated throughout the media, contrasting various instances of Islamic particularism and primitivism with markers of Western universality, including access to beauty parlours, the wearing of cosmetics, listening to Western music, watching Hollywood films, and owning and watching a television set.

These examples of the politics of affect at work in the media explain how the saturation of the public sphere and the media with 'invisible ideology' allows a particular group or field (America, the middle class, the 'silent majority', capitalism, the market) to occupy the empty space of the 'global democratic community'; a discursive space opened up and maintained by the doxa of globalization.

It is important, however, not to jump to conclusions about the Americanization or Westernization of the public sphere because of its saturation of the global media. Just as the native South Americans converted to Catholicism under the Spanish imperialism (as we mentioned in Chapter 2) but 'took it somewhere else' and made a use of it that was not European, so too the fact that young men around the world may wear baseball caps back to front does not mean that they have necessarily been interpellated by a particular form of ideological imperialism. It could as easily suggest that they are taking something and making it their own. Contemporary popular music, for instance, may be dominated by American musicians and labels, but across the world young musicians are making music that picks up their styles and forms, but inflects it with local sounds, local stories and local interest. The Australian Aboriginal group Yothu Yindi is a case in point, where within the framework of rock music is a powerfully present indigenous sound, including instrumentation, vocals and the obligatory video clip. What is perhaps their most famous song, 'Treaty', is peculiarly local, since it ignores the usual topics of love and sex, drug culture and police brutality, and instead issues a call for a treaty between the government of Australia and the indigenous people. Informed by global (for which read American) media and culture, this band has taken the forms somewhere else (to their own place) and made of it something that is expressly not American or global, but Australian-Aboriginal.

Held and McGrew pick up this point, and note that although there is a saturation tendency within the global media, the fact that Western images are broadcast so widely does not necessarily mean that everyone is interpellated according to the Western hegemony. Rather, the fact that communication technologies have such a wide reach means they also have the capacity to highlight cultural difference, and to remind citizens of other countries and other cultures of the particularities of their own traditions, tastes and values. Perhaps in consequence:

> national (and local) cultures remain robust; national institutions continue in many states to have a central impact on public life; national television and radio broadcasting continues to enjoy substantial audiences; the organization of the press and news coverage retains strong national roots; and foreign cultural products are constantly read and reinterpreted in novel ways by national audiences. (Held and McGrew, 2000: 16)

And nor, despite our arguments above, is there just one press. Although the global media are marked, as we pointed out, by concentration and deregulation, there are still small independent presses; the internet still provides alternative voices and alternative views on global politics; and even mainstream media outlets do at times take a position that opposes the hegemony. Douglas Kellner points out that though the United States media were almost entirely supportive of George W. Bush in his first months in office, the global press, including such luminaries as the London *Times*, the *Guardian Weekly* and *Der Spiegel* printed scorching critiques of Bush's unilateralism and 'arrogance' (Kellner, 2001). All the same, these can best be read as exceptions that prove the rule that the *de facto* public sphere which is the media is subject to the forces of commoditization and universalizing that render the global public sphere a site for the imposition of Western values and Western interests.

Conclusion

Up to this point we have tried to describe and trace the relationships between the state, democracy, the public sphere and the media, and in particular to look at how the supposedly 'inalienable' public sphere of civic society, and the 'empty space' of democracy, have been alienated and occupied by the interests of globalization, the market and America/the West. We suggested that this was tied up with two main processes: the domination of the media by the market; and the media coming to 'stand in' for the public sphere. What this means, in effect, is that the identity of the contemporary public sphere has largely come to be determined by the logics, rationales, values and orientations of the market. The question that needs to be addressed, however, is: how did market logic vampirize and suffuse Western culture to the point where, as Frow puts it, 'Something important is . . . disappearing' (1999: 2)? The answer is clearly tied up with developments in global communication technology, but as we suggested in earlier chapters, technology is not of itself an explanation for anything. It is always developed and utilized within, and comes to be valued and understood in terms of, specific social, cultural and political contexts. In the final chapter we will address these issues in more detail, and consider what is available at the level of activity and politics 'after globalization'.

8

Globalization, Counter-memory, Practice

We have argued in the previous chapters that globalization can be understood as a grid of discourses, practices, relations and values that passes over and transforms virtually every aspect of contemporary life. This does not mean it is all-encompassing, of course; some of the claims made against it – that the nation-state has become irrelevant, that there is no alternative to the economic system that dominates world markets, that everyone across the globe is part of a giant communication network – are exaggerated. But it is evident that this grid of globalization has changed the world and relations between its parts. Nations are more closely connected with one another, especially with others in their area, than was the case a century ago. The 'turn to the local' has changed the way individuals understand their community connections and obligations, and forced nations to reconsider their relation to what is one of the central reasons of state: the management of populations.

The combination of corporate and national economic interests has also pushed the world into what Manuel Castells terms a 'network' in which communication and business can (indeed, must) be undertaken, and the rise of transnational and international companies, organizations and 'policing' mechanisms has vitiated the territoriality and autonomy that were once considered attributes of nation-states. In short, the passing of the old Soviet bloc and Cold War politics has been replaced by the politics, ideology and institutions of the 'new world order', determined, regulated and policed by international political, economic and cultural institutions.

In this chapter we contextualize the rules and their identity by examining the practices and discourses of this new world order in terms of its relationship to both theoretical (i.e. neo-liberalism) and politico-economic (i.e. neocolonialism) contexts. Particularly, we investigate the ways in which this new world order has instituted itself by working counter to memory, in the obfuscating or erasure of history. We argue, though, that history is reasserted from time to time, and that the rules are redeployed, rearticulated and redirected, particularly as and when social demands draw attention to, and potentially trans-form, the dominant set of discourses, practices and ideologies in a given moment.

Disaffection and 'imperialist reason'

In the middle of the US bombing of Afghanistan, an article appeared in the *New York Times* written by Fawaz Gerges, a Professor of Middle East and International Affairs working at an American college. Part of it read as follows:

> While the world awaits a determination of Osama bin Laden's fate, many Arabs and Muslims are coming to terms with his destructive legacy. People in that part of the world are fed up with losers who often abuse their political naivete . . . Bin Laden had hoped that by killing thousands of innocent Americans he could make the US lash out angrily and murderously against Muslims, thus precipitating a clash of civilisations. But the Bush administration did not play into his hands . . . Bin Ladenism taps into the Arab sense of victimisation . . . Arabs and Muslims must take charge of their political destiny by seizing the initiative from bin Ladenism and charting a new, liberal, humanist path. Blaming the other – the West – is an easy escape from addressing the real

conditions that give rise to and sustain backwardness, underdevelopment, extremism and intolerance. (Gerges, 2002: 7)

Gerges fits in perfectly with the idea of the 'inflected representative' who is often chosen by the media to 'speak for' a group; he is clearly Arabic and possibly a Muslim (which makes him an 'authentic' spokesperson), but also Westernized, educated and sympathetic to America and American values, and therefore by extension reasonable, civilized and authoritative. Although the article seems to be directed at an Arabic or Islamic audience ('Muslims must take charge of their destiny'), its actual addressee is America and the West; and its message, quite simply, is that 'It's not your fault, it [11 September] has nothing to do with you.'

In this version of events, the 'real' cause of Arabic or Islamic disaffection is not American imperialism or the US support of Israel (although Gerges does refer, briefly, to the need for America to reassess 'the efficacy and fairness of its foreign policies'), but Arabs themselves: they are backward, underdeveloped, naive, extremist, intolerant, self-pitying and deluded, all conditions and characteristics which give birth to, and provide the context for, 'bin Ladenism'. In this view America has achieved, and is an exemplar of, civilization: the Bush administration's refusal to 'lash out' demonstrates this. (And this was written, extraordinarily, during the American bombing of civilian groups in Afghanistan, and while Secretary of State Donald Rumsfeld was more or less asserting America's right to kill anyone it didn't like.) In order for Arabic and Islamic states and peoples to join the universal family of 'modernity', Gerges suggests, they must take the 'liberal, humanist path'; in other words, they must become like America and Americans.

The article functions, in the context of the circulation of texts and intertexts that help us understand 11 September, as another 'piece of the real', a testimony – in this case from 'one of them' – that authenticates and evinces the truth of George W. Bush's claim that America was fighting for good against evil, for civilization against barbarism. The specific contexts (social, historical, political, colonialist, imperialist, Orientalist) that could be brought to bear on the events of 11 September are elided, both in Gerges's article and in Bush's rhetoric, in favour of this inflection of the 'universals' of globalization, civilization and progress by American values, politics and interests. But this can be articulated only if history and its particularities are effaced.

Bourdieu and Wacquant write with regard to the 'imperialist reason' of globalization:

> A kind of fictional axiomatization fit to produce the illusion of pure genesis, a game of preliminary definitions and deductions aimed at substituting the appearance of logical necessity for the contingency of de-negated sociological necessities, tends to obfuscate the historical roots of a whole ensemble of questions and notions. (Bourdieu and Wacquant, 1999: 41–2)

Their point is that if we behave as though all world relations and international practices are just 'the way things are', 'the way they've always been', then this becomes a commonsense view of the world, based on a forgetting of the historical roots of contemporary disaffection. Lewis Lapham, for instance, writes that 'the United States invariably chooses for its allies the despots who operate their countries on the model of a prison or a jail' (Lapham, 2001: 10). If we forget this, there is no context in which to make sense of attacks on America, or America's responses to such attacks.

The 'forgetting' of history is an effect of what Claude Lefort terms 'invisible ideology'. As we discussed in Chapter 7, this refers to an all-encompassing set of discourses on the social that become social discourse, largely through the mass media, which work constantly to produce a way of seeing the world, and seeing one another, of attesting 'to the permanent presence of the "between-us", the *entre nous*' (Lefort, 1986: 19). The role played by the media in the constitution of national communities is now reprised, in a sense, on a global scale, so that the bonds of the 'between-us' are not just within national boundaries, but stretch across nations and hemispheres. Wherever we look we see others who are 'like us', and to whom we have responsibilities; and, of course, we see others who are not like us, and to whom we owe little or nothing.

Like Lefort, Bourdieu identifies the media as central to this production of a global community and its 'truths' of identity; Lefort's 'set of discourses' translates, in Bourdieu's writing, as 'the great new global vulgate that endless media repetition progressively transforms into universal common sense' (Bourdieu and Wacquant, 1999: 42). Whatever the terminology, the effects are the same; whether we term it a set of discourses or a global vulgate, the hegemony of the market in the Western public sphere is ensured, and that hegemony works to produce an identification between, say, America and civilization, modernity and progress. In other words, it is reasonably unproblematic to move from a situation where one set of values and narratives (encapsulated in Gerdes's 'liberal, humanist path') comes to stand in for and explain the whole global community. After all, that community and, in effect, the doxa of the globalization of the world are by and large a post-Enlightenment Western invention. But what it doesn't entirely account for is the way in which this hegemony works to 'efface itself'; that is, how a set of values and imperatives (the market) cannibalize something (civic society, the public sphere) of which it is a product.

Bourdieu offers a starting point with his references to the obfuscating of historical contexts. This reduces the difference of 'the other' – which in the present situation is represented by the Islamic community – to the status of an adjunct of, or stage in a path to, 'the same' – the global community, represented by America, the market and the West. This is not all it effects, though; it also covers over the fact that, as Lefort points out with regard to democracy, the West was never 'the same', never 'itself'.

Simulation and 'the real'

How, then, did history come to be neutralized in order to facilitate the erasure of difference within the West? One theorist

191

whose work offers an answer to this question is the French sociologist Jean Baudrillard, who has offered a thesis that the Gulf War did not take place. What he meant by this startling statement is that this military exercise was conducted as a simulation of a war; the war itself, and military events such as bombings, troop movements or negotiations, existed for people outside the area of engagement as media events, rather than conventional military activities. The American performance artist Laurie Andersen referred to the 'Superbowl coverage' of the war, a metaphor which reflects the media production of war as entertainment. And the way in which America and its allies prosecuted the war, which resulted in very low Allied causalities, allowed civilians outside Iraq to thrill to the nightly fireworks over Baghdad, without the dread and grief which would have been attendant on the probable deaths of their own loved ones. In this war we can identify what Baudrillard refers to as the 'simulacra': first comes the representation in 'signs', or cultural texts (here, news reports), and only after this can we experience the 'reality' of (the idea of) the war.

Like Lefort and Bourdieu, Baudrillard sheets much of this writing-out of historical particularities, and enshrining of 'invisible ideologies', to the work of the media in disseminating our picture of the world. But Baudrillard adds an account of the role played by the new communication technologies, in explaining the 'disappearance' of the inalienable dimension of culture and society. For Baudrillard, the new technologies do away with the need for material objects; which vitiates the ability of things and signs to make and hold meanings, or of discourses to establish ethical principles of evaluation, because the material world disappears into a world of virtuality:

> Everything begins with objects, yet there is no longer a system of objects. The critique of objects was based on signs saturated with meaning, along with their phantasies and unconscious logic as well as their prestigious differential logic. Behind this dual logic lies the anthropological dream: the dream of objects as existing beyond and above exchange and use, above and beyond equivalence. (1988: 11)

The logic here is straightforward enough. Signs are the means by which we both represent the world and inflect it with the 'fantasy' of non-economic value, a dimension 'beyond and above exchange and use'. Once signs are emptied of meaning (and disconnected from the 'real'), they become undifferentiated, and effectively interchangeable. But if signs are interchangeable, undifferentiable and without meaning, then so is the world and 'everything that is the case' of the world – including the notion of a public sphere, time, history, culture, the earth, religious beliefs, ethics, sexuality, all forms of identity, and the human body. Baudrillard writes again:

> The body as a stage, the landscape as a stage, and time as a stage are slowly disappearing. The same holds true for the public space: the theatre of the social and of politics are progressively being reduced to a shapeless, multi-headed body. (Baudrillard, 1988: 19)

What this means, in effect, is that in lieu of stable meanings grounded on verifiable objects, events and practices, we have a mass of proliferating information that is no longer subject to processes of verification. And this renders the domination of society and culture by the market much more explicable: if there is too much information for us to digest, let alone verify and analyse, then we can only be free-floating, atomized individuals, disconnected from ideas of truth or continuity. This is not to say that all regimes of value have disappeared: the notion of the inalienable individual subject continues to have valence; but even this has no future because, in the end, disconnected from the real, it has nothing behind it.

The other aspect of the production of a subject outside time and place is that it effectively does away with the possibility of, and the need for, history. Baudrillard writes that history has in fact become impossible, because it is simply one more sequence of stories told endlessly over and over, and told without and outside their original contexts. This happens, he writes, because communication technologies require the dismantling, or the fracturing, of all stories:

> Every set of phenomena, whether cultural totality or
> sequences of events, has to be fragmented, disjointed, so that it
> can be sent down the circuits; every kind of language has to be
> resolved into a binary formulation so that it can circulate not,
> any longer, in our memories, but in the luminous, electronic
> memory of the computers. . . . No history can withstand the
> centrifugation of facts or their being short-circuited in real
> time. (1994: 2)

So there is, for Baudrillard, a connection between the 'real-time' proliferation and circulation of texts and events and the erasure of meaning; and real-time global communication technology effects the disappearance of time and place in precisely the way that proponents of globalization have claimed. But the globalists locate this phenomenon within the teleological – that is to say, meaningful – narrative of neoliberal 'progress and freedom' which works to transform time and space 'for the better'. Their point is that time and space connote difference, so their trans-formation effectively does away with the negative consequences of difference: poverty, ignorance, superstition, hunger, barbar-ism and terror. The collapse of space and time will, in this reading, effect the universalism of the world, and particularly of Western values, so that instead of difference we will all be 'the same'.

Baudrillard, on the other hand, understands the collapse of time and space not as a real phenomenon, but as a simulation of meaning, progress and freedom, and of space and time. He identifies not an exchange of time and space for the benefits claimed by the proponents of globalization, but a retreat into the virtual, where images and information circulate ceaselessly and take the place of all those narratives, values, ideas and meanings that seemed inalienable (the nation-state, the human, the public sphere, the general interest) and now are disappearing, or being 'disappeared'.

Convincing as Baudrillard is in explicating the phenomena associated with globalization, there is an obvious flaw in his apocalyptical thesis that the world, time/space, values, meaning and politics are pure technological simulation. The flaw is that he pretty much swallows – hook, line and sinker – the idea of the emptying of meaning and the disappearance of difference. And yet, as we have seen with our examples taken from the events and aftermath of 11 September, there has been no shortage of either. Meaning is quickly inserted into events and texts; difference always reasserts itself in the face of social, cultural, political and economic interaction. The fact that al-Qaeda attacked specifically US targets shows that one group, at least, remains unconvinced about the end of meaning and politics. The Bush administration's response to the attacks was also predicated on the continued existence of meaning, politics and difference: its aims to build and promote an undifferentiated world, signalled by terms such as 'the global community', 'the forces of civilization' or, more generally, 'humanity', have as their obverse the 'world of difference', because they depend upon binaries such as civilization/barbarism and, less overtly, the West/Islam.

Restructuring the world order?

We can also take issue with Baudrillard in one other important area – the imbrication of technology and politics. The French theorist Paul Virilio shares many of Baudrillard's assumptions regarding, say, the 'technical aspects' of the relationship between globalization, technology and history, the concomitant transformation of time/space, and the scope and (historical) significance of those changes:

> Implicitly doing away with the 'historic' time of politics – more precisely, of geopolitics – and exclusively promoting the 'anti-historic' time of the media, the general spread of real-time information causes a radical divide beside which the industrial revolution will pale into insignificance. (1997: 70)

He recontextualizes that relationship, however, and the 'radical divide' it brings into being, in terms of what we could call 'a new order of politics':

The global metropolitics of the future electronic information superhighways in itself implies the coming of a society no longer divided so much into North and South, but into two distinct temporalities, two speeds: one absolute, the other relative. The gap between developed and underdeveloped countries being reinforced throughout the five continents and leading to an even more radical divide between those who will live under the empire of real time essential to their economic activities at the heart of the virtual community of the world city, and those, more destitute than ever, who will survive in the real space of local towns, that great planetary wasteland that will in future bring together the only too real community of those who no longer have a job or a place to live. (1997: 71)

Virilio points not just to the technical aspects that characterize the new world of time/space compression, the retreat of the state and 'global transformations' but, most importantly, to what we could call the 'cultural politics' of the imbrication of technology and/as ideology.

Ankie Hoogvelt provides a similar representation of the world in terms of its reorganization, by the processes of globalization, into a kind of 'class' system defined not by geographical location, but by degrees of 'bankability', and hence of freedom and prosperity. She writes that the world's population is divided into three classes, or 'circles', the first of which is of course the 'elites', those who are 'bankable'. The second class is made up of 'workers and their families' who are not bankable, because they 'labour in insecure forms of employment', vulnerable to the effect of the globalized market place and the speed of investment and disinvestment, which at one moment provide work and access to commodities, and then as suddenly disappear elsewhere, leaving them bereft. The final group in Hoogvelt's 'architecture' is made up of those who have no role to play in the global economy, no connection with technologies, and are thus 'effectively excluded from the global system' (Hoogvelt, 2000: 358–9).

It is tempting to think of, and characterize, this 'new ruling class' scenario in terms of the kinds of explanations put forward by anti-globalization protesters: as being explicable in terms of

US imperialism, the rule of capitalism and the market, the dominance of transnational corporations, the hegemony of technologically literate bureaucracies or the neocolonial universalism of the West. All these narratives can be applied to, and used to help explicate, the different moments, sites, events, trends and practices which have brought, or threaten to bring, this new world (class-based) order into being. But while each of them may individually appear to offer a coherent explanation for the effects of globalization, they tend to undermine the possibility that the other narratives can equally act as driving forces of that transformational process. If the villain of the piece is capitalism 'of and for itself', for instance, then what do we make of US imperialism, or Western neocolonialism? And if we continue to look to capitalism as the villain of the piece, what do we make of the nationalistic aspects of supposedly transnational corporate activities?

We could accept Wallerstein's explanation that capitalism both works within, and identifies with, the institutions, identities, discourses and boundaries of nation-states when it is in its interest to do so. But this raises the theoretical issue, articulated by the American writer Kurt Vonnegut in his novel *Mother Night*, that 'we are what we pretend to be'. An American corporation that aligns itself with US imperialism to further its own ends (say, with regard to being complicit in the overthrowing of a government, or by providing information to secret service agencies) is something other than capitalism 'of and for itself'.

There is also a sense in which all the fields and identities we referred to (capitalism, the United States, the West) fold into one another much of the time. Jean-Marie Colombani's declaration that 'after this we are all Americans' was both journalistic bombast and a very accurate 'prediction' of how, say, EU countries would go along with, and help facilitate, US policies in Afghanistan and elsewhere, at least for a while, even where they clearly were not the Europen Union's policies of choice. And the close identification between the United States and capitalism (best articulated in the expression 'The business of America is business') means that when American politicians and diplomats, or bureaucrats from the WTO, the World Bank or the IMF, push for, say, the deregulation of communication and media spheres around the world, they are simultaneously 'doing the work' of transnational media corporations such as Time-Warner and News. This is not necessarily something that is carried out as a conspiracy; it is often the case that there is a seamless bond (in the form of shared values, ideologies, dispositions and goals, not to mention Castells's 'network logic') between states, corporations and bureaucracies that translates into mutually advantageous activities and policies. Manuel Castells claims, for instance, that:

> It is essentially wrong, as leftist critics often argue, that the International Monetary Fund is an agent of American imperialism or, for that matter, of any imperialism. It is an agent of itself, fundamentally moved by the ideology of neoclassical economic orthodoxy, and by the conviction of being the bulwark of measure and rationality in a dangerous world built on irrational expectations. The cold-bloodedness I have personally witnessed of IMF technocrats' behaviour in helping to destroy Russian society in the critical moments of transition in 1992–95 had nothing to do with capitalist domination. It was, as in Africa, as in Latin America, a deep-seated, honest, ideological commitment to teach financial rationality to the people of the world, as the only serious ground to build a new society. (1997: 269)

In order to make sense of the politics of globalization without reducing its many manifestations to a single explanation or characterization, we need to return to two concepts that we have used throughout this book – Bourdieu's notion of doxa, and Frow's reference (put forward as a characterization of postmodernism) to contemporary cultural events, activities, theories and meanings being processed by a 'grid of power' and a 'prescriptive network' (1997: 15). The two concepts come together at the end of Frow's essay 'What was postmodernism?', an analysis that is in many ways highly relevant to the question of globalization. Frow refers to the idea of postmodernism as 'conceptual machinery' that inflects and informs a whole genre of writing and thinking:

> As Gerald Graff says, 'it is difficult to take the concept seriously yet not easy to dismiss it', because 'once a certain number of people believe that a concept like the Post-Modern marks a real change in the cultural climate, the change becomes a reality to be reckoned with'. (1997: 63)

The concepts of postmodernity and globalization are both characterized by a vast body of theoretical, analytical and descriptive texts, and the 'globalization industry' boasts the extra dimension of various forms of quantitative proof and evidence. Essays on globalization, for instance, include everything from comparisons with the *belle époque* of 1870–1914 to the number of television sets or McDonald's restaurants in sub-Saharan Africa as evidence of its reality and its effects. The main difference between the two 'discursive grids' is that whereas the postmodernism grid tends to remain primarily within the fields of academe and cultural production, the latter is far more ubiquitous. A quick check of any text that purports to provide a comprehensive account of globalization will turn up references to economics, culture, the media, technology, governance, democracy, the state, time and space, education, demographics, the environment, labour and trade unionism, poverty, architecture and many other topics. This means the doxa of globalization has the potential to impact far more dramatically on the lives of large numbers of people.

If we go back to the point we made in Chapter 1 about 'the politics of naming', we can appreciate how globalization can be understood primarily as a discursive regime, a kind of machine that eats up anyone and anything in its path. We drew attention in that chapter to three related aspects. The first was that the 11 September attacks could be understood as a response to a set of politics associated with globalization. The second was the way in which the activities that occurred after 11 September made use of the notion of globalization to build a 'global coalition against terror'. The third issue focused on how this coalition was inflected by various players to promote their own interests – including senior American politicians, the Pentagon and the CIA, the media, Afghanistan's Northern Alliance, and the governments of Israel, Australia, Britain, Pakistan and India.

What these issues point to is the way in which different organizations and agents use the notion of globalization as a means of justifying and imposing their interests on others. In this scenario, globalization functions as a set of texts, ideas, goals, values, narratives, dispositions and prohibitions, a veritable template for ordering and evaluating activities, which is 'filled in' or inflected with the interests of whoever can access it. Of course some organizations, such as the United States or large transnational corporations, are more likely to be able or inclined to use the doxa of globalization to 'make things happen', simply because they are in more powerful positions than is, say, Bangladesh, or a local cheese factory. In some ways the more an organization is in a position to impose its interests on others, the more it needs to call up globalization and its values and narratives to justify or recontextualize whatever forms of violence it uses to achieve its ends. As Foucault writes, apropos of Nietzsche's notion of the 'will to power', social rules:

> are by no means designed to temper violence, but rather to satisfy it . . . The nature of these rules allows violence to be inflicted on violence and the resurgence of new forces that are sufficiently strong to dominate those in power. Rules are empty in themselves, violent and unfinalized; they are impersonal and can be bent to any purpose. The successes of history belong to those who are capable of seizing these rules, to replace those who had used them, to disguise themselves so as to pervert them, invert their meaning, and redirect them against those who had initially imposed them; controlling this complex mechanism, they will make it function so as to overcome the rulers through their own rules. (1986: 150–1)

An example of this kind of agonistics, and the different 'results' that are achieved, can be seen in the fight by the peoples of East Timor and Chechnya to gain independence from Indonesia and

Russia, respectively. In both cases the state branded the pro-independence movement as a 'terrorist organization' – much as Indonesia continues to do with the Aceh separatists, Iraq and Turkey with the Kurds, India with Muslim Kashmiris, Sri Lanka with the Tamils, and Spain with the Basques. The Timorese consistently appealed to the West through the use of the 'capitalized ideas' of human rights and democracy, appeals which were routinely ignored by states such as Australia and the United States, which clearly felt that their interests were best served by supporting Indonesian sovereignty. A combination of events – a weakened, post-Suharto Indonesian government, and the representation in the Western media of the brutal violence of the pro-Indonesian militia – turned things round; the Australian and US governments suddenly developed a strong interest in, and commitment to, the (violated) human rights of the Timorese people. In Chechnya, on the other hand, the Russian invasion was taken off the agenda as an issue for the United States and its Western allies once President Putin brought his nation into the 'global coalition', and designated the conflict in Chechyna as another front in the war against terrorism.

There is a second aspect – another side, if you like – of this relationship between globalization and agents (nation-states, corporation, citizens), which is played out in (Castells's explanation of) the behaviour of those IMF technocrats in Russia. Previously we have emphasized how agents have intentionally 'inhabited' or identified with the idea of globalization (and its values, ideals and practices) for political purposes; in other words, we suggested that they are cynically playing the game to further their interests. But Castells insists that the IMF technocrats 'really believed' that what they were doing (paving the way for the rule of the market) was 'good for Russia'. If this is the case, then it is an example of globalization 'using agents'; in other words, we could say that the neoliberal ideology most strongly associated with globalization has a kind of life of its own, creates subjects 'in its own image' and gets them to do its bidding. In other words, the (political) struggles between groups as to what is meant by terms such as 'human rights', 'democracy', 'freedom' and 'civilization' (or for that matter 'terrorism', 'evil' and 'barbarism') produce not only winners and losers, but sceptics and, most importantly of all, believers, who are 'made' and, in turn, go out and (re)make the world. The work of IMF technocrats in Russia, from this perspective, can be located within what Bourdieu refers to as 'the new conservative revolution' constituted by imbrication of neoliberalism and globalization.

Historicizing practice

This revolution, of course, has its own history, based on 'the oldest ideas of the oldest capitalists' (Bourdieu, 1998a: 34); and so too, whether agents are cynically deploying the values and logic of globalization in their own interests, or being 'embarked' as agents of globalization, both are themselves subject to historical contextualizing and analysis. Karl Polanyi provides a historical context for neoliberalism which is instructive in our thinking about globalization. He writes that nineteenth-century economic liberalism was 'Born as a mere penchant for non-bureaucratic methods' (1957: 135), and developed into something that possessed a 'crusading passion', and 'a militant creed' (1957: 136). From its early beginnings, it became a dominant and dominating force that established the competitive labour market, the automatic gold standard and international free trade as tenets of the economy and as 'a coherent whole' (1957: 137) that brought all trade under its logic. In this respect the development of economic liberalism was very like Castells's 'network logic': every part and aspect is interdependent and draws strength from all the others in the network, but also inherits their weaknesses and liabilities, and thus can function only in terms of the logics and trajectories of the network as a whole. So, too, economic liberalism eventually vampirized the British economy, British society, and to a certain extent the globe, simply because it resembled one of those spaceships in science fiction films which are travelling at such an extraordinary speed that they require a lifetime to turn around.

Polanyi's argument is that the manifestation of liberalism as self-regulating market economics, and the forms of global economic activity it gave birth to in the period 1870-1914, can be characterized in terms of two main features: the ascendency of the English middle classes, and the fact that neoliberalism and its policies acquired an almost religious state. Where Polanyi was less perceptive is in his presumption that the 'institutional separation of politics and economics' (1957: 254) had 'proved a deadly danger to the substance of society' (1957: 255) because it facilitated both the Great Depression and the rise of fascism, and that therefore the self-regulating market would be contained, and phased out. But he is prescient in noting – and warning – that, regardless of the failures of economic liberalism, it had become so established in the system of social organization that it would not easily be dislodged.

Polanyi was writing in 1944, but his arguments about economic liberalism still hold true as a description of neoliberalism in the twenty-first century. The contemporary changes in demographics, labour, the environment, the sovereignty of the nation-state, the 'Americanization' of culture, and the compression of time/space seem like our 'runaway train', or spaceship that cannot be turned; and developments in technology seem as irresistible to people today as the steam engine, dynamite and moving pictures presumably did to people in the nineteenth century. But we need to recall two points. Firstly, as we explained in Chapter 3, technology is never neutral, natural or necessary; that is, it has no life of its own. Developments in technology are always the product of historical contexts and forces. The kinds of technology that are developed, the uses to which they are put, and the interests they serve, are all open-ended – if heavily influenced and weighted – social, cultural and political questions. That this 'question of technology' might be beginning to surface, at least under certain circumstances, was evinced by the debate in Britain about the government selling multimillion-dollar weapon systems to African countries steeped in poverty and largely devoid of communication, education, welfare and health infrastructure; or again, by the widespread call, in many Western states, for a global ban on genetic cloning.

Secondly, the neoliberal ideology which is at the heart of globalization is predicated on what we might call its 'hijacking' of the Enlightenment principle of freedom, read in terms of the unrestricted circulation of ideas, things, people and money. But, quite clearly, the consequences of a freedom enjoyed by a relatively small elite class are, as analysts such as Bauman, Bourdieu and Virilio point out, a loss of freedom for the great majority of the people of the world. The neoliberal version of 'freedom of circulation' very much resembles the American communication models that dominated textbooks in the second half of the twentieth century, which presumed that the flow of communication was independent of notions such as power or cultural literacy. Those American communication models were highly idealized: they never actually explained, at a practical level, what communication was, how it happened, or the factors that informed it. Neoliberal versions of the contemporary world, epitomized in the calls for the abolition of trade barriers so as to ensure a level playing field for world trade, or the creation of a free and unrestricted labour market, suffer from this same deficiency. What these demands ignore, among other things, are the various power differentials and relations which inform not just communication practices but also the ability of developing countries to compete with the West, and the ability and willingness of corporations to use their power over workers to erode wages, conditions and security.

Antisocial tendencies, and the return of the social

Such factors seem to be largely irrelevant in the face of the saturation of the public sphere by neoliberal ideology, which naturalizes technological developments and their uses as natural and irresistible, and which narrativizes the freedom of the few as a (necessary) prelude to the freedom of all. And yet there are two reasons why this is not necessarily the case. Firstly, following Polanyi, we can suggest that the tenets, discourses, policies, institutions and practices that are the product of and perpetuate neoliberal ideology are essentially antisocial. What do we mean by this? At one level, the processes and politics of globalization function to 'undo' social structures and institutions in states too weak to resist them. Ankie Hoogvelt (2000: 359) writes that this is exemplified in the developing world, and particularly in Africa, where the effects of globalization have been dropped over the after-effects of colonialism. Because of the divide-and-conquer approach of so many colonial administrators in Africa, few of the postcolonial African nations have been fully successful in crafting a unified state out of the various ethnic identities. Globalization and its economic pressures, including the structural adjustments imposed by the IMF or the World Bank, have further weakened the ability of the states to manage themselves. And the civil breakdowns that have been apparent in places like Rwanda or Zimbabwe are manifestations of this combined pressure.

But it is not only in developing states that this 'antisocial' tendency is played out. The retreat of the state under the effects of globalization has also brought about a retreat of the social more generally. As we suggested in our previous chapter, the rule of the market has no place, in effect, for the maintenance of those areas and sites that a community designates as inalienable. The result is that the identities of communities and individuals are reduced to market logic, and to the status of 'a thing'. This was as true for the nineteenth century as it is for the contemporary world but, as Polanyi explains (1957: 75–6), the social and political ravages brought about by economic liberalism provoked what he sees as a more or less inevitable 'social backlash', a series of 'protective responses' that grew directly out of the excesses of *laissez-faire* economics. The usual suspects were, of course, involved: labour unions, political parties and politically influential groups such as landowners. The results were seen in the introduction of interventionist legislation, which varied from state to state, depending upon local circumstances; in Britain and Germany, intervention predominantly took the form of labour and tariff policies, while in the New World the restriction of immigration played a more significant role.

Polanyi also points out that the supposedly 'anachronistic state' played an even more significant role in terms of monetary policy. As protectionism increased around the globe, and states suffered the economic and social roller-coaster rides that accompanied it, global monetary flows became even more important in guarding against, and overcoming, the economic vicissitudes that threatened to cause debtor states and companies to default on their payments, stop the flow of trade, bring about a downturn in business activity, increase unemployment, close off immigration or bring on inflation. In other words the system of global economic activity that prevailed in the period 1870–1914, and in some cases until the Great Depression, came to depend on a monetary system which was predicated on, and unthinkable without regard to, the nation-state. As Polanyi writes, 'If money now avowedly ruled the world, that money was stamped with a national die' (1957: 202).

Let's return, for a moment, to Manuel Castells's characterization of the contemporary globalized world as 'the network society'. Castells's point is that the various systems in which human activities occur – economic, political, cultural, social, environmental and military – are all closely interconnected and mutually dependent. And the same goes at both macro- and micro-levels, with regard to, and across, the practices specific to a cultural field such as corporate activity, education, health or sport. Everything and everyone must be 'in', the argument goes, because otherwise it is 'out' and simply unable to compete or function. If it is out, it will lack the information, resources, capital, speed of access, contacts, technology and infrastructure necessary for it to remain up-to-date and therefore viable.

Polanyi demonstrates in *The Great Transformation* (1957) that something comparable characterized the globalized world of 1870–1914. His argument, however, is that while 'network logic' in a sense gave rise to and facilitated the apparently relentless expansion of globalization, it also worked to bring about its demise. In response to the social vicissitudes that were the result of the triumph of liberal ideology, the state, its peoples, pressure groups and institutions intervened – in different ways at different times and in different places – to roll back the takeover of society by the market. Once this rollback had commenced, it gradually unravelled all the threads that constituted the network that had made globalization such an irresistible force in the first place, until there was nothing left to keep the system going but the authority and sovereignty of the state, manifested, in its most extreme form, in the use of military might to keep things circulating.

While Polanyi is writing about events and trends that took place around a century ago, it all sounds very familiar. We have many parallels in the economic sphere to the pressures caused by a global economy: the Enron collapse of 2002; the economic and political instability in Argentina; the Asian economic crisis of 1998–99; and perhaps most importantly the extraordinarily high (and in the long term unsustainable) level of US government and domestic debt; governments are variously involved in bailing out the failed market ventures to protect national capital. We also have the evidence of the failure of neoliberalism and its 'freedoms' to provide the sort of society that people want. Even in America, the heart of neoliberal ideology and 'small government', as many commentators and *vox pop* individuals pointed out after 11 September, it was not corporate might but 'big government' – particularly in the form of the New York firefighters and police officers – that mobilized to protect citizens. This has shaken, if only temporarily, the 'truth' of neoliberalism and its freedoms. Lewis Lapham writes that prior to 11 September the United States depended upon 'four pillars of imperishable wisdom':

> 'Big government is by inclination Marxist, by definition wasteful and incompetent' . . . 'Global capital is the eighth wonder of the world, a light unto the nations and the answer to everybody's prayers'. . . . 'the art of politics is subordinate to the science of economics' . . . 'History is at an end'. (Lapham, 2001: 8)

He goes on to write that 'all four pillars collapsed'. Big government swooped in to rescue and soothe the population; global capital wilted in the face of the attacks, the art of politics became suddenly far more relevant, locally and internationally, than economics; and history had re-emerged, violently, to protest its erasure. Society, in other words, reawoke to lay claim to the sorts of truths by which people – both the terrorists and the American public – wanted to live.

There are many other areas where we can detect this 'return of the social' to which Polanyi refers. The most obvious examples are the demonstrations against the institutions, policies and players of globalization – the United States, the WTO, the IMF, the World Bank. We have referred, on numerous occasions, to the protests and protesters at Seattle, Melbourne and Genoa, which were clearly aimed at the agents of globalization, but also at governments which were seen to be in the service of somebody or someone other than their citizens. This culminated in the chaotic situation in Argentina in early 2002, when hundreds of thousands of so-called 'ordinary people' took to the streets protesting about, and seeking to overturn, the economic policies imposed on them by the IMF. The seriousness of the protests, and the level and resilience of the disaffection, meant that cosmetic changes – the replacement of one President committed to a continuation of IMF policies by another of the same ilk – were not enough to end the protests. Rather, all classes were affected and (temporarily) united as a society against the perceived 'antisocial' policies of the IMF.

Much the same anti-globalist reading could be applied to the issue of immigration or the flow of people, which O'Rourke and Williamson single out as being the one factor that played a role consistent with the argument that globalization produced international convergence. In the nineteenth century, convergence more or less ceased to be an issue once the New World (the United States, Canada, Australia, Argentina) closed its door to migration, mainly in order to protect the wages and conditions of labour. As we noted in previous chapters, globalization advocates usually make claims about the contributions of free trade, technological developments and capital circulation to convergence:

> but in fact mass migration was the cental force. Capital flows were mainly an anti-convergence force (Scandinavia being an outstanding exception), in that they raised wages and labor productivity in the resource-abundant New World, while

lowering them in the resource-scarce Old World . . .
Furthermore, relatively little of the late nineteenth-century
convergence is likely to have been the result of technological
catch-up or human capital accumulation . . . the central
elements of the modern convergence models . . . Convergence
explanations based on technological or accumulation catch-up
in closed economy models miss this point. The millions on the
move in the late nineteenth century did not. (O'Rourke and
Williamson, 1999: 165–6)

Nor, one might add, did the millions on the move at the end of
the twentieth, or the beginning of the twenty-first, centuries. But,
as we noted in earlier chapters, there has been a backlash across
the world against migration. We pointed out, in Chapter 1, how
the situation in Australia during the election of 2001 mirrored
this fundamental 'discrepancy' within globalization, with, on
the one hand, a government enthusiastically committed to free
trade, deregulation, privatization and the global war against
terrorism; and, on the other, the same government resorting to
discourses and practices that allowed the incarceration of
hundreds of refugees (including unaccompanied children) in
out-of-the-way, razor-wire-enclosed camps, or their deportation
to relatively inaccessible places such as Nauru or Papua New
Guinea, all in the name of sovereignty and the protection of
society. Australia is only one (although an egregious) example of
this tendency; anti-immigrant political forces and attitudes have
surfaced in Italy, Germany, Britain, France, Austria, Switzer-
land, Scandanavia and the United States. And as a corollary, and
in parallel with events in the 1920s and 1930s, there has been an
upsurge in neofascist or overtly racist activity in Britain, France,
Russia, Germany, Austria and Australia – all in the name of the
preservation of the social unit.

Memory and the media

Perhaps the most important place where this notion of the social
unit 'of and for itself' is playing itself out in contradistinction to

globalization doxa is in the military/political sphere. The globalization that Polanyi describes was always predicated, to some extent, on the power of nation-states such as Britain, Germany, France and the United States. At the same time there is something seriously amiss about needing to send in gunboats to facilitate the 'free flow' of trade and capital, and the payment of debts. Doubtless it was easier to reconcile gunboat diplomacy with the religion of *laissez-faire* in the nineteenth century, but it is certainly problematical in the contemporary world. The sight of American troops patrolling the streets of Buenos Aires in order to restore order and ensure the payment of Argentina's foreign debt would do little to convince, say, Argentinians of the disinterestedness of the agents of globalization, no matter how much the US troops believed in what they were doing. In a sense the events that occurred after 11 September can perhaps be seen as one of the last grand performances of globalization, played out as it was somewhere between the enthusiastic support and complicity of the global media, on the one hand, and con-servative Americans' denunciation and repudiation of it, on the other.

This brings us to another important question we need to address, which is the extent to which the global media's take-over of the public sphere can continue to circulate, sell and prop up globalization's various discursive performances, institutions and practices. We pointed out that the media, at least in the West, have had the ability to spread and facilitate the doxa of globalization. They do this in a number of ways. Firstly and most obviously, they effect what Bourdieu would call a 'satur-ated reproduction' of the discourses of neoliberalism, repeatedly using, and thereby naturalizing, terms such as 'restructuring' (a.k.a. mass sackings), 'labour reform' or 'flexibility' (a.k.a. the erosion of wages and conditions) and deregulation (a.k.a. lack of accountability). Secondly, and to pick up on Claude Lefort's notion of 'invisible ideology', they facilitate communication on important social issues like the environment, poverty, unem-ployment, making sure that every possible group, no matter how small or radical, is represented. What this does is transfer the realities of political difference to the homogeneous and largely apolitical space of the television or radio current affairs genre, where everything is talked about and, in the process, dissolved. Thirdly, and as a corollary, the media employ the politics of affect to discipline the responses of audiences by contextualizing images, personalities or events in term of almost instantly recognizable and applicable intertextual narratives.

Events after the attacks of 11 September certainly testify to the efficacy of these techniques, and not just in America. The extraordinary orchestration of the performances of patriotism that characterized American public life were impressive, but in a sense they were not only irrelevant with regard to, but may in fact have contributed to undermining, the more general discursive performance (by the media, Tony Blair, Colin Powell) of globalization as a disinterested, teleological march towards, and defence of, civilization. As we mentioned earlier, with regard to nineteenth-century globalization, sending in gunboats – or, in this case, bombing Afghanistan back to the Stone Age – tends to vitiate claims of the naturalness, irresistibility and disinterestedness of the processes of globalization.

Moreover, the very strengths of the techniques that enable the media to occupy the public sphere, and effectively stand in for and direct public speech on any range of issues, also constitute a serious weakness. As Claude Lefort points out, one of the characteristics of invisible ideology is that social and cultural institutions move from a position of speaking with authority 'on the social' to being simply one within the social, and therefore speaking without authority. This explains why television stations are always trying to commoditize a particular newsreader, personality or journalist as having authority, articulated in terms such as '(s)he tells it like it is' or is 'the one you can trust'; and exemplified, for instance, by CNN employing a crew of middle-aged, serious-looking, deep-voiced clones to report on and analyse the events of 11 September. This practice has its successes, but it is always basically baseless; that is, the authority given rests on nothing, and like John Donne's 'death' is 'slave to fate, chance, Kings and desperate men' (Donne, 1968: 84).

This loss of authority both stems from, and is symptomatic of, a transformation in the status of narratives, discourses and language itself. As Foucault demonstrates, the authority wielded by any form of representation or explanation is always tied to, and dependent upon, a place or an institution such as the church or a university. The contemporary media are faced with a paradox; as Lefort suggests, they become 'one of us', and therefore give up authority. But equally they are, in their increasingly global manifestations, *not* one of us; the images, narratives and explanations come from the global CNN, ESPN, Time-Warner, AAP, Reuters – that is, from nowhere. Michel de Certeau traces what has, since the Enlightenment, been a gradual 'emptying out' of the authority of language and representation, and its accompanying, contemporary consequences:

> Two centuries of linguistic analysis have shown that language does not make manifest the presence of things, no longer yields presences, and no longer produces a world of transparence. Rather, it is an organized place that allows things to happen. It does not give what it says: it lacks being. . . . Mass media internationalise anonymous broadcasts, aimed at everyone and true of no one, according to the law of a market of signifiers that furnishes an indefinite margin of profit to its directors. The market can only hope to produce oblivion among its consumers. (1997: 30)

What Certeau points to is the curious situation whereby no one can be free of the effects of the media – because they 'capture' public speech and the public sphere – but no one really believes their narratives, explanations or images. But oblivion isn't good enough; on the contrary, it can be fatal, as Slavoj Zizek makes clear in his analysis of the fall of Nikolai Ceaucescu, the former dictator of Romania, writing that the turning point in the collapse of his rule, which resulted in his own execution, was the fact that the Romanians would no longer play his game or support his version of events. Zizek writes that the beginning of the end of the Soviet Union was 'the sudden awareness of the subjects that, in spite of the tremendous force of the apparatuses of repression, the Communist party is actually powerless, that it is only as strong as they, the subjects, make it, that its strength is their belief in it' (1992: 40–1).

Conclusion

What is clear from events in the contemporary world – from the collapse of the Soviet Union, through the anti-IMF demonstrations in Buenos Aires, to the political demonizing of Afghani refugees in Australia – is that there is a huge disjunction between the doxa of globalization, promulgated through and naturalized by the media, and what people (dis)believe. This 'belief gap' should be, and to a certain extent is, accentuated by what Karl Polanyi refers to as the backlash by the various forces of the social unit against neoliberalism. But as Zizek points out, and as Polanyi was only too well aware, the articulation of this position has often been left, at least within the political sphere, to the more extreme, and sometimes fascist or racist, elements or institutions of society.

Zizek notes that the radical right seemed to have been transformed into a version of the radical left of the 1960s, taking on the role of demonizing the state, while the 'exact counterpoint to this is a Leftist like Pierre Bourdieu, who defends the idea of a unified Europe as a strong "social state", guaranteeing the minimum of social rights and welfare against the onslaught of globalization' (1999: 355). And yet while this may seem highly ironical to Zizek, it is perfectly in keeping with the social processes and trends outlined by Polanyi in his explication of the demise of nineteenth-century globalization. The state, particularly the democratic state, has no inherent meaning of its own; it is perfectly 'available' for appropriation, and for (re)naming. So, to turn neoliberalism on its head, what the social in its many manifestations is increasingly demanding from the state and other institutions is freedom, not from the interference or intervention of the state, but from what Bourdieu refers to as the 'utopia of unlimited exploitation' (1998a: 94). In other words, what the social is demanding is freedom from the insecurity, dehumanization and misfortune of lives lived as members of armies of standing reserve available to, and at the mercy of, the practices and discourses associated with the name of globalization.

Glossary

affect   Term used to designate emotions and attitudes produced in textual and other interactions. Hardt and Negri (2000) extend this to discuss what they term the **'affect industries'**, especially the media and advertising: industries designed to construct a sense of attitude in their consumers.

archaeological   The term used by Michel Foucault to refer to the process of working through the historical archives of various societies to bring to light the discursive formations and events that have produced the fields of knowledge and discursive formations of different historical periods.

biopower   The technologies, knowledges, discourses, politics and practices used to bring about the production and management of a state's human resources. Biopower analyses, regulates, controls, explains and defines the human subject, its body and its behaviour. For Michel Foucault it is associated most particularly with official institutions that construct spaces and ways of regulating (and so producing) people – schools, hospitals and prisons.

Bretton Woods   An international system of monetary management, based on a series of multilateral agreements and developed in 1944 to fix and stabilize foreign exchange rates following World War II; associated with the estabishment of the International Monetary Fund (IMF) and the World Bank.

capitalism   Currently the dominant system for the organization of economies; characterized by the private ownership of the means of production, and reliance on the market to direct economic activity and distribute economic goods and rewards. Its founding principle is the pursuit of self-interest through competition (see **Marxism**).

convergence theory   Term associated with the Swedish economists Eli Heckscher and Bertil Ohlin, who developed it in reference to post-World War I commodity price convergence and income distribution effects; refers to the idea that increased circulation of trade, capital, technology, education and people necessarily leads to convergence of inequality across different nations.

cultural capital   A form of value associated with culturally authorized tastes, consumption patterns, attributes, skills and awards. Within the field of education, for example, an academic degree constitutes cultural capital.

cultural field   Term associated with Pierre Bourdieu, which refers to all those things in a society – institutions, rules, rituals, conventions, categories, designations, appointments and titles – which constitute an objective social hierarchy, and which produce and authorize certain discourses and activities. Cultural fields are always the site of conflict about what constitutes capital within that field, and how that capital is to be distributed. Examples of cultural fields include art, sport, the economy, education and other major social institutions which operate in relative autonomy from the general social field.

discourses   The forms of language associated with, and which express the values of, particular cultural fields. A legal discourse, for example, expresses the values and beliefs of the field of law.

doxa   Pierre Bourdieu's term for a set of core values and discourses which a field articulates as its fundamental principles and which tend to be viewed as inherently true and necessary. For Bourdieu, the 'doxic attitude' means bodily and unconscious submission to conditions that are in fact quite arbitrary and contingent (see **ideology**).

Empire   Coined by Hardt and Negri (2000), the term refers to both a system and a hierarchy which organizes the global world and orders it within their logic. Empire is constituted by, and constitutive of, the imbrication of the economic, political and cultural aspects of contemporary life.

Enlightenment, The   Both a collection of ideas and attitudes (concerning reason, justice, equality, progress and rationality) and a series of political events (starting with the French revolution). Historically, the Enlightenment sought to replace the old order of absolute sovereignty, injustice, ignorance and superstition with an order based on reason, rationality and equality. The Enlightenment can be understood as being based on an interrogation of how and what and why things are, and as a particular self-referential attitude to oneself and one's time.

endocolonialism   Paul Virilio's term for the new form of colonialism where social and economic inequalities are not exported 'to the colonies' but are accentuated within colonialist states such as the United States and the United Kingdom (see **Empire**).

exocolonialism   The traditional form of colonialism, characterized by an imperial centre which controlled and directed politics, economic and social organization throughout the empire (see **Empire**).

foreclosure   Usually associated with psychoanalytical theory; a process whereby certain feelings, desires, ideas and positions are both unthinkable with regard to, and simultaneously constitutive of, identity.

G-8   The Group of Eight, an international, informal organization compromising eight of the main industrialized countries (Canada, France, Germany, Italy, Japan, Russia, the United Kingdom and the United States) which meets annually to discuss economic policies.

global convergence The tendency, facilitated by communication technologies, to bring together different communities, institutions, media.

globalists 'Believers', in globalization, in the sense that for them it is a real and significant historical development.

habitus A concept that expresses, on the one hand, the way in which individuals 'become themselves' – develop attitudes and dispositions – and, on the other hand, the ways in which those individuals engage in practices. An artistic habitus, for example, disposes the individual artist to certain activities and perspectives that express the culturallly and historically constituted values of the artistic field.

hegemony The way states and state institutions work to 'win' popular consent for their authority through a variety of processes which disguise their position of dominance.

hyperreality Artificially heightened, exaggerated form of realism which permeates much of contemporary culture, whereby fabrications seem to be more real than material reality – and better (more interesting, more beautiful, more efficient) than the original.

ideology A practice whereby a particular group within a culture attempts to naturalize their own meanings and values, or pass them off as universal and as common sense (see **doxa**).

informationalism Associated with the pre-eminence of knowledge, information and communication in the globalized world; a shift towards the production of 'immaterial goods' such as information and networking; and the transformation of how the world understands time and space.

Keynesianism An economic perspective developed from the work of British economist John Maynard Keynes, which argues against the classical capitalist view that the market is a self-regulating system capable of delivering prosperity. Keynesian economists encourage government intervention to ensure the smooth and equitable working of the market.

Glossary

Marxism A way of understanding the world that focuses on economic relations and class conflict; includes as an objective the attainment of a Communist system of economic organization, whereby the means of production are held in public ownership (see **capitalism**).

mini-systems Term associated with Immanuel Wallerstein; where division of labour and economic exchange occur only within a discrete group (see **world-systems**).

modernity As used in disciplines like philosophy, historiography and sociology, generally refers to that period of (Western) history which dates from the Enlightenment to the present, and which is characterized by scientific rationality, the development of commerce and capitalism, the rise of education, surveillance, urbanism and atheism.

neoliberalism A way of understanding the world as committed to a particular idea of freedom, in the form of the unfettered circulation of capital and goods. Aspires to the liberation of money and entrepreneurship from social contexts and their obligations.

Neomarxism A way of understanding the world which draws on **Marxism**, but which is cautious of grand narratives (of which Marxism is one), and gives more emphasis to the cultural aspects than the economic organization of society.

Orientalism A term associated with Edward Said; it provides the tools through which the world is divided up into us/them, rational/irrational, centre/periphery, the West/the rest.

politics of naming The notion that powerful discourses shape everyday life; discourses which simultaneously name, and thus help bring into being, what they are supposedly designating or describing.

postmodernism Variously understood as a period of time (from about the 1960s), a way of thinking or a set of cultural practices that followed, and in many ways draw on, modernist notions. Associated with pastiche, irony and relativism.

public sphere   Like 'civil society', related to but distinct from, and exceeding, national government. The public sphere is an important aspect of how people understand themselves as members of communities, because it appears at least to be a site in which the interests of 'the people' take precedence over the interests of power.

sceptics   Writers on globalization who consider that it is not a new feature of sociopolitical organization, and that it is principally ideological rather than material.

sovereignty   The combination of political control, administrative functions and regulatory mechanisms that characterize the individual nation-state, and that state's right to control activities within its borders.

standing reserve   Martin Heidegger uses this term to explain that because modern technology is capable of producing an excess, of forcing nature to yield product, it always produces a store available for human use. He uses the example of an airliner waiting on the runway; it is standing reserve because its identity is 'the possibility of transportation' and it is simply waiting to be put to use. But, he goes on to argue, human beings are also part of the standing reserve, part of what is put to work in the great technological machine.

symbolic violence   The violence which is exercised upon individuals in a symbolic, rather than a physical, way. It may take the form of people being denied resources, treated as inferior or being limited in terms of realistic aspirations. Gender relations, for example, have tended to be constituted out of symbolic violence which have denied women the rights and opportunities available to men.

technē   Term associated with Martin Heidegger, who uses it to refer to all activities involving human skill (artisan craft, intellectual thought, artistic imagination and creation).

technological determinism   The notion that technology is independent of social contexts, and simultaneously imposes itself on to society and transforms it.

technology For Sigmund Freud, simply an extension of our natural organs to get things done. Includes tools and machinery, and is often associated with progress; for Foucault, refers firstly to the ways in which societies pacify, dominate and regulate subjects, and secondly to 'technologies of the self' which allow individuals to shape their own bodies and thoughts.

turn to the local The tendency in contemporary society for communities to focus attention and loyalty on local traditions, values and practices, at the expense of national or international considerations.

universalism The attribution of universal standing and significance to contingent attitudes and issues; often seen in writings and media statements to extend to the entire world values that in fact may have very local meanings. To treat a set of values derived from a particular field as though they are universally applicable across every field. For instance, academics may attempt to universalize the value of contemplative reflection and regard it as a form of behaviour to which everyone should aspire.

Westphalia model Named for the signing in 1648 of the Peace of Westphalia, which ended the Thirty Years' War in Europe. A condition of the Peace was the recognition of sovereign states with clear geographical boundaries and recognized governments which held the monopoly of force over their territory. It changed the previous system of government and forms of identification because of this institution of territoriality and autonomy.

world-systems Term associated with Immanuel Wallerstein; where economic exchange occurs across political and cultural barriers (see **mini-systems**).

Bibliography

Adas, Michael (1989) *Machines as the Measure of Men: Science Technology, and Ideologies of Western Dominance*. Ithaca NY: Cornell University Press.

Afrol News (2001) 22 June, http://www.afrol.com/News2001/eri005 war victims.htm (accessed 25 February 2002).

Alcorn, Gay (2001) 'No end in sight', *The Age* (Melbourne), 4 December, p. 13.

Alleyne, Mark (1997) *News Revolution*. New York: St Martin's Press.

Anderson, Benedict (1983) *Imagined Communities*. London and New York: Verso.

Appadurai, Arjun, ed. (1986) *The Social Life of Things: Commodities in Cultural Perspective*. Cambridge and New York: Cambridge University Press.

Appadurai, Arjun (1997) *Modernity at Large: Cultural Dimensions of Globalization*. Minneapolis MN: University of Minnesota Press.

Australian (2001a) 'Taliban isolated as terror net tightens' (AFP/The Times) 26 September, p. 1.

Australian (2001b) '5 million Afghans at risk' (John Zubrzyohti and Megan Saunders) 27 September, p. 1.

Barber, Benjamin R. (1992) 'Jihad versus McWorld', *Atlantic Monthly*, 269, pp. 53–65.

Baudrillard, Jean (1983) *Simulations*, trans. Paul Foss, Paul Patton and Philip Beitchman. London and New York: Semiotext(e).

Baudrillard, Jean (1988) *The Ecstasy of Communication*, trans. Bernard and Caroline Schutze, ed. Slyvere Lotringer. New York: Autonomedia.

Baudrillard, Jean (1993) *The Transparency of Evil: Essays on Extreme Phenomena*, trans. James Benedict. London and New York: Verso.

Baudrillard, Jean (1994) *The Illusion of the End*, trans. Chris Turner. Cambridge: Polity Press.

Bibliography

Bauman, Zygmunt (1998) *Globalization: the Human Consequences*. Cambridge: Polity Press.

BBC News (2002) 2 February, http://news.bbc.co.uk/hi/english/world/americas/newsid 1796000/1796034.stm (accessed 6 February 2002).

Beck, Ulrich (2000) 'What is globalization?' in David Held and Anthony McGrew (eds) *The Global Transformations Reader: an Introduction to the Globalization Debate*. Malden MA: Polity Press, pp. 99–103.

Beynon, John, and Dunkerley, David, eds (2000) *Globalization: the Reader*. London: Athlone Press.

Blanchot, Maurice (1986) *The Writing of the Disaster*. Lincoln NE: University of Nebraska Press.

Bourdieu, Pierre (1977) *Outline of a Theory of Practice*, trans. Richard Nice. Cambridge: Cambridge University Press.

Bourdieu, Pierre (1990) *The Logic of Practice*, trans. Richard Nice. Stanford CA: Stanford University Press.

Bourdieu, Pierre (1998a) *Acts of Resistance: Against the New Myths of our Time*, trans. Richard Nice. London: Polity Press.

Bourdieu, Pierre (1998b) *On Television*, trans. Priscilla Pankhurst Ferguson. New York: New Press.

Bourdieu, Pierre (1998c) *Practical Reason: on the Theory of Action*. Cambridge: Polity Press.

Bourdieu, Pierre (2000) *Pascalian Meditations*, trans. Richard Nice. Cambridge: Polity Press.

Bourdieu, Pierre, and Eagleton, Terry (1994) 'Doxa and common life: an interview' in Slavoj Zizek (ed.) *Mapping Ideology*. London: Verso, pp. 265–77.

Bourdieu, Pierre, and Wacquant, Loic (1992) *An Invitation to Reflexive Sociology*. Cambridge: Polity Press.

Bourdieu, Pierre, and Wacquant, Loic (1999) 'On the cunning of imperialist reason', *Theory, Culture and Society*, 16 (1), pp. 41–58.

Burnett, Sara (2001) *Leo's page*, 24 July, http://interstice.com/leo/ (downloaded 29 March 2002).

Busch, Andreas (2000) 'Unpacking the globalization debate: approaches, evidence and data', in Colin Hay and David Marsh (eds) *Demystifying Globalization*. Basingstoke: Palgrave, pp. 21–48.

Calhoun, Craig (1997) *Nationalism*. Buckingham: Open University Press.

Castells, Manuel (1996) *The Rise of the Network Society*. Malden MA: Blackwell.

Castells, Manuel (1997) *The Power of Identity*. Malden MA: Blackwell.

Castells, Manuel (2000a) *The Rise of the Network Society*, second edition. Oxford and Malden MA: Blackwell.

Bibliography

Castells, Manuel (2000b) 'The global economy', in David Held and Anthony McGrew (eds) *The Global Transformations Reader: an Introduction to the Globalization Debate*. Malden MA: Polity Press, pp. 259–73.

Castells, Manuel (2000c) 'The network society' in David Held and Anthony McGrew (eds) *The Global Transformations Reader: an Introduction to the Globalization Debate*. Malden MA: Polity Press, pp. 76–81.

Certeau, Michel de (1984) *The Practice of Everyday Life*, trans. S. Rendall. Berkeley CA: University of California Press.

Certeau, Michel de (1997) *Culture in the Plural*. Minneapolis MN: University of Minnesota Press.

Chomsky, Noam (1996) 'Media and globalization: interview transcript', *Third World Network*, 1 July, http://www.corpwatch.org/issues/PID.jsp?articleid=l 809 (downloaded 10 April 2002).

CNN (2001a) report, 21 June, http://www.cnn.com/2000/WORLD/africa/06/21/con go.killing.fields/ (accessed 25 February 2002).

CNN (2001b) report, 12 September, http://www.cnn.com/2001/US/09/11/white.house/ (accessed 25 February 2002).

Colombani, Jean-Marie (2001) 'After this act of terrorism we are all Americans', *Guardian Weekly*, 20 September, p. 33.

Costello, Peter (2001) Transcript of interview with Neil Mitchell, Radio 3AW, 20 September, http://www.treasurer.gov.au/tsr/content/transcripts/2001/124.asp (accessed 12 March 2002).

Crary, Jonathan (1990) *Techniques of the Observer: on Vision and Modernity in the Nineteenth Century*. Cambridge MA: October/MIT Press.

Danaher, Geoff, Schirato, Tony, and Webb, Jenn (2000) *Understanding Foucault*. London: Sage.

Deleuze, Gilles (1988) *Foucault*, trans. and ed. Sean Hand. Minneapolis MN: University of Minnesota Press.

DeLillo, Don (2001) 'In the ruins of the future: reflections on terror and loss in the shadow of September', *Harper's Magazine*, December, pp. 33–40.

Donne, John (1968) Holy Sonnets, in Helen Gardner (ed.) *The Metaphysical Poets*. Harmondsworth: Penguin.

Donzelot, Jacques (1979) *The Policing of Families*. London: Hutchinson.

Eisenstein, Z. (2000) 'Cyber inequities' in John Beynon and David Dunkerley (eds) *Globalization: the Reader*. London: Athlone Press, pp. 212–13.

Foucault, Michel (1973) *The Order of Things: an Archaeology of the Human Sciences*. New York: Vintage.

Foucault, Michel (1984) *The Foucault Reader*, ed. Paul Rabinow. London: Penguin.

Foucault, Michel (1986) *Language, Counter-memory, Practice*, ed. Donald Bouchard. Ithaca NY: Cornell University Press.

Bibliography

Foucault, Michel (1997) *Ethics: Essential Works* I, ed. P. Rabinow. London: Penguin.

Frow, John (1997) *Time and Commodity Culture: Essays in Cultural Theory and Postmodernity*. Oxford: Clarendon Press; New York: Oxford University Press.

Frow, John (1999) 'Res publica', <http://home.vicnet.net.au/~abr/ FebMar99/fro.html> (downloaded 17 January 2002).

Fukuyama, Francis (1992) *The End of History and the Last Man*. London: Hamish Hamilton.

Gerges, Fawaz (2002) (no title) *The Age*, 9 January, p. 7.

Goldenberg, Suzanne (2002) 'Cash not pity, now needed by women of oppression', *Canberra Times*, 18 January, p. 12.

Goodman, Ellen (2001) 'Our charmed life has gone forever', *Guardian Weekly*, 20 September 2001, p. 31.

Halliday, Fred (2000) 'Global governance: prospects and problems' in David Held and Anthony McGrew (eds) *The Global Transformations Reader: an Introduction to the Globalization Debate*. Malden MA: Polity Press, pp. 431–41.

Hardt, Michael, and Negri, Antonio (2000) *Empire*. Cambridge MA: Harvard University Press.

Harvey, Pharis (1998) from 'Globalization: responses from below', *Globalization and Human Rights*, January. PBS on-line transcript, <http:// www.pbs.org/globalization/corporations.html>.

Hay, Colin, and Marsh, David, eds (2000) *Demystifying Globalization*. Basingstoke: Palgrave.

Heidegger, Martin (1977/1993) 'The question concerning technology' in *Basic Writings*, revised and expanded edition, ed. David Farrell Krell. London: Routledge, pp. 311–41.

Held, David (2000) 'International law' in David Held and Anthony McGrew (eds) *The Global Transformations Reader: an Introduction to the Globalization Debate*. Malden MA: Polity Press, pp. 167–71.

Held, David, and McGrew, Anthony, eds (2000) *The Global Transformations Reader: an Introduction to the Globalization Debate*. Malden MA: Polity Press.

Hoogvelt, Ankie (2000) 'Globalization and the postcolonial world' in David Held and Anthony McGrew (eds) *The Global Transformations Reader: an Introduction to the Globalization Debate*. Malden MA: Polity Press, pp. 355–60.

Hou Hanru (1999) 'On the mid ground: Chinese artists, diaspora and global art' in *Beyond the Future: the Third Asia-Pacific Triennial of Contemporary Art*. Brisbane Qld: Queensland Art Gallery, p. 191.

Bibliography

IMF (2000) *Globalization: Threat or Opportunity?* International Monetary Fund, 12 April, http://www.imf.org/external.pubind.htm (downloaded 13 January 2002).

James, William (1967) *The Writings of William James*. New York: Random House.

Jameson, Fredric (1992) *The Geopolitical Aesthetic: Cinema and Space in the World System*. Bloomington IN: Indiana University Press; London: British Film Institute.

Karmack, Elaine Ciulla (2000) 'Globalization and public administration reform' in Joseph S. Nye, Jr, and John D. Donahue (eds) *Governance in a Globalizing World*. Cambridge MA: Visions of Governance for the Twenty-first Century; Washington DC: Brookings Institution, pp. 229–52.

Kellner, Douglas (2001) *Grand Theft 2000: Media Spectacle and a Stolen Election*, http://www.gseis.ucla.edu/faculty/keliner/kellner.html (downloaded 12 April 2002).

Kellner, Douglas (2002) *September 11, Terror War, and the New Barbarism*, http://www.gseis.ucla.edu/faculty/kellner/kellner.html (downloaded 12 April 2002).

Kelly, Paul (2002) 'No escaping migrants', *Weekend Australian*, 30–1 March, p. 28.

Klein, Naomi (2002) 'No logo', *Media Report* (transcript), 17 January, Australian Broadcasting Commission, <http://www.abc.net.au/rn/talks/8.30/mediarpt/stories/445871.htm> (downloaded 14 February 2002).

Krasner, Stephen D. (2000) 'Compromising Westphalia' in David Held and Anthony McGrew (eds) *The Global Transformations Reader: an Introduction to the Globalization Debate*. Malden MA: Polity Press, pp. 124–35.

Krauthammer, Charles (2001) 'Unilateralism is the key to our success', *Guardian Weekly*, 20–6 December, p. 22.

Kristof, Nicholas (2001) 'Our duty now is to Afghan women', *The Age*, 13 December, p. 15.

Lapham, Lewis H. (2001) 'Res publica', *Harper's Magazine*, December, pp. 8–11.

Lee, Gregory B. (1996) *Troubadours, Trumpeters, Troubled Makers: Lyricism, Nationalism and Hybridity in China and its Others*. Durham NC: Duke University Press.

Lefort, Claude (1986) *The Political Forms of Modern Society: Bureaucracy, Democracy, Totalitarianism*, ed. John B. Thompson. Cambridge MA: MIT Press.

Lefort, Claude (1988) *Democracy and Political Theory*, trans. David Macey. Minneapolis MN: University of Minnesota Press.

Bibliography

Marx, Karl (1977) *Selected Writings*, ed. David McLellen. London: Oxford University Press.

Massey, Doreen (2000) 'Time-space compression' in John Beynon and David Dunkerley (eds) *Globalization: the Reader*. London: Athlone Press, pp. 58–60.

Mattelart, Armand (1994) *Mapping World Communication: War, Progress, Culture*, trans. Susan Emanuel and James A. Cohen. Minneapolis MN: University of Minnesota Press.

Mattelart, Armand (1996) *The Invention of Communication*, trans. Susan Emanuel. Minneapolis MN: University of Minnesota Press.

Mattelart, Armand (2000) *Networking the World, 1794–2000*, trans. Liz Carey-Libbrecht and James A. Cohen. Minneapolis MN: University of Minnesota Press.

Mattelart, Armand, and Mattelart, Michele (1992) *Rethinking Media Theory: Signposts and New Directions*, trans. James A. Cohen and Marina Urquidi. Minneapolis MN: University of Minnesota Press.

Milmo, Dan (2001) 'New York gets back to business', *Guardian Weekly*, 17 September, http://media.guardian.co.uk/attack/story/0.1301,553498, 00.html (accessed 12 March 2002).

Mouffe, Chantal (1993) *The Return of the Political*. London: Verso.

Nader, Ralph (1998) 'Globalization: responses from below', *Globalization and Human Rights*, January. PBS on-line transcript <http://www.pbs. org/globalization/corporations.html>.

Negroponte, Nicholas (1996) *Being Digital*. London: Hodder and Stoughton.

Nye, Joseph S., Jr, and Donahue, John D., eds (2000) *Governance in a Globalizing World*. Cambridge MA: Visions of Governance for the Twenty-first Century; Washington DC: Brookings Institution.

Ohmae, Kenichi (2000) 'The end of the nation state' in John Beynon and David Dunkerley (eds) *Globalization: the Reader*. London: Athlone Press, pp. 238–41.

O'Rourke, Kevin H., and Williamson, Jeffrey G. (1999) *Globalization and History: the Evolution of a Nineteenth-century Atlantic Economy*. Cambridge MA: MIT Press.

Polanyi, Karl (1957) *The Great Transformation*. Boston MA: Beacon Press.

Polanyi, Michael (1983) *The Tacit Dimension*. Gloucester MA: Doubleday.

Polanyi, Michael, and Prosch, Harry (1975) *Meaning*. Chicago: University of Chicago Press.

PREM Economic Policy Group and Development Economics Group (2000) *Assessing Globalization*, World Bank Briefing Papers, April, http:// www.worldbank.org/html/extdr/pb/globalization/index.htm (downloaded 13 January 2002).

Bibliography

Rybczynski, Witold (1983) *Taming the Tiger: the Struggle to Control Technology*. New York: Viking Press.

Shah, Hemant (2000) *Journalism in an Age of Mass Media Globalization*, November, http://www.idsnet.org/Papers/Communications/HEMANT_SHAH.HTM (downloaded 12 April 2002).

Shanahan, Angela (2001) 'We've changed but our values haven't', *Australian*, 13 November, p. 13.

Smith, A.D. (1990) 'Towards a global culture?' in Michael Featherstone (ed.) *Global Culture: Nationalism, Globalization and Modernity*. London: Sage.

Smith, Adam (1776/1937) *An Inquiry into the Nature and Causes of the Wealth of Nations*. New York: Random House, Modern Library edition.

Sum, Nga-Ling (2000) 'Globalization and its "other(s)": three "new kinds of orientalism" and the political economy of trans-border identity' in Colin Hay and David Marsh (eds) *Demystifying Globalization*. Basingstoke: Palgrave, pp. 105–26.

UNDP (2000) 'Globalization with a human face' in David Held and Anthony McGrew (eds) *The Global Transformations Reader: an Introduction to the Globalization Debate*. Malden MA: Polity Press, pp. 341–7.

Virilio, Paul (1997) *Open Sky*, trans. Julie Rose. London and New York: Verso.

Virilio, Paul (2000) *The Information Bomb*, trans. Chris Turner. London and New York: Verso.

Wallerstein, Immanuel (2000) 'The rise and future demise of the capitalist world-system' in John Beynon and David Dunkerley (eds) *Globalization: the Reader*. London: Athlone Press, pp. 233–8.

Weekly Telegraph (2001) 'I was a Taliban torturer – I crucified people' (Christine Lamb) 3–9 October, issue 532, pp. 1 and 3.

Williams, Raymond (1980) *Problems in Materialism and Culture: Selected Essays*. London: Verso.

Woods, Ngaire (2000) 'Order, globalization and inequality in world politics' in David Held and Anthony McGrew (eds) *The Global Transformations Reader: an Introduction to the Globalization Debate*. Malden MA: Polity Press, pp. 374–99.

Zizek, Slavoj (1992) *Enjoy your Symptom! Jacques Lacan in Hollywood and Out*. New York: Routledge.

Zizek, Slavoj (1996) *The Indivisible Remainder: an Essay on Schelling and Related Matters*. London: Verso.

Zizek, Slavoj (1999) *The Ticklish Subject: the Absent Centre of Political Ontology*. London and New York: Verso.

Zizek, Slavoj (2001) 'Welcome to the desert of the real!' 15 September, http://web.mit.edu/cms/reconstructions/interpretations/desertreal.html (downloaded 17 September 2001).

Index

Index

Also Available

Understanding Foucault

Geoff Danaher *Central Queensland University*,
Tony Schirato *University of Otago, Dunedin* and
Jennifer Webb *University of Canberra*

'An ideal introduction, accurate and easy to follow thanks to its excellent prose and simple, lucidly explained examples from popular culture' - *Toby Miller, New York University*

Understanding Foucault is a lively and accessible introduction to the main themes of this influential thinker's work.

Richly illustrated throughout with examples drawn from popular culture, the authors cover all the issues dealt with by Foucault, including: power, knowledge, subjectivity, and sexuality.

Not available for sale in Australia or New Zealand
2000 • 192 pages
Cloth (0-7619-6815-6) • Paper (0-7619-6816-4)

Understanding Bourdieu

Jennifer Webb *University of Canberra*,
Tony Schirato *University of Otago, Dunedin* and
Geoff Danaher *Central Queensland University*

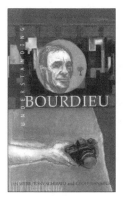

'Bourdieu's work is formidable - the journey is tough. Follow this French foreign legion - take an apple, take a hanky - but take this book' - *Peter Beilharz , La Trobe University*

This book aims to explain Bourdieu's work in a lively and accessible style with extensive reference to popular culture, as such it is an ideal primer for all beginning sociology and cultural studies students.

2002 • 204 pages
Cloth (0-7619-7462-8) • Paper (0-7619-7463-6)